FOUR LIVES
IN PARIS

Hugh Ford

With a Foreword by
Glenway Wescott

NORTH POINT PRESS
San Francisco

North Point Press
850 Talbot Avenue
Berkeley, California
94706

For Julie, Sam, and Annie

CONTENTS

PREFACE

When I began this project a few years ago, I aspired to do what Lytton Strachey had accomplished in his short biographies of four notable Victorians. I admired the boldness with which Strachey attacked the myths that threatened to obscure that era and the people who made it. I admired particularly the form of portraiture he created, which illuminates a century that had already been abundantly documented.

In his preface to *Eminent Victorians* (New York, G. P. Putnam's Sons, 1918) Strachey announced that the history of the Victorian Age could not be written because too much was already known about it. Recognizing this problem, Strachey then proceeded to solve it by attacking his subject in "unexpected places" and by directing a "revealing searchlight into obscure recesses" in pursuit of "characteristic specimens" of the age. The "specimens" are an ecclesiastic, a woman of action, an educator, and a man of adventure. Their portraits he composed and presented as corrective "Victorian visions to the modern eye."

There are, I believe, important similarities between what Strachey had done and what I intend to do in this book on the *expatriate age*—the twenty-year period between world wars when Paris became the resident workshop for artists from all over the world. Much has also been written about the expatriate age and particularly about the Americans who settled in Paris in the twenties and thirties. Some would say too much. But we may know less about this extraordinary artistic and social phenomenon and about the many gifted people who contributed to it than is commonly realized, since this subject is circumscribed by the experiences and opinions of a few celebrated authors who resided in Paris at various times and by the theories and interests of numerous critics and biographers who, with some important exceptions, were not members of the generation that produced, in Malcolm Cowley's felicitous phrase, America's "second flowering."

It is true that those literary giants who will forever be associated with Paris—Ernest Hemingway, Gertrude Stein, Ezra Pound, F. Scott Fitzgerald, and Henry Miller—all did much of their best work there. Few cities have inspired tributes as affectionate and literary as *A Moveable Feast, The Sun Also Rises, The Autobiography of Alice B. Toklas, Paris France, Tender Is the Night*, "Babylon Revisited," *Tropic of Cancer*, and *Black Spring*. These paeans are ample illustration of what Janet Flanner meant when she called Paris "the greatest refreshment." Partly because of the success of their writing and partly because these authors were and remain fascinating personalities, their powerful portrayals of expatriate life in Paris and France have done much to shape attitudes about this era. Time and fame have granted these few a daunting legendary prominence that has greatly overshadowed their contemporaries' evocations of Paris and the life that American expatriates and others pursued there.

Each of the four American men and women who appear in this book— the composer George Antheil, the critic Harold Stearns, the short story writer and novelist Kay Boyle, and the editor Margaret Anderson—represents a different and characteristic aspect of expatriation, a distinct perspective. Together they provide the comprehensiveness and the depth that an understanding of this era requires.

In Paris, American composer George Antheil boasted that he would revolutionize the musical world. The French called him *sauvage*; Antheil named himself the "bad boy of music." Supported by an American patroness and courted by Ezra Pound and James Joyce, he climaxed his European career with celebrated performances of the notorious *Ballet Mécanique*. The composition that electrified Paris drew jeers in New York and ended his ambition to become America's foremost composer.

Harold Stearns, famed as the spokesman for America's disenchanted, abandoned a rising career as a social and political critic for what he hoped would be a productive life in Paris. Contrary to his expectations, Stearns lapsed into a routine of pleasurable apathy that eventually led him to dissipation and physical collapse and finally resulted in repatriation and a return to his once promising position as a writer.

Kay Boyle, one of the longest-staying expatriates, returned to America in 1941 after nearly two decades in France. In the stories and novels she brought to publication in the thirties, she drew on the experiences of her formative years in the twenties—a failed marriage to a Frenchman, a liaison with the doomed poet Ernest Walsh, residency in Raymond Duncan's commune, and a harrowing spree among writers and artists in Montparnasse.

Margaret Anderson, pioneer feminist and founder of the *Little Review* and the first person to publish James Joyce's novel *Ulysses*, left the complacent literary life of America for an aesthetic adventure in France. With her theatrical friend and lover Georgette Leblanc, she pursued a life of organized inspiration, ceaselessly searching for originality and depth of feeling and for the elusive ideal of spiritual perfection.

Spared the relentless attention that has turned their illustrious contemporaries into simplified legends, the lives of these Americans have retained a seminal quality that makes discovering them an exciting event, like coming on "unexpected places" and finding truths not before perceived. These Americans responded in unexpected ways to the creative opportunities Paris provided. The impact of the city on them was as powerful as it was on their more famous colleagues. Their lives contain some of the answers to the abiding questions of why so many Americans went to Paris, what they accomplished there, and what they discovered about themselves and about their native country.

bert Channick for sending me letters and a picture of the late Evan Shipman; Elizabeth Clark for sharing her memories of Margaret Anderson;
Harry Clark for giving me a rare copy of Harold Stearns's *The Street I
Know* (New York, Lee Furman, Inc., 1935) and for maintaining a friendly interest in the progress of this book; Morrill Cody for his recollections of
Margaret Anderson and Harold Stearns and for many hours of stimulating conversation about Paris in the 1920s; Malcolm Cowley for information about his friendship with Harold Stearns and for the photograph of
himself; Professor Noel Fitch for sharing her impressions of George Antheil; the late Ralph Jules Frantz for an account of Harold Stearns's career
as the *Paris Tribune*'s "Peter Pickem"; the late Judge Sidney Goldman
for his colorful account of George Antheil in Trenton; Dr. Hans Heinsheimer for animated and precise descriptions of George Antheil; Professor Mathilda Hills for information about Margaret Anderson and George
Antheil; Eugene and Betty Husting for their warm hospitality and sup-
portive assistance; David Jackson for his abiding interest in this project
and for his assistance in finding information about Harold Stearns; Professor Frederick Kiley for providing a first edition of Margaret Anderson's
The Fiery Fountains (New York, Hermitage House, 1951); Professor
Martin LeBeau for his careful reading of the typescript; the late George
Lechner for his good company and enthusiastic interest in this book;
the late Julien Levi for perceptive comments on Harold Stearns; Jim
McGraw for supplying useful information about Harold Stearns; Susan
and Ian MacNiven for generously sharing their collection of Kay Boyle
letters; Arthur McTighe for recollections of his uncle, George Antheil;
the late Anna Newman for spirited accounts of George Antheil's childhood in Trenton; Peter Roth for providing me with a copy of his honors
thesis (University of Pennsylvania) on the early career of Harold Stearns;
Mabel Schirmer for perceptive recollections of George and Boski Antheil;
George Seldes for his hospitality and for many memories of Harold
Stearns; the late Solita Solano for introducing me to Margaret Anderson
and for her assistance in the preparation of the early versions of the portraits of Margaret Anderson and George Antheil; Virgil Thomson for allowing me to read his copies of Antheil's letters and for sharing his re-
membrances of the composer; Mark Turbyfill for helpful assistance in
Chicago and reminiscences of Jane Heap and Margaret Anderson; the late
Sara Ullman for recollections of Harold Stearns; Apple and Clover Vail
for their interest in this book and for providing photographs of their father
and mother, Laurence Vail and Kay Boyle; Professor Jeanne K. Welcher

for sending me a copy of her article "Harold Stearns's Brief Halcyon"; the late Bill Widney and his wife, Kay, for their warm hospitality and for generously providing me with written descriptions of George Antheil, Harold Stearns, and Margaret Anderson, and for witty and informative vignettes of other Americans in Paris.

To the many librarians who took a lively interest in this project and provided services that made the usual entanglements of research less burdensome, I extend my deepest thanks to: David Koch, curator of the Rare Book Collection, Morris Library, Southern Illinois University; Stanley Mallach, curator of the Fromkin Memorial Collection, University of Wisconsin-Milwaukee; Charles E. Greene, Harvey S. Firestone Library, Princeton University; Ellen S. Dunlap, Carolyn Harris, and Sally Leach, all at the Humanities Research Center, University of Texas; Saundra Taylor, curator of manuscripts, Lilly Library, Indiana University; Jo August Hills, curator of the Hemingway papers, Kennedy Library, Boston; Dr. Lola Szladits, curator of the Berg Collection, New York Public Library; Veronica Cary, former director of the Trenton Free Public Library; Wayne D. Shirley, manuscript librarian, Music Division, Library of Congress.

I should also like to express lasting thanks to: Jacques Baron, Erskine Caldwell, Linda Claus, Norman Gates, Maurice Grosser, Gertrude Hamill, Elizabeth Hagedorn, Stephen Longstreet, the late Walter Lowenfels, Carl Miller, Lewis Mumford, William L. Shirer, Sandra Spanier, and Elaine Sproat.

I am greatly indebted to the National Endowment for the Humanities for a senior fellowship. I should also like to express my gratitude to the Research Committee of Trenton State College for generous allowances of time and financial support and to the MacDowell Colony for a peaceful sojourn in that stimulating retreat.

I am in special debt to Ben Raeburn for his abiding interest in this book; I am everlastingly grateful to Therese Ford, who shared in the making of this book from its inception; and my affectionate thanks to Julie Groff Ford for her support and assistance during the final stage of the writing and her fertile title-making ability.

For permission to quote material herein, I am indebted to Peter Antheil for quotations from the letters of George Antheil; Mrs. Cary Bok for quotations from the letters of Mrs. Mary Louise Bok; Kay Boyle for quotations from her letters and writings; the Society of Authors for quotations from the unpublished letters of James Joyce; Mrs. Betty Lechner for quotations from the letters, manuscripts, and writings of Harold Stearns;

Elizabeth Clark for quotations from the letters and writings of Margaret Anderson; New Directions Publishing Corporation for "Previously Unpublished Excerpts from the Letters of Ezra Pound, Copyright © 1984 by the Trustees of the Ezra Pound Literary Property Trust, used by permission of New Directions Publishing Corporation, agents."

FOREWORD

I made my voyage to Paris in stages. After living in Chicago, where I attended college, worked for *Poetry* magazine, and wrote my first poems, some of which my lifelong friend, Monroe Wheeler, published, I settled in Greenwich Village, which I liked and where I was happy to be away from a number of people who had made me unhappy. In 1921, Monroe and I set out from New York for England, bearing letters of introduction (provided by Harriet Monroe) to the Sitwells, Ford Madox Ford, and Raymond Mortimer. In London, to our great distress, our money began to run out, and unable and unwilling to return home, we pondered how we could stay on, if not in England, then somewhere else. Monroe, with his usual insistent intuition, went to the German Consulate and inquired whether it was true that one could live on very little in Germany. The German official blustered that we Americans only wanted to exploit a country we had already damaged. Monroe replied that, on the contrary, he had a poet on his hands (me) who wanted to learn the language in order to translate Heine. His nationalistic pride touched, the official recommended Wiesbaden. So it was by way of England and Germany that we went to Paris.

Before I had ever seen Paris, I was intensely interested in books about the city and about France. As I found later to be true, Paris looks as though it was planned by an architect. Certainly it is a city that tries to look unified. I had heard that the French were tolerant and that Parisians, especially, were open-minded, curious, and inquisitive about foreign artists who brought with them different ways of living. A writer in Paris could, I learned, do whatever he wanted, no matter who he was or where he came from, no matter how scandalous his behavior might be. Paris was also a place where one could afford to live for a long time on very little, and for a writer this was important.

If it interests the reader to understand us—the creative men and women who went abroad during the twenties—let me extend a caution against the sentimental view that our relationships constituted a homogeneous and fond society of friends in gay Paree. We were not in mercenary or monetary competition with each other; only rarely was money at stake in the literary life of those days; we maintained, I think, a commendable truthfulness, impartiality, and courtesy concerning each other's works. None of us was apt to praise another's work because of personal fondness; on the other hand, our liking for any piece of writing was not often inhibited by any dislike of the author. But in any matter of opinion, theory of form or style, concept of psychology, theology, sexual morals, or (toward the end of the decade) politics, many of us were fighters, indeed dirty fighters.

In Paris I became acquainted with some of the American literary luminaries who made that city a shining cultural capital in the twenties. First, there was Ernest Hemingway, who was immensely good-looking, animated, and hardworking. The French used to say he had *esprit*—a rather light, pointed, and quotable way of talking. He was, I believe, an incredible genius, but he was never a very happy one, nor a very intelligent one. He had a bad tongue, and he more than once used it to play mean tricks on me. Before that happened, we were together occasionally, and one spring I played bridge with him and Ford Madox Ford and Monroe Wheeler.

One notable thing about Hemingway was that he did not understand character at all, especially the character of women. He had no perception of the delicacies or differences of behavior. Certain traits of his character—the combination of enthusiasm and perfectionism about people, with a vengeful disillusionment when he found out what he thought they were really like, a lack of perception of causes and effects in human nature and behavior, and, in consequence, some sentimentality and occasional wild lapses into melodrama—kept him from ever writing an altogether first-rate novel. Consequently, his short stories are better than his novels. He often achieved perfection in scenes about innocent childhood in Michigan, about the heat of battle, or bouts of heavy drinking, or exploits when fishing, on safari, or in the bullring—matters often less outwardly motivated, with little or no future in them and no direct derivation from the past. These are nuggets of pure experience set apart from all the matrix of the world.

Then there was Gertrude Stein, who was a far more beautiful woman than Jo Davidson or others ever made her out to be. She was handsome, in a modernistic way, and had a delectable voice, mannish but velvety, and a marvelous laugh, which came from deep inside her. Contrary to what others have said, I do not believe Gertrude Stein had a sense of humor. She had no jokes, although she enjoyed listening to those told by others. It was her blessed, lifelong co-resident, Alice B. Toklas, always less subjective and more worldly than she, who contributed touches of realism and humor and wit to the conversation.

Gertrude (like Hemingway) had a narcissistic temperament—an excessive consciousness of her position, her pedestal, her niche in literary history. It is true that she took a benign interest in the work of young writers and painters and composers. Hemingway especially derived from her idiosyncratic example and clever precepts a good part of his magical colloquialism that has enriched English and American literature. But she could also be scornful of young creators and their work, particularly when she felt she had been reproached or when she worried too much about her status and her future. She accused Hemingway, who drew much closer to her than I, of having a yellow streak. What she meant by that, and what she said about me, came to the same thing. In *The Autobiography of Alice B. Toklas*, she wrote: "There was also Glenway Wescott but Glenway Wescott at no time interested Gertrude Stein. He has a certain syrup but it does not pour." There was truth in this. My writing career had started with a bang, but I had found that I was not a facile writer and I had slowed up. Hemingway's method—a powerful perfectionism that carefully fit every one-syllable word into place—and mine—an inhibited sweetness and diffidence when I had pen in hand—were reproaches to her, a rivalry with her, who wrote with such extraordinary, one might say scandalous, facility.

When I think of Ezra Pound, what I remember first is the afternoon in 1923 when Mina Loy took me to call on him. I suppose I was unprepared for that meeting and for the man. He was young looking, but his face had an unpleasant pallor. His eyes looked strange, like those of some old bird. His hair and beard were carrot-red. His expression was often tentative, dreamy, fatuous. He seemed unable to sit still, jumping from chair to chair, from chair to couch, throwing himself down flat on his back and kicking his legs in the air; and all these extraordinary acrobatics were going on in the middle of sentences. Ezra never seemed to finish what he was saying. He would interrupt himself, splintering his syntax into fragments. He was decidedly a man who did not appear to be normal.

Of those who have taken the greatest liberties with the English language, Pound, in my opinion, has done the least amount of damage, and Joyce, the most. Potentially the most original writer of this century, Joyce got the wicked idea of ruining the language by mixing it with other languages. He frittered away his great talent doing this evil thing, and he very nearly succeeded. Gertrude Stein did not try to ruin the language; she simply disarranged syntax. She left the language intact. Ezra Pound, who (I believe) is a better artist than Joyce, wrought more literary art with less syntax than anyone I can think of. The *Cantos* is the greatest magpie nest in all literature. It is like Burton's *The Anatomy of Melancholy*, but without the syntax that sustains the latter. His mind was ever wandering, ever fluctuating, roving, distractable; thus his subjects, so often didactic and self-promotional, are compulsively juxtaposed, and his two obsessions—banking and politics—function as leitmotifs. Of his greatest disabilities Pound made an enormous strength.

I could write a good deal about the Americans Hugh Ford has chosen for his book *Four Lives in Paris*, but apart from the brief comments that follow, I wish only to say that they are among the most representative figures of those who made Paris their home and workshop during the twenties, and that their lives abroad, as they are described in this book, provide valuable insights into the complex and much misunderstood subject of expatriation.

The one I feel closest to among the people in this book is Margaret Anderson. Along with Harriet Monroe, the founder of *Poetry* magazine, Margaret profited from the courage of Ezra Pound, who kept both women on their marks by setting an example of boldness and staying power. It saddened me to discover, when I read *My Thirty Years' War*, Margaret's first autobiographical book in which she recounted the history of her avant-garde magazine, the *Little Review*, that she regretted never having published anything by me in the magazine, because, as she explained, she had liked what I had done as much as anything that had appeared in America, with the single exception of Hemingway's work. What she had forgotten was that she had published a poem of mine, "Old Style of Garden," in the spring (1924) issue of the *Little Review*. The only thing worse than not being published is being published and then having your publisher forget she published you.

In Paris Margaret disagreed with me when I called my writing "old-fashioned." She argued that it could be called that only in the sense of its having "more accretions than are fashionable." By accretions, Margaret meant "those strata of personal experience which some people manage to acquire out of little and others fail to acquire out of much." That may have been why she praised my second novel, *The Grandmothers*, which I had written in eighteen months.

Sometimes I wonder why Margaret did not try to be more of a writer, even though she insisted she could never be one. She did write, and her books are ravishing to read. She did not try to fool you and make them seem better than they were, and they fulfilled their promise and potential. Margaret settled for what she could do and what she wanted to do, and she enjoyed doing it. She probably wrote in front of a mirror, since she loved looking at herself. Her famed beauty—masculine when I first knew her in Chicago, and then, as she realized her influence and the use she could make of it, suddenly very delicate and even voluptuous—was comparable only to that of her friend Djuna Barnes, who in Greenwich Village made as great a stir as Margaret did in Chicago.

I learned about Harold Stearns from Duff Twysden, the vivacious lady with whom Hemingway fell in love and on whom he modeled the character of Brett Ashley in his novel *The Sun Also Rises*. She and Mary Butts were close friends, and I was Mary's friend. Mary introduced me to Duff and we got on perfectly. In those days in Montparnasse, Duff and Harold Stearns were the two most celebrated gamblers on horses. Duff always considered herself to be the best, and Harold, even though he was the distinguished horse-racing columnist for the *Paris Tribune*, to be a close runner-up.

One of the great modern types, here and in France, I believe, is the drunk. In France no one expects much of anybody who drinks, but in America the drinker is supposed to drink *and* to produce. Some American writers have done it, but the management of drinking and what is expected of the drinker are very different in France. The feeling there about conduct and morals is not like ours in America. Europeans may make dissipation work, but Americans, whether at home or abroad, usually go to hell and become social problems. The French do not genuinely go to hell. It is a way of life, and at the same time, they are absolutely determined to do their work. No one abused himself physically more than Baudelaire. But he watched everything he was doing, and he stopped short of becoming dangerous to himself and to his friends. At that point he wrote one of the most perfect bouquets of poetry ever written. He was a controlled drunk.

Harold Stearns tried to be a Baudelaire and he should not have done so; if he had been a Frenchman, he would not have. He fell between two stools. He was trying to be a writer in Paris, or he said he was, and to go on drinking at the same time, and he could not do it.

George Antheil is another interesting type—a person who goes to a foreign country to be supported by that country and then returns to his own country and fails. Stranded, without any physical or spiritual home, he wastes away. Some people cannot survive because they cannot find a home for themselves. Antheil thought that if he gained a European reputation, he would be assured of an American audience. He also made the mistake of depending too much on those who said they admired him and his music. Aaron Copland, although he studied in Paris with Nadia Boulanger, remained in America for the most part and was successful there. Virgil Thomson, Antheil's companion in Paris, worked himself out of France. It is regrettable, but understandable, that so few have recognized that George Antheil was two people: a hardworking composer and a self-seeking publicist who mistakenly tried to build a career on sensation and spectacle.

It was while living in Villefranche, near Nice on the French Riviera, that I again met Kay Boyle. I had known her earlier in Paris when she was a young novelist, and I had found for her in a poem by Marianne Moore a few lines from which she took the title for her first novel, *Plagued by the Nightingale*. She was a companion of Ernest Walsh, the co-editor (with Ethel Moorhead) of a little magazine called *This Quarter*. Walsh was dying of tuberculosis and was confined to a wheelchair. He knew that he would not live much longer, and he had asked Kay to arrange a meeting with me. I do not remember what we talked about, but I do remember that Kay looked after Walsh with the solicitude of a mother.

Kay Boyle was more "abroad" than the rest of us; she was more "French"

than I. She was also what we all wanted to be: a person living a full life
without ever seeming to get tired. She did not pick out her men to be
helpful to her or to be helpful to them. It is impossible to conceive of any
difference in her life making any difference in her writing. She wrote just
as well as she could from the start, and by that I mean she wrote quickly,
loosely, and romantically. She was as good as she could be. Her work
maintained just the right balance of inspiration.

The south of France was not an especially friendly place, but it was very
sociable, enchanting and foolish at the same time. It was wonderful if you
could afford it. Close by, in Nice, lived Isadora Duncan, the first American to captivate the French. When she died in an automobile accident,
Monroe and I sat up all night with her body until Raymond, her brother,
arrived from Paris. She was a marvelous, wild woman. Monroe and I
stayed in the Welcome Hotel, in Villefranche, with co-residents that included, at various times, Mary Butts, Clive Bell, Paul Robeson and his
wife, and most important for me, Jean Cocteau, to whom Katherine Harvey introduced me. Cocteau was the best teacher who ever lived. He made
me read everything of French literature, beginning with the classics of the
seventeenth and eighteenth centuries. Having done that, I used to love
to startle the French with my knowledge of their literature. In Chicago,
while employed as an office boy by Harriet Monroe, I read modern French
poetry, and with the extensive study I made of the French classics under
Cocteau's (also Jacques Guerin's) direction, I could brazenly boast that I
knew more about French literature than Ezra Pound, who concentrated
on the Provençal troubadour poets.
    French literature enchanted me. It was balanced and precise and all of a
piece. The French make it so. Their writers are always tacking themselves
onto an older generation of writers, who are, I suppose, their literary
father figures. In France I began to see that I had only superficial relations
with those of my generation who lived abroad. I have always believed that
my generation has not been strongly influenced by our immediate elders
as the French have and that we have not had any great effect on one another. The longer I remained in France, the more I felt myself being influenced by French writing.
    The way the French lived moved me, too. I was unlike my compatriots. I
saw little of the Americans in Paris and a great deal of the English and the
French. I think that Americans like myself who were intimate with the

xxii   FOUR LIVES IN PARIS

French, socially as well as sexually, had an experience that had a lasting effect. They learned that the French in love are very different from other people in love. They make you behave the way you are supposed to behave, to be responsive. They certainly have a desire to rule.

All the Frenchmen I knew acted a role. I suppose they did it for each other, and they certainly did it in their families. When one got to know a few Frenchmen, in one way or another, one might have believed that one had met the devil. I know I did. If anyone came to Paris with any interest in the arts, as I did, there were French people ready to take him up. They are very conscious of the benefits of foreign creators. I was launched by a society of men of all sorts in Paris.

Why one decides to return to one's native land is often as difficult to explain as why one decides to leave it. Perhaps I felt I had stayed abroad too long. Certainly I knew there would be war in Europe. The portents were every-where, and I wrote about them in a book called *Fear and Trembling*, which very few people read when it appeared in 1932 and even fewer heeded. There were other reasons to return to America. My future sister-in-law, Barbara Harrison, had fallen seriously ill, and Monroe who, with her, had begun publishing luxury books under the imprint of Harrison of Paris, foresaw that rising costs would make continuation of the business unprofitable.

How strongly I had been influenced by my sojourn in France became clear once I had returned to the United States. I found that I was not only thinking in French, I was also dreaming in French. Worse, I felt as though I had lost part of my language, a serious loss for a writer and one that explained why I had had difficulties with the two books I had written just before leaving Europe in 1933. It was a sobering impasse. What relieved it and contributed to my growth as a writer was reading Somerset Maugham, who, with Colette and Ford Madox Ford, belongs to my tree of heroes. Reading Maugham gave me back more than my language. From him I learned techniques that I had always found troublesome, especially dia-logue. When Maugham detected that I was trying to imitate Cocteau, he gave me a piece of advice I never forgot. "Glenway, you'll never live long enough in France to know what Frenchmen know." He was right, and I stopped what I was doing, but I have retained the best of what France gave me.

Expatriation, particularly the expatriation of writers in France, is one of the keys to our present American culture. Of late, a legendary feeling about it has developed. Some of us who have been homebodies for years still enjoy a little luster for having been there at the same time as Hemingway, Pound, Gertrude Stein, and Henry Miller. It was our education.

GLENWAY WESCOTT
Rosemont, New Jersey

FOUR LIVES
IN PARIS

GEORGE ANTHEIL

I am a man and an artist,
and not a vaudeville show.
(from a letter to
Mary Louise Bok)

The young man who bounded up to the front door of a large, gray rambling mansion near Bernardsville, in rural New Jersey, looked more like a lightweight boxer than a musician. Short, barely over five feet, he had stocky legs, muscular arms, a broad chest, and fingers like sausages. His nose, stubby and flat, was the only blemish that marred a round face so comely that schoolmates had called him "Angel Face." His blue eyes, set wide apart, were fixed and intense. His straight blond hair he wore short. Confidently, he put down a cardboard valise stuffed with music paper, pencils, India ink, and rulers, shook hands firmly with his hosts, strode across the room to a piano, and began beating upon it a compelling mechanical music. Two hours later he stopped, thanked his captivated listeners for their invitation and attention, and announced that he had informed his parents in Trenton that henceforth his address would be Bernardsville. The audacious young guest was George Antheil. The admiring hosts were Georgette Leblanc, Margaret Anderson, and Allen Tanner.

For the opera singer Georgette Leblanc (better known at the time as the estranged wife of the writer Maurice Maeterlinck), coming to New York had been a disaster. Lured by the promises of large rewards from the

Hearst newspapers for her memoirs, she had scarcely settled down in the city and begun to write when the offer was withdrawn. On the verge of penury and depression, she had retreated to Bernardsville, where her life was rejuvenated by two new friends, the attractive and mercurial editor of the *Little Review*, Margaret Anderson, with whom she would live for the next twenty years, and a handsome, young friend of Margaret's named Allen Tanner, who had brought the two women together. It was also Tanner who, after listening to Muriel Draper's rhapsodic account of Antheil's playing, had invited the pianist to their sylvan hideaway. His acceptance note had intrigued them: "I will come with pleasure since you are interested in modern *musics*." That he intended to stay he had now made clear.

Antheil moved into the East Room, an appropriate place, since his habit was to rise with the sun and work all day. Georgette complained that they all suffered under his manner of composing. "He would choose a theme of five or six notes and repeat it insatiably for hours on end. He seemed to hypnotize himself with certain vibrations." All noticed that he seldom stopped to eat, a feat that defied explanation until Tanner discovered a nearly empty sack of green apples and several cans of baked beans missing from the pantry. These, along with frequent imbibings of peppermint oil to soothe a rambunctious stomach, remained his daytime staples.

Each of the friends worked alone, not meeting, except occasionally for a brief lunch, until teatime. Dinner, prepared and served by Georgette's faithful *dame de campaigne*, Monique, appeared at nine, and afterward the "great hours" began. Georgette sang, George performed a "work in progress," Allen played Debussy or Chopin or Scriabin. Margaret, sitting apart, listened in her own "lyrical manner." Two o'clock signaled the hour of "stories and laughter" and a light supper. At four o'clock the revelers retired.

George was not as incurious about his new companions as he pretended to be. His letters from Bernardsville to his close friend Stanley Hart quivered with thrilled observations. Margaret was almost beyond imagining, certainly the most congenial being he had ever seen, a person of great sincerity, intellect, pure emotion, and, at times, almost Rabelaisian sensuality. Her every emotion was an "exquisite gesture of herself." Georgette was equally hard to describe. Although she possessed a "very great soul" and was "the most charming woman of forty" he had ever known, she lacked the sophistication of a woman. Hers was "not a baby-like imitation of unsophistication—but the *real thing*." To think of her as "anything but a child" was impossible. Tanner, who had ventured to supervise his work, time, and even exercise, and who had clothed him in baggy trousers and a checkered sports jacket out of his own sketchy wardrobe, held mysteries. He never laughed, only smiled a strange smile. On the pianoforte he was a "burning genius."

Of George his hosts formed opinions, too. Tanner identified a haunting beauty in his complex and weighty sonatas. For Georgette, everything about him substantiated her first impression: he was a genius. Margaret, more circumspect, found George "unprepossessing," except for his vitality and concentration. That he was a master of harmony there was no question, and most impressive was his "intense and immense" output: a concerto for piano and orchestra, an intricate composition inspired by Brancusi called *Golden Bird*, a strange piece entitled *Serpent*, and early versions of what would become his *Mechanisms*. George, she wagered, might be the first of their group ready for Europe.

Two months after it began, the caravansary Georgette had provided in the peaceful New Jersey woodlands folded. Margaret and Allen returned to New York to seek a concert manager for Georgette. George hurried off to Philadelphia to resume his studies. Behind remained Georgette and Monique.

George Antheil has too much competitive spleen. So remarked Jane Heap, Margaret Anderson's friend and co-editor of the *Little Review*. He could hardly dispute the reproach. Nor could he deny that it existed in the generous measure Jane suggested. Tanner had noted that George reduced other composers and musicians to bothersome rivals who blocked his way and would sometime have to be pushed aside. Beneath the puckish exterior was an aggressive spirit. Like Horatio Alger's trusting heroes, whose adventures he had absorbed with pure and unquenchable faith, Antheil grew up believing he would be famous. Even more, famous *and* sensational. He never doubted that he would outperform his rivals, who by the time he was twenty included Igor Stravinsky, Arnold Schönberg, and a composer exactly his age, Aaron Copland. He put absolute faith in what he rightly considered his superior musical powers and in what he mistakenly believed was an inexhaustible supply of energy. Life, as Horatio Alger had convincingly demonstrated, consisted of more than just the daily struggle to exist; it was a challenging, even heroic, contest that demanded courage, honesty, imagination, character, excellence—and luck. Glorious victories awaited the persistent and bold. True, Alger preached that the struggle always counted for more than the rewards. But that stern lesson was only for the timid and irresolute. For George Antheil a future that withheld the fruits of struggle was inconceivable.

A child of the century, George Johann Carl Antheil was born on July 8, 1900, in Trenton, New Jersey, then as now a gray industrial city spread along the banks of the fabled Delaware River and populated mainly by laborers who, like their fathers, took mute pride in the city's slogan: "Trenton Makes, the World Takes." What Trenton made the most of at the turn of the century was steel—Roebling Steel. From the Roebling mills of south Trenton, a short distance from the Antheil home, came not only the wire cables that hold up the Brooklyn Bridge, but a machine-produced cacophony—hums and screeches, clanks and clunks—that Antheil would one day transmute into a symphony. Like the English artist L.S. Lowry, who spent a lifetime painting the grimy townscapes of the industrial north, Antheil drew inspiration from a raw, pulsating mechanical environment.

George discovered in his aunt's piano the same stimulating combination of sound and mechanics. So compelling was this complex instrument that for his third Christmas he demanded a piano of his own, a large one, like Auntie's. While waiting, he transformed his mother's sideboard ("horrible piece of furniture") into a makeshift "piano," thumping and drumming on it by the hour, all the while admiring himself in a mirror. Christmas arrived but not the big piano he expected. Santa had deposited instead a toy piano with hardly an octave. It simply would not do. Without a word, he picked up the despicable instrument, disappeared into the cellar, and chopped it to pieces. The licking that ensued he bore tearlessly. Either he would have one like his aunt's, or he would have nothing. Years later he made the dismembered toy a symbol of his music. "Either big music or the little music gets chopped up, and I get a licking." Apart from convincing his parents he possessed a firm single-mindedness, the episode revealed a less endearing trait: a proclivity to retaliate against anybody he suspected of deluding him. It was a trait that time and events would strengthen.

When, at the venerable age of ten, George received his first real piano, having earlier abandoned the violin, he immediately became a curiosity: a pupil fonder of composing than of practicing. Often the problem in households where such musical industry prevails is how to live with the zealous aspirant without losing one's wits. The solution the Antheils favored was flight, usually into the neighborhood streets. Against her son's efforts to perfect a particularly dissonant piece, his mother, Wilhelmina, a strict, deeply religious woman, waged a relentless campaign of castigation. "George," she remonstrated, "music should soothe, not irritate. Yours is too discordant. It irritates me, your father, the neighbors, and it will irritate your audiences." Such strident compositions violated all her cherished musical opinions. George retorted that neither she nor his father, Henry, a pliant, tolerant man, knew anything about music, certainly nothing about his music, and to prove his point he named dozens of people who understood what he was doing and approved, including his German nanny, for whom he had set to music a melodramatic story she had told him of two dancers who consummated their love by flinging themselves from a window.

Wilhelmina had almost exhausted efforts to redirect her son along traditional musical paths when Henry ordered George to report for work in the family shoe business (Antheil's Friendly Shoe Store). If his son were required to earn part of his musical education, thereby reducing the time for composing, he would have to concentrate almost entirely on his teachers' assignments. But George turned the shoe store into a studio, going about the place making an audible humming noise, and at moments of unbearable inspiration, vanishing into the storeroom, where he would commit snatches of a burgeoning song to the butts of shoe boxes. Once he sent an indecisive customer away with one tan and one black shoe. When the angry man returned with the mismatched shoes, George explained to his father that it seemed the only way to satisfy a person unable to make up his mind. It soon became apparent that even commerce could not deflect the torrent of music flowing from their son, and the vanquished parents were on the verge of relinquishing their last proprietary rights when Henry acted again. This time he purchased a summer home at Washington's Crossing, a pastoral settlement a few miles from Trenton and immediately below McKonkey's Ferry, where General Washington landed after his icy expedition across the Delaware. For the family, the hermitage provided quietude and rest. For George, it became a seething composing outpost.

After Bernardsville, Antheil traveled to Philadelphia to see the man he affectionately called his "musical godfather," an Old World teacher and a former student of Liszt's named Constantine von Sternberg. From him George had already received a thorough theoretical training in counterpoint and harmony as well as countless admonitions to practice restraint, to adhere to the classical virtues of simplicity, balance, and moderation, and above all, to shun the purely sensuous effects of Ravel and Debussy. "Speak your own language," he urged his young charge, "not bad French."

Beware of extremes, be modern but not modernistic, use harmony only when the reason for using it is clear, and follow the examples of Bach and Beethoven, who expressed feeling and thought in great simple statements. Similar advice had also come from Josef Hofman, soon to become the first director of the Curtis Institute of Music, who advised the "musical voluptuary" to restudy Beethoven's early sonatas and then write a few first movements with close adherence to the master's form. Neither instructor had irritated George as much as the composer Ernest Bloch, a teacher at the David Mannes Music School in New York, who dismissed his compositions as empty and pretentious and refused, despite Sternberg's recommendation, to accept him as a student. Stunned, Antheil retreated to Trenton, mastered his chagrin, and in an orgiastic burst, composed music for five songs, at the same time showering Bloch with letters beseeching him to reconsider his decision. Months passed. Bloch finally relented, listened to his new compositions, and accepted him.

Antheil's lifelong problem—lack of money—beset him when he returned to Philadelphia. His parents' stipend barely covered expenses, and if Bloch had not refunded a portion of his tuition when he discovered George had been starving himself so that he could remain his pupil, he would have run out of funds almost at once. George took his problem to Sternberg. Do not succumb to false pride and take some trivial job to pay for your training, the old man warned. Remember, Wagner relied on Liszt. Advertise for support and never work gratis. Seek aid, always avoid menial drudgery, and go on studying, alone, and rewriting your compositions, again and again, until your work has "consistency" and "definiteness." But when such inspiring advice failed to produce the needed assistance (the American Academy in Rome rejected him), Sternberg armed his impecunious pupil with a sealed letter and dispatched him on a mission that would change his life.

Mary Louise Bok, philanthropist and patron of the arts, was the daughter of Cyrus H. K. Curtis, founder of the Curtis Publishing Company. Her mother, Louise Knapp Curtis, edited the *Ladies' Home Journal* from 1883 to 1889, when Mary Louise's husband, Edward Bok, became the editor. It was to Mrs. Bok's mansion in Merion, Pennsylvania, on Philadephia's Main Line, that Antheil carried Sternberg's letter. It read in part:

> I am morally certain to have discovered in the bearer of this—George Antheil—one of the richest and strongest talents for composition

that I have ever met here or in Europe. Its possessor is scarcely more than a boy, of good parentage, well bred, pure minded, and of impeccable character. His father went to the limits of his means to foster and develop the boy's talent; but he can go no further and the boy has now to face the struggle for existence. For this struggle, however, he is by his unworldly disposition and lack of experience utterly unfit, and even if he were not so, it would be a pity if so great a talent as his should be frittered away in some kind of routine occupation, such as playing in the "movies" or in a "cafe" and thus lose the fine lustre of its *noblesse*—which nothing could ever bring back.

Now, what he needs are the means to hide himself for a year or two in some secluded spot . . . where, living the simplest possible life, he could devote himself to his work without having to earn money for his bodily maintenance.

Believe me, my dear Mrs. Bok, that I did not send the boy to you . . . with any thought of asking you for monetary aid and I *know that such is not his purpose.* . . . Let me ask you . . . not to take for audaciousness what was prompted by my natural love of a talent which, under halfway favorable conditions, is likely to reveal itself as "genius."

Years later, in a letter to Mrs. Bok, George recounted in mock storybook language his version of the momentous visit to her home: "I came to your door at Merion, on that cool late autumn day of 1921. I was really very hungry. You put ten dollars into my hand, and you had no means of knowing whether I had one jot of talent." With considerably more than that bounteous amount, George left Merion. He had Mrs. Bok's pledge of $150 a month for one year, in return for light teaching chores at the Philadelphia Settlement Music School, forerunner of the Curtis Institute that she would establish in 1922.

With Mrs. Bok's bounty, Antheil purchased a new wardrobe, a mahogany walking stick, and a pair of English gunmetal shoes. Without her assistance, he acquired an awe-inspiring English accent. With a Philadelphian called Abraham Lincoln Gillespie, who contrived a likeness to his namesake by growing a beard, speaking slowly, and looking impressive, and whose notoriety in Paris would one day rival Antheil's, he shared an expensive midtown apartment, which Gillespie had clandestinely furnished with lawn furniture expropriated on midnight raids into the city's plush suburbs. At the Settlement School, George taught theory and studied

George Antheil and Margaret Anderson, Bernardsville, N.J.

intermittently with George Boyle, who endeavored (on orders from Mrs. Bok) to turn him into a concert pianist. The rest of the time he spent composing, practicing, amusing himself with Gillespie, and conducting a desultory romance with a sixteen-year-old socialite named Annette Williams, daughter of a prominent Germantown physician. Only the demands of his "artistic life," he informed Stanley Hart, prevented him from falling convincingly in love with her. But by the end of the year, his flirtation with Annette had alternately smoldered, flared up, descended, glowed again, and expired.

As his romance collapsed, so did the seductive attractions of Philadelphia, a disenchanting experience Sternberg abetted by admitting that the "chiefest charm" of the city where he had labored thirty years before attaining a position of independence would always remain the hourly trains to New York. Certainly the opportunities New York offered had not been lost on Antheil. There, thanks partly to Margaret Anderson and Georgette Leblanc, his name and music were becoming known. On occasional visits, he had tried out a few of his own promotional ideas, usually without successful results. Arthur Rubinstein told Tanner of an encounter with Antheil that had left him more perplexed than impressed. "So you know Antheil," Rubinstein said. "Well, he is a most extraordinary chap; thought he had left his gloves in my room this morning; he was showing me some new music of his, and, can you imagine, he has been phoning me every half hour since, reminding me in a very peculiar tone of voice that he'd forgotten them. To such a point that I'm beginning to wonder if I didn't steal them, so I keep looking . . . inside the piano, under the bed . . . in the water closet, everywhere, trying to find where I hid them . . . if I did." With Muriel Draper, George fared better. His "greatest efforts" had left her weeping with excitement and exclaiming that someone had at last come to "collect the reigns [sic] and be the horseman of the East." A reaction only slightly less exuberant came from visiting Polish composer Karol Szymanowski, who called *Golden Bird* a "most extraordinary orchestration." With such accolades resounding in his ears, George posted an end-of-the-year report to his patron that was memorable for its restraint and uncanny accuracy: "Everything is beginning now—little by little."

In Mary Louise Bok, Henry and Wilhelmina Antheil had a confederate. She too believed George ought to be a concert pianist. George professed to be in agreement ("I am turning to more work on the piano, for I secretly want to be a concert pianist"), but he could not resist divulging that Leopold Stokowski had asked to examine his work and that Rubinstein had called him one of the "most radical and interesting composers now alive" and, in a spurt of hyperbole attributable to the recipient, by far the most interesting personality in America. Although composing would remain "a ruthless impellation," he assured her that his admiration for the "ultra-modern" faddists was limited to their catalytic effects. They jolted people out of "their smug musical holes." Mrs. Bok would have to understand that, having mastered the techniques and styles of his contemporaries, he now looked forward ("not many months from today") to creating music of his own.

In the spring of 1922, the pianist Leo Ornstein, one of the ultramodernists, separated from his manager, Martin H. Hanson. It was an opportunity Antheil was determined to seize. For a month he practiced sixteen to twenty hours a day, stopping only to bathe his blistered hands in fish bowls on either side of his piano stool. Hanson was impressed. In his judgment, Antheil was ready to make his debut. He was also certain that recitals could be scheduled in London, Berlin, and other cities. Only time (Hanson would leave for Europe in less than two months) and money (the cost would be steep) could keep him in America.

The letter of petition George dispatched special delivery to Mrs. Bok two days after playing for Hanson was a masterpiece of persuasion, self-congratulation, and cringing deference. Hanson, he began, had predicted that a European tour, undertaken without delay, would be a critical and financial triumph. Besides challenging the belief that America lacked serious composers, a successful tour would undoubtedly launch his career at home. If Mrs. Bok thought he wanted to go abroad just to show off his compositions, he predicted that "his piano playing alone" would astonish her. Whatever conquests awaited him could be attributed to her "real and honest" friendship. As for the cost of the tour, he confessed that he had lacked the courage to ask Hanson.

Hanson's follow-up letter to Mrs. Bok contained an enthusiastic appraisal of Antheil's talent and his moral character ("I feel the lad is amazingly honest") and two sets of figures: a small tour for $3,900 and a more extensive one for $6,400. Mrs. Bok selected the larger.

Her decision, proclaimed George, had made him a new man, more confident but also more cautious. "I plan to draw attention to myself as a pianist. I plan it all, and give but little to chance or indisposition." Preparing his repertoire consumed the weeks before departure. In addition to the mainstays of his program—Chopin, Debussy, and Bach—he included three piano sonatas—*Golden Bird, Nocturne,* and *Chinese Dragon*—a "very modern, post-Stravinsky rhythmically" sonatina for pianoforte, and a collection of short pieces dating from as early as 1915. In New York, Margaret and Georgette hosted a farewell party. George played for an audience of journalists and "distinguished-looking Frenchmen." Later the same day he bid a teary good-bye to Wilhelmina and Henry, who would not see their son again until the spring of 1927, five years hence, when he would perform in Carnegie Hall.

Antheil's first and only concert in London in late June received mostly negative reviews. The critics that Hanson had invited George had dismissed as decidedly not the "proper kind." One accused him of copying Leo Ornstein's methods, another detected the influence of both Debussy and Stravinsky, and a third found Antheil's compositions "clever" but unrelated to their titles. Only the correspondent for *Musical America* called him a pianist of "first rank" and a composer with "a powerful talent."

Showing true Horatio Alger–like optimism, George extracted several benefits from the performance. The "indolent" English had at least learned his name and knew he was serious. While he may not have conquered London, he had accomplished something better: he had incensed it. The reviewers' scorn for his unorthodox music would strengthen the reputation of notoriety essential to the world's first "Futurist-terrible," an appellation George considered appropriately self-descriptive and iconoclastic. The London experience reinforced his resolve to play his work wherever he performed, and when Hanson informed him that he had been invited to the first International Festival of Modern Music in Germany, George concluded that someone had not only watched over him but had taken charge of his destiny.

But any hope that the event was part of a divine plan to acquaint the world with the compositions of the world's first "Futurist-terrible" was destroyed when he reached the country estate of the festival's organizer, the Prince of Furstenburg, and found that only Germans, Austrians, and a few Czechs and Hungarians had been invited. No new works by Ravel, Milhaud, Stravinsky, Honegger, Bliss, Bloch, or by young Germans such as Hindemith or Krenek appeared on the program. Furthermore, Antheil quickly concluded that his nationality made him an outsider. So low was the opinion of American music among the participants that even the few who deigned to speak to him were patronizing or snobbish. The rest ignored him. The few performances he endured George dismissed as boring and soporific, mostly "sterile Brahms with traces from Debussy and Schönberg," the "unilluminated music" of a "bunch of Hochschule boys." Obviously, the would-be "Futurist-terrible" needed more hospitable audiences.

On July 4, 1922, George entered Berlin. The city swarmed with Russian emigres, among them Ivor Stravinsky and Pavel Tchelitchew. The place existed in a state of siege. Everywhere he heard rumors of revolution. Filth, starvation, and shameless luxury—the same volatile ingredients that ignited the French Revolution, virtually guaranteed revolt. "I am in the forbidden city," he informed Stanley Hart. "It is a strange city, giving off the perfume of luxury and perfumed orgy. It is the city of Dr. Caligari." For a pittance, a Russian princess would be his mistress, and for almost nothing he could pick the prettiest prostitute from among the hordes roaming the streets, where it was often unsafe even for a man to walk alone or accompanied, as he learned one evening when Stravinsky and he were set upon by half a hundred streetwalkers. Stravinsky, George reported, coolly deflected their demands by telling them they had just come from entertaining half a dozen girls each.

No impecunious and obliging princess became Antheil's paramour, however. His choice was a twenty-year-old Russian actress named Valla, "fiercely beautiful," with hair of "wild black silk" and a face like a Madonna. It was impossible for him not to propose to this personification of "old Russia with all of her mystery and vice." To George's astonishment she accepted. A month later, however, she vanished, and George, satiated with the girl he had chosen because she was the wildest, most devilish creature in Berlin, retreated to a quiet and distant suburb.

Others succeeded the exotic Valla—a Kikomoro dancer; Mary, the Rachel of Ben Hecht's cynical novel *Erik Dorn* (1921); Maryla, the bisexual mistress of the artist Dungert (a "strange misshapen soul"); and, briefly, the eccentric poetess Baroness Elsa Freytag von Loringhoven, who inconsiderately ended their liaison with threats of blackmail. None, however, matched another "beautiful and strange creature" George spied one day at a café on the Kurfurstendam. Her face, "savagely and boyishly beautiful," reminded him of "the sound of a Mongolian death gong." Young and diminutive, "like the Mongols from whose race" he surmised she came, she walked like a boy and wore her hair like a boy. Eugene Berman, an American endocrinologist studying homosexuals confined to Berlin hospitals, confessed he had never before seen "such a remarkable creature," but he hinted that she might not be "sexually normal," perhaps a lesbian like Jane Heap, who also had a boyish appearance and the look of a Mongol. For several months this remarkable person—Boski Marcus—seemed more an apparition than the virile woman George would eventually subdue and love.

Such scintillating distractions notwithstanding, Antheil followed Hanson's advice and continued his musical studies with Artur Schnabel. At Der Sturm hall, a focal point for German Futurists, he presented a program of his music that read like a "plumber's catalogue." In November he hired a young director named Dornberg to conduct his *First Symphony*.

If performance is the supreme test of a composition, this one revealed all its flaws. The enthusiastic reception that followed, George correctly observed, was less for his music than for Dornberg, who had valiantly conducted the Berlin Philharmonic orchestra through a novel and difficult work. For two days, critics feasted on his failure. It was his second bruising encounter with music critics, and like the English, the Germans demolished his work, *not* for what it was but for what it was not. He concluded that because he had avoided atonality, the current German rage, and sufficient play of counterpoint, the Germans had pronounced his work a failure.

With the two concertgoers he wanted most to impress, George both won and lost. Boski Marcus disliked his music and vanished immediately after the concert. But Igor Stravinsky stayed behind and congratulated him. Any compliment from the man he idolized generously compensated for the critics' gibes or Boski's rebuff. What Stravinsky actually said to him, or what Antheil imagined he said, he duly reported to friends. "Stravinsky," he told one, "has discovered me. He has proclaimed me a great talent and invited me to Paris to live and study with him." To Mrs. Bok he confided: "Stravinsky says I have a terrible musical intelligence, one dangerous to coming generations . . . as dangerous as an anti-Christ."

Allen Tanner once observed that George Antheil often imposed himself on those he would eventually oppose. Stravinsky was one. More than anybody else, George wanted to be like Stravinsky. He admired Stravinsky's eclectic mind, his ability to do many things in many different ways. He had succeeded because he had a "magnificent intelligence, a consummate technic [sic] and cleverness—above all, he was a man—a soul—an enormous sensibility," the equal of Picasso, Joyce, and Léger. A genius few dared to imitate, Stravinsky stood alone among modern composers. To be with this peerless artist became an obsession, but sooner or later even a fawning, deferential disciple becomes annoying, and when Antheil's unannounced visits exceeded the invitations Stravinsky extended and

Allen Tanner, Georgette Leblanc, George Antheil, Bernardsville, N.J.

threatened his privacy, the composer, now out of patience, would post a notice on his door sufficiently blunt to deter even the intrepid Antheil: "Mr. Igor Stravinsky is not at home today, this week, this month, this year, or any other year."

Despite such rebuffs, meeting this genius had been the greatest event of George's life, and saying farewell to Stravinsky was a deeply emotional experience. At the Friedrichstrasse Bahnhof, Antheil remembered, the two men wept and embraced, and Stravinsky, after the Russian fashion, kissed him on both cheeks and asked that the time before their next meeting be short. Had it not been for Boski, they might have met again soon, for in Paris, Stravinsky, as promised, notified George that he had arranged a piano recital for him during Christmas week.

The predicament occasioned by the good news was excruciating. An appearance under Stravinsky's "beneficient sponsorship" could have lasting benefits. But how, George wondered, would it affect his career? Would he thereafter be too closely identified with Stravinsky? While he deliberated, the truant Boski unexpectedly reappeared, and in a tractable mood, she agreed to spend her vacation from Berlin University with George, but not in France, where her Hungarian passport was invalid. The choice was agonizing: either Paris and the Stravinsky-arranged recital or Poland (where Boski's passport was valid) and Boski. In the end pulchritude triumphed over performance. A few days before Christmas, the happy couple entrained for Poland, while Stravinsky in Paris vainly waited for his friend's confirmation. George's peccadillo put a strain on their friendship that practically ensured its eventual collapse.

In January 1923, Antheil and Hanson left on the first of two tours to major cities in Germany, Austria, and Hungary. Everywhere George insisted on being billed as a "Futurist-terrible." Everywhere his reputation as the *enfant terrible* of modern music preceded him, for George inundated the cities on his schedule with raucous manifestos proclaiming the inevitable triumph of modernism in the arts. Everywhere curious crowds flocked to see the "Futurist-terrible." What they saw was a young man who looked more like a timid seminarist (he now wore his hair in bangs) than the notorious figure who incited riots wherever he appeared. His boyish appearance combined with a cultivated shyness and a slightly contemptuous manner belied the music that thundered from his piano. Everywhere audiences and critics eschewed thoughtful criticism and lapsed into jeremiads or panegyrics. For his "mass of caricatures" of modern composers, Rudolph Kastner (*Berlin Morgenpost*) consigned the "clownish Antheil" to vaudeville. Correspondent Albert Noelte, in the Philadelphia *Musical Courier*, found his dadaist titles (example: "Mechanisms interrhythmic, cubistic, eliptrocentric, and planetary, psycholliptic, sensurorhythmid") intimidating. In Vienna, where a howling, screaming crowd nearly drowned out his playing, one critic labeled his music the "image of these crazy times." Another swooned over his renditions of Chopin and Debussy, and a third admired his "splendid technique and hurling rhythm." From Munich came uniformly rave reviews: an "excellent pianist with a fluent technique bordering on high grade virtuosity and a most sensitive touch," a "musically gifted" pioneer of "positive ugliness" with a "fine polished technique, completely unapproachable."

In Budapest, where the audience, including Bartok, had come to the theater seeking amusement, George met the Schnitzler family, wealthy and respected burghers, to whom Boski had timidly confessed she was related. "Papa" Schnitzler congratulated George, but Boski's uncle, the renowned playwright Artur Schnitzler, maintained a frosty silence.

From these performances, George returned to Berlin exhausted but bursting with triumph and arrogance. The noisy receptions his "crazy compositions" (Hanson's term) generated everywhere fueled his ambition to be the pathfinder of a new musical line that would influence his generation as deeply as Debussy and Stravinsky had influenced theirs. In a fervor of productivity, he composed a synthetic jazz sonata. Berliners were enthralled. Next came *Sonata Sauvage*, a portrait of Boski Marcus as "a Mongolian-Hungarian amazon riding over an ancient 'pusta' full tilt"; then *Jesus Christ Sonata* (perhaps inspired by delusions of being an anti-Christ; and then *Mechanisms*, in eight movements, which would gestate into *Ballet Mécanique*. In these works, he explained to Mrs. Bok, he had written of things never before expressed. He had gone beyond being an accomplished pianist; he was now a "superpianist." Furthermore, he had nearly realized a second ambition: "to become a great and good composer."

What he eventually admitted to his patron was that he was nearly broke, and that if she did not act (he requested $300), he would be stranded without a penny. After that, a loan of $1,000 or $2,000 might enable him to gain momentum as a "noted and notorious . . . ultramodern pianist-composer." That accomplished, probably within a year, he would be an American success, for with his European reputation, American critics would be afraid to assail him as they had Leo Ornstein. There were other compelling reasons for remaining in Europe, too. Since America was not yet ready for his music, he might wait years before having a work performed there. Were he to return now, it would take two years to earn enough money to pay for his debut, and during that time he would lose the momentum he had built up in Europe. He would be forgotten.

Mrs. Bok cabled $500, and offered another $500 and boat fare to New York if he wanted to return. "Poor sense," she chided, had brought him to the "edge of pennilessness." He could not go on "reaping concert plaudits and appearances ad lib—being indefinitely backed by a woman." She had expected him "to make connections" that would lead to solvency, by teaching and writing if necessary. George made only a few protestations before accepting the $500 gift.

The exchange rate that had made Germany a financial haven had by the early twenties shifted to France, where one dollar bought twenty-five francs. With a three-course meal including wine available for three francs, Paris was packed with Americans eager to enjoy life on slim wallets. Outbreaks of anti-Americanism in Germany had often erupted during George's engagements, and in Berlin there were ugly encounters with tough bullies who prowled the streets on the lookout for foreigners. Also, the city George had called a "perfumed orgy" had turned stale; the grimness, dissipation, and crime were increasingly blatant and sordid. With Boski his problems had also intensified. While physically and mentally they belonged together, spiritually they occupied different worlds. When they were happy, Boski was like an elixir, and George worked like a slave and made "marvelous things." But Boski could be recalcitrant. When he was drawn into political and philosophical arguments with her friends, usually against his will, she would often side against him. Even alone they frequently quarreled. Once after she had denounced his music, sensational concerts, conversation, clothing, even the expensive nightclubs where he took her to make an impression, he had angrily sent her away, certain she would regret the outburst and return. But the "most beautiful and strange creature in the world" did not come back. She nearly succeeded in killing herself with an overdose of morphine. During a painful convalescence, Boski reciprocated his love. In April they decided to go to Paris, where, if they pooled their money, they might live for months. The alternative, remaining in Germany, would certainly reduce them to pauperism.

On the day George selected to enter Paris, June 13, the new Ballets Russe season, featuring two Stravinsky works, *Pulcinella* and *Les Noces*, opened. The new arrivals, strolling along the crowded Boulevard St. Michel—Boski begowned and George swathed in a Savile Row full dress suit and a cape of his own design—looked more like caricatures out of "le high life" than near paupers. *Pulcinella* disappointed Boski, but it infected George with a slow-maturing musical disease—neoclassicism. Both applauded *Les Noces*, a "big, bustling percussion piece" the composer had orchestrated in Berlin the previous year. George condensed Stravinsky's achievement into three words: piano, percussion, machine. "The double pianos are played as percussion instruments—without nuance. Here at last the piano seems to have come into its dignified own. The piano is a machine and at its best when treated as one." Backstage, Stravinsky greeted George warmly and invited him to Pleyel's (the huge piano manufacturer's establishment where Chopin once practiced) the next day to hear the electronic pianola version of *Les Noces*.

Assuming that the composer's friendly manner meant that he held no grudge against him for failing to turn up in Paris for the recital at Christmas, George was astonished when Stravinsky began avoiding him and even refusing to answer his calls and letters. From the American composer Theodore Chanler came this explanation. At a party honoring Stravinsky after the performance, guests had asked him if it was true that he had been so impressed by Antheil and his compositions that he had seen no one else in Berlin. Stravinsky replied that this was untrue and that George had of course exaggerated the amount of time he had spent with him, even suggesting that the composer had extended his visit in order to see more of him. He admired Antheil's playing, but he scarcely knew his compositions. The reply delighted everybody. "Ah, that's just what we suspected," they chorused, "a four flusher." It was "an inexplicable anti-Antheil landslide," Chanler concluded. At a concert a few days later, George and his hero spied each other. Neither spoke, but Stravinsky's steely monocle, George remembered, bore "straight through" him.

Remaining in Paris necessitated a move to cheap quarters, and what George found could hardly have been more spartan: a single room with barely enough space for a piano, even if he had been able to afford one. For the next four years, it would serve as studio and residence, and for the rest of his life, it would be the only place George would call home. Below the miniscule flat at 12 rue de l'Odéon was a bookshop called Shakespeare and Company. The proprietor, Sylvia Beach, a small, self-assured woman, had just finished the prodigious labor of publishing James Joyce's opus *Ulysses*; along with the author, Beach was basking in the post-publication publicity that would make her a celebrity almost as well-known as Joyce and make her bookshop the most famous in the world. Living at 12 rue de l'Odéon, even in a cramped *entresol* and without a piano, promised so many rewards that any personal or professional inconveniences would be insignificant by comparison. There he would be privy to all that was happening in artistic Paris, for Sylvia and her companion-friend Adrienne Monnier, whose bookshop devoted to Franco-American writing was across the street, had made their establishments gathering places for artists from all nations.

The couple standing before her, holding hands, in no way prepared Sylvia for the future. George seemed "a mere kid." He even wore his hair in bangs—a Berliner affectation that photographer Man Ray hustled to capture for posterity and profit. (In Man Ray's portrait, Antheil stares back at the viewer with a look of defiance and truculence sweetly tempered by a hint of puckishness and comic aplomb.) Boski looked even younger and spoke broken English. Two things immediately united George and Sylvia: New Jersey, where both had grown up, Sylvia in the hushed confines of her father's Princeton rectory; and James Joyce, whom Sylvia had seen almost daily during the production of *Ulysses*. That book, in fact, had already figured in George's plans, for, as he revealed to a startled Miss Beach, he intended to ask Joyce for permission to set it to music. It must have occurred to Sylvia that if her new tenant ever realized his ambition, he might someday be as famous as Joyce.

Although moving to the rue de l'Odéon relieved Antheil's financial problems, it did not solve them; unless something was done, he would again face the bleak prospects he had faced in Berlin. The situation demanded action. He again appealed to Mrs. Bok for money, contending that if he was nearly broke, it was only because Hanson had mismanaged the funds she had entrusted to him. Naive and inexperienced, he had not spied out what he labeled Hanson's Machiavellian tactics, until now, when, alas, the money had vanished.

While awaiting Mrs. Bok's reply, he approached Margaret Anderson and Georgette Leblanc, who had finally arrived in Paris in May and had taken a flat in the rue Vaneau. As expected, they offered practical ways to advance his career, but not the money to implement them; they introduced him to Paris's oldest musical potentate Erik Satie and to a "Mephistophelian red-bearded gent" named Ezra Pound. George paid far less attention to Satie than to Pound, who after listening to George expound his musical theories and advancing a few of his own, asked to visit George soon. Was it possible, George wondered, that this "discoverer of genius," who had done so much for Joyce, Eliot, and Wyndham Lewis, might also do things for him? He did not have to wait long for the answer. The next morning George gave his new admirer a private recital. When Pound asked to see his musical writings, George heaped on him all the pronunciamentos, declarations, and jottings he had written for the *Little Review* as well as miscellaneous scribblings—an anthology of unconventional ideas. Incontestably new (for Pound) was his theory that "harmony . . . was a matter of what preceded and what followed." That concept would become the controlling idea of "The Treatise on Harmony," the main essay in a musical miscellany Pound began to assemble almost immediately.

Pound had more on his mind. There was an unfinished opera (*Le Testament*) he had begun in London and had worked on desultorily ever since. George agreed to help him put it into shape. There was also Olga Rudge's emerging career. From Ohio like Natalie Clifford Barney, in whose elegant salon she would soon perform, Miss Rudge had come to Europe at the age of nine. Her concerts in London from 1916 to 1920 had been generally well received, but it was her repertoire of modern violin works by Pizzetti, Respighi, Malipiero, and Lili Boulanger that had charmed Pound. When the poet and his wife, Dorothy Shakespear, moved to Paris in 1921, Miss Rudge had followed.

As Pound saw the situation, Antheil was "full of talent but ridiculed by the public. Everyone was waiting to see 'which way the cat would jump' before committing themselves to his peculiar music so as to receive immediate or future advantage from it." If a joint concert could be arranged in which Antheil performed with Miss Rudge, the "cat" might be made to jump quickly and predictably. Antheil would receive serious consideration. Miss Rudge would perform works by a promising new composer. Had George written anything for violin? No, but he would happily start at once. By mid-autumn he had prepared two violin sonatas, both "as wildly strange as [Miss Rudge] looked, [and] tailored to her special appearance and technique." Pound, delighted with the results, scheduled the premiere performance at the Paris Conservatoire.

Throwing in his lot with Pound was not without risks. It meant acquiescing to a "revolutionary" whose grasp of music at times seemed to George only semi-informed. It also meant collaborating with one who had scarcely taken pains to hide his ulterior motives. For it was apparent that in him, the "unrecognized" American composer-musician, Pound had found a weapon with which to humiliate his enemies. Antheil personified all that Pound believed—and wanted others to accept—was "true" about modern music. Now, certain that the "cat" would jump in a direction he had prearranged, Pound anticipated the rich returns soon to be his to exploit.

The event that catapulted George from near obscurity to sudden notoriety, however, was arranged not by Pound but by Margaret Anderson and Georgette Leblanc. For a film titled *L'Inhumaine*, the director Marcel L'Herbier had invited to the largest theater in Paris, the Théâtre des Champs-Élysées, an audience of "extras," well-known artistic celebrities. In a scene in which Georgette portrayed a temperamental prima donna who had antagonized her public, these extras would create a ruckus that would send her rushing from the stage. It occurred to Margaret and Georgette that this was an ideal opportunity for George to make his Paris debut. An audience so enlightened would doubtlessly be enthusiastic. With the cameras turning, Georgette appeared on stage and sang; as directed, the "illustrious extras" bellowed their resentment. The outraged prima donna stormed into the wings. Next came George. A few bars of the *Airplane Sonata* brought the audience to its feet, howling, whistling, yelling, and acting more riotously than the most unruly crowds in Vienna or Budapest. Eric Satie broke into violent clapping and yelling. Milhaud ("green with envy") tried to stop him, but Satie pushed him aside, exclaiming *"Quel precision! Quel precision! Bravo!"* Jean Cocteau, Man Ray, Francis Picabia, and Picasso applauded loudly. James Joyce, alone in a box, expressed quieter approval, but Ezra Pound and Fernand Léger erupted into boisterous shouts. Margaret and Georgette, delighted with the spectacle, added their acclamations, as did Sylvia Beach and Adrienne Monnier, nearly overcome by their first full exposure to Antheil's music. *Mechanism*, a strident exercise in discord, brought the show to an aural and physical climax. Spectators in the gallery began hurling cushions into the orchestra, and as though on cue, the police suddenly appeared to restore calm.

A beaming, confident Antheil basked in the acclaim the *succès de scandale* had produced. He omitted any mention of the invited extras in the report he sent to Mrs. Bok, saying only that he had "become famous in a night!" He had. It may have been George's understanding that the cameras would be turned off while he played. If so, he could assume that the lively response his performance produced was genuine rather than the required antics of an invited audience. When he later learned (as he claims in his autobiography) that L'Herbier had not stopped filming the au-

The house in Bernardsville

Ezra Pound and George Antheil, Paris, 1924

dience's reactions during his performance, he accused the director as well as his old companions of trickery. From Margaret came denial; neither she nor Georgette was guilty. George, she asserted, had known of the cameras from the start. In view of their past services to him, even to accuse them of such a thing was monstrously ungrateful.

The success of the concert–cum–variety show at the Champs-Élysées, whether contrived or not, was not lost on Ezra Pound. Antheil, he announced, would make another appearance with Olga Rudge at the Paris Conservatoire in December. Meanwhile, Antheil could be seen and heard at a recital that Pound had persuaded Natalie Clifford Barney to sponsor. George commissioned Chester McKee to conduct the *Symphony for Five Instruments,* a strange mixture of jazz and discords, written for flute, trombone, trumpet, bassoon, and viola. The piece made little impression on Miss Barney's undefined musical tastes, although she and her distinguished retinue bore the proceedings with polite self-control. When asked to explain his intentions in the piece, George replied he had tried to express the "rhythm of modern America exactly as it appears to a neurotically sensitive ear"; the combination of jazz and "anarchistically strange chords and discords" formed the basic "idea of the American rhythm." Miss Barney and her friends had neither seen nor heard the last of George Antheil.

As the December performance approached, Pound planted promotional notices in the two Paris-American dailies, the *Herald* and the *Tribune*. His claims for his latest "discovery" combined typical generosity and indiscretion. In the serious vocation of "specializing in men of genius," Antheil interested him more than anyone since Gaudier-Brzeska. Granted, Antheil was extremely young, Pound told a *Herald* reporter, but already he was Stravinsky's "most formidable opponent for the heavyweight built music."

Among the notables attending the Antheil-Rudge recital were the Joyces, Jean Cassou, Fernand Léger, Jean de Gourmont, Marcel Duchamp, and Ford Madox Ford. If they came for surprises, they got them; and one reviewer observed that the denizens of Montparnasse had departed satisfied. The bold or confused laughed, but others struggled to express their feelings: "It was the speech of the free untrammeled spirit." "It was a rebellion against the awful tyranny of tradition." All agreed that Antheil's violin sonatas, performed by Olga Rudge with the composer at the piano, were serious works; but a short composition and arrangement by Pound were presumably beneath critical mention. Pound's only skill, wisecracked one critic, was as a page turner for the two musicians. The *Herald's* Louis Schneider discerned in both sonatas "a kind of fantastic, primitive melopoeia, conceived according to a definite rhythm, which grows exacerbated like those bizarre tambourine accompaniments of Arab or Moroccan musicians when . . . they play to the native ballet dancers." Alongside the sonatas, Schneider ventured, a jazz band would seem melodious. A brief notice in the rival *Tribune* noted that Antheil, by hitting the piano keys with his wrist, palm, and fingers, had succeeded in drawing from the instrument only a few "strange barbaric sounds." The writer had also attributed the composition to Pound, an error that prompted the poet's pithy suggestion that the "perfect critic," when not able to attend a concert, "should always refer to the printed program." From the offending critic, Irving Schwerke, came a tardy review dimissing Miss Rudge's performance with faint praise and ridiculing Pound's efforts to crash Parisian music circles with inane arrangements and compositions. On Antheil, however, he discharged his heaviest salvos. The contriver of a "conceited art," to which Miss Rudge had mistakenly sacrificed herself, Antheil had managed in the violin sonatas to divide listeners into those who classified what they heard into "music pure and absolute" and those who dismissed it as "degenerate noise and crash." The exchange was the opening skirmish in a protracted struggle between Schwerke and a protective Antheil-Pound clique that consistently dismissed the critic's unfavorable reviews as exercises in pique.

The partners closed the year with joint proclamations. Pound announced that his musical miscellany titled *Antheil and the Treatise on Harmony* would soon emerge from Bill Bird's Three Mountains Press and would prove that Antheil was Stravinsky's strongest competitor. From Antheil came notice that he had begun a revolutionary work called *Ballet Mécanique*. Both assured the growing audience of titillated amusement seekers and serious followers that the team of Pound and Antheil would provide more and greater events in the new year.

The only thing George lacked at the start of 1924, besides money, was a piano. For a while he used Pound's, but complaints from the poet's wife ended that arrangement, forcing George to confine his composing again to a clavier. Just as frustrating for George was trying to find a way out of his dismal financial impasse. His instruction of two wealthy young Americans brought in some money, but he resented losing time in teaching. Performing at the Princess de Polignac's soirees or for the select audiences at Paul Poiret's private theater or at the Rosenberg Galleries, he earned little more than the publicity churned out by the press agents who usually organized the programs. Ironically, Hanson, whom George continued to blame for his plight, helped resolve George's financial problems. Conveniently forgetting the charges he had often made against his erstwhile manager, George appealed for help to Hanson, who obligingly informed Mrs. Bok that Antheil was hard up and recommended granting him a monthly allowance of $50 or $100. Mrs. Bok split the difference and put George on a stipend of $75 (later increased to $100) and continued this for the next seven years. George told no one the allowance had been Hanson's idea, and after Mrs. Bok's first check arrived, he again urged her to extract the money that Hanson had misappropriated from tour funds. It was an opportunity to repeat both the boast that on almost no money at all he had "become famous as a pianist and composer" and the promise that henceforth he would try harder to earn a living; if he could not, he would swallow his pride and "do what greater names" than he had done— "to work under financial protection, when it comes, and when it does not come, to work anyhow and take chances."

Antheil's snappish tone doubtlessly sprang from a sense of increased self-importance and pride and a determination to be no longer trifled with or patronized. Hanson's perfidy would eventually be exposed, and the manager would be made to ante up the "missing" money. He felt as much aversion for Stravinsky, another who had betrayed his trust. Now that he had gained support from those who had abandoned the Russian composer, he envisioned himself locked in a contest that would decide who was the "world's greatest composer," Stravinsky or Antheil, lone survivors of countless skirmishes that had eliminated all rivals. "I must win it," he confided to Mrs. Bok. Hyperbole was his chosen weapon. As he privately vilified Stravinsky the man, George publicly extolled Stravinsky the creator. "Stravinsky is the greatest living composer," he wrote in the *Paris Tribune* in February 1924. Unlike Schönberg, whom he considered a fallen rival, Stravinsky was an "undeniable original," the "only pass through the mountains" that cut aspiring composers off from "the music of the future." His genius must be recognized, but it was also necessary to go beyond him and engage in that ceaseless friction with the master's contributions from which the music of the future would emerge. With the gauntlet dropped and the defender warned, George sounded the challenger's battle cry: "Salute to Stravinsky, the next to be hated!"

George's personal contest with Stravinsky dramatized what Ezra

Pound had often said about the importance of Paris. Besides stimulation and challenge, the place abounded with new artistic theories, ideas, and expressions as well as the competition that furnished the impetus for perfection. As a proving ground, George informed Stanley Hart, Paris demanded the best one had. ("Art can only be wooed by the daring, the quick, and the infinitely sincere.") In Paris, he continued, he was composing the most radical music ("so complete and certain") of his life.

But he was also discovering that Paris could be a treacherous place. Charlatans, always ready to attach themselves for profit to genuine creators, were everywhere. Even old friends could not be trusted. Since learning that Georgette Leblanc had begun singing his early songs—an obvious attempt, in his opinion, to capitalize on his rising fame—Antheil revised his once high estimate of the *Little Review* and its editors and supporters. The magazine now seemed nothing more than an extension of Greenwich Village, which he had long considered to be the "greatest fraud on earth." As for the editors, they mistakenly tried to graft onto American life a European culture already lagging a decade behind the times. Artistically, they were "whores," and the *Little Review* had become a shelter for every "poor downtrodden artist" (that is, fakes). That he had once allowed the editors to pamper him was bearable only because he now realized they had always fastened on the oppressed ultramodern artist with the intention of using him to demonstrate their avant-garde tastes. In his revanchist mood, he reduced Margaret, Jane, Georgette, and their supporters to the status of faddists, no better than the bogus artists who inhabited Montparnasse—all of them poor, suffering, complaining, and burning with some particular genius to fulfill. Their efforts revealed only "the infinite capacity to copy the genius of others." The whole lot did not contain a genius. Even those with talent did not know they had it, and the rest could not disguise their cozenage or hide it from themselves. To listen to them haggle and complain like "a lot of aping monkeys, just as though they *were* artists" was abominable.

When Ernest Hemingway, who presumably had escaped consignment to simian obscurity, wrote a jeering remark about Antheil in the *Transatlantic Review*, he bristled. Before the magazine appeared, Hemingway had sent Antheil an offprint of the article, a tribute to Joseph Conrad, and had offered to remove the remark if he found it offensive. "Living in a world of literary politics," Hemingway had written, "where one wrong opinion often proves fatal, one writes carefully. I remember how I was made to feel how easily one might be dropped from the party, and the short period of Coventry that followed my remarking when speaking of George Antheil that I preferred my Stravinsky straight. I have been more careful since." George, Hemingway ventured, would probably not care what he had written, since publicity of any kind was after all publicity. Although more disturbed than he revealed, Antheil said nothing until the article appeared. Then in a burst of spleen, he denied plagiarizing Stravinsky, contending that critics in London had accused him of copying Debussy; in fact, he added sarcastically, his practice was to imitate a different composer everywhere he played. To Miss Beach, who coddled Hemingway as much as she did Antheil, he complained that Hemingway was a very dumb person ("among the dumbest") who had to have something to talk about in order to appear smart. Hemingway's remark amused him at first, and considering the source, he had seen no reason to ask the author to drop it. Now its imbecility outraged him. From Sylvia, he turned to Hemingway, toning down his ire but complaining that the gibe had stirred up old foes like Arthur Moss. Restrained and apologetic, Hemingway recommended that Antheil ignore Moss and remember that plenty of dirt would come to both of them without them doing it to themselves. As for the crack about "Stravinsky straight," he had said it carelessly earlier in the year and had made some listeners angry. He had remembered the occurrence while writing the Conrad article, and the point he wanted to make was that he had been rebuked for making a bon mot about Antheil and Stravinsky, not that Antheil had ever copied Stravinsky.

None of the accusations Moss and the others made bothered Antheil more than being labeled an ultramodernist. Despite having previously exploited the designation for its réclame, he now fulminated tirelessly against it. The term signified a smart, arty performer of new tricks who turned out stylish nonsense. Modernity was more than a lacquer spread over a flimsy structure. One had to feel it. From now on he would simply call himself a composer, but as he explained to Pound, one with an awesome responsibility. "Outside of yourself and myself, there are no composers today. Stravinsky, a great artist like Picasso, has stopped, or at least like Picasso is repeating. . . . I can prove by a sort of supermathematics that your music is the only new center, musically, of the age. It is newer than mine, but I am clever enough to know it." As the first American Pound had ever endorsed (an honor Antheil reiterated in conversation and correspondence), George confidently contemplated a future thick with stunning successes. Meanwhile, the uninitiated would have to be prepared for the compositions of the future.

For a program entitled *Musique Americaine*, dedicated to the signing of the Declaration of Independence, Pound hired a small room in the Salle Pleyel and dispatched invitations to selected friends. There would be no admission fee, for he had discovered that the most propitious way to launch new music was to invite the public but not to permit anyone to pay. The program included his own *Fiddle Music* and *Musique de XV Siecle* (dug up in Perugia) as well as Antheil's *Second Violin Sonata* and the premiere performance of *Quatour à Cordes*. On hand to hear the products of the "two musical conspirators" were Sylvia Beach and Adrienne Monnier; James Joyce, who brought his son, Georgio, in hopes of converting him to modern music; Hemingway and Djuna Barnes; and perhaps making their final appearance at an Antheil concert, Jane Heap and Margaret Anderson. This time critic Irving Schwerke came in person. His comments, predictably irreverent, were in Antheil's case acrimonious. Contrary to the program notes, he found that the four selections were not iconoclastic, revolutionary, or "very rough on tradition." Although rummaging for inspiration in the music of the past was scarcely a new practice, Pound's were the only pleasing compositions. Antheil's contributions demonstrated again his foolish striving to say something "revolutionary" rather than something that might be truly new. The *Second Violin Sonata* reaffirmed his refusal to recognize the piano as a musical instrument. As for the quartet for string instruments (*Quatour à Cordes*), it raised dissonance and scorn for original melody, euphony, emotion, and straight thinking to depressingly new heights.

In July George began composing music for the ballet-in-progress by Fernand Léger called *Ballet Mécanique*. The score, he boasted, would exceed in discordance and tension Stravinsky's *Le Sacre du Printemps*. Then Léger changed his mind and decided to make an abstract film, the objective of which was to provide "percussion in pictures," an illusion achievable by using static objects repeated and reflected in mirrors and special lenses (Léger credited Dudley Murphy and Ezra Pound with the instrument that abetted this process) that would create a moving and separating effect and, like music, a definite rhythm. George's score would be heard simultaneously with the objects Léger amassed for the various sequences—wine bottles, a strawboater, a pendulum, metallic discs, a cockatoo, and still lifes of the model Kiki and of Antheil himself. But practicality proved stronger than invention, and after several unsuccessful attempts to synchronize images and music, Léger abandoned the plan and released the film, without George's music, under the title *Ballet Mécanique*.

As arresting as *Ballet Mécanique* were two other compositions, both as radically diverse as the sources that inspired them. The "banal," a concept derived partly from Stravinsky's *L'Histoire du Soldat*, was the basis of the *First String Quartet*, George explained to Mrs. Bok, to whom he dedicated it. More precisely, what he sought was the representation of the "drunken energy of mediocrity" exemplified in the sounds of a "third-rate string orchestra in Budapest [where George admitted spending very unhappy evenings] trying to harmonize . . . mongrel Hungarian, or would-be Hungarian themes . . . [and] doing it with brilliant success—getting away with it." The other work was called *Cyclops*, which originated from Joyce's suggestion that the "Cyclops" episode in *Ulysses*, with its barroom fight and noisy pursuit into the street, would make an ideal subject for Antheil's talents. It would be a new kind of musical force and quite different from *Le Sacre du Printemps*, George explained, a "dynamic" not an opera at all. The performers, hidden from view, would sing into microphones connected to amplifiers located throughout the auditorium. Joyce would provide a ballet arrangement, which would interpret in pantomime the action of the episodes as they progressed. Considering the difficulty Antheil had had trying to synchronize several pianos for *Ballet Mécanique*, it is not surprising that *Cyclops*, for which he attempted to hook up eleven pianos as well as various mechanical instruments to a twelfth piano that played the master roll, was fraught with insurmountable technical problems.

The promotional publicity Pound and Antheil orchestrated throughout the year reached a climax of mutual congratulation in autumn with the publication of Pound's miscellany, *Antheil and the Treatise on Harmony* (printed by his friend Bill Bird and entirely subsidized by the author) and George's adulatory article on Pound, "Why a Poet Quit the Muses." Both propounded the same premise: Pound and Antheil were teetering on the brink of musical eminence. Ezra Pound, claimed Antheil, had become what he wanted to be all his life: a composer of music unlike any during the last four centuries. Granted, *Le Testament*, which Antheil had orchestrated while Ezra "sang the score and tapped on his desk," had suffered from an annoying technical gawkiness, but it was nonetheless a gaunt, spare work, throbbing with new richness. The poet turned composer was a "gold mine of new technical means," far more accomplished than his contemporaries, for example Stravinsky, who fed off the attainments of the "old masters."

About Antheil, Pound was even more laudatory, although only the Antheil section of his miscellany bore directly on the composer. The mar-

Allen Tanner, Georgette Leblanc, George Antheil, Bernardsville, N.J.

ginalia Antheil supplied (at Pound's request) for the William Atheling segment do little to illuminate Pound's oblique ramblings extrapolated from the fortnightly columns of music criticism Pound wrote for A.R. Orage's *The New Age* from 1917 to 1920. The most original and valuable part, "The Treatise on Harmony," had, Antheil raved, "with one stroke [brushed] away a world of imbecilities carefully cultivated and cherished by impotents since the time of Bach." Rarely, he claimed, had he read such "a clear and simple statement on the theory of harmony."

Although Pound relied on Antheil for most of his material, he succeeded in creating the impression that he was Antheil's equal, if not his better. For Antheil the effect was unfortunate, since he appears in the article as one whose work reflects the author's own purportedly hard-won theories. As a result, Pound seems far more advanced than Antheil and therefore more competent to determine his musical eminence. Pound's conclusions, none too well presented in an essay that suffers from poor organization and multiple redundancies, amount to the following: Antheil, besides rhythmic precision, notes rhythms with an exactitude that "we may as well call genius." Like Stravinsky, he takes "hard bits of rhythm" and notes them "with great care," often inventing new mechanisms, "solid objects," and constructions working in time and space. Both composers write "horizontal music," that is, music with strong lines as opposed to atmospheric music. Antheil makes the piano a percussion instrument, like the xylophone and cymbalo. His use of modern machines, "without bathos" (Pound mistakenly claimed), is without precedent. (Pound overlooked the fact that Satie's ballet *Parade* [1917], which Pound had heard himself in London, employed sirens, a steam engine, an airplane motor, a dynamo, Morse Code apparatus, and typewriters.)

Pound also included a catalogue of critical remarks Antheil had published about other composers, which antagonized many of them and later embarrassed Antheil, as well as a sketchy biography that, considering its hyperbolic inaccuracies, must have been heavily edited by the composer. Antheil, concluded Pound, was "possibly the first American or American-born musician to be taken seriously." A creator of music that could not have been written at an earlier time and an interpreter of his age who did not stoop to rhetoric, Antheil was an original who fashioned a musical world of "steel bars, not of old stone and ivy."

Confused by the author's extravagant claims or by the awkward organization and ponderousness of the book, readers questioned Antheil about what Pound meant. Almost no one pretended to understand the book, but this hardly mattered. What really counted, Antheil asserted, was that the "most intelligent" defense of him ever to appear had finally been written. Nothing, as Pound himself had said, could be as harmful as obscurity, and such a compilation of "very high aesthetics," whether comprehensible or not, could scarcely be ignored. Antheil's name was now linked to Pound's forever. But a year after the book appeared, Antheil wished that Pound had never written it. Its profuse praise of George and vicious criticism of other composers sowed an "active distaste" for the name *Antheil*.

The longer George stayed abroad the more ambivalent his views of America became. He excoriated America for faults ranging from a paucity of well-stocked libraries to an abundance of speakeasies. In statements that echoed Harold Stearns, George declared that he too was no longer proud to be an American. The country was uncivilized. Its art was in the "baby-garde." Only fools believed in "an all-American art." No one could make an art by himself. Yet, paradoxically, the future of the arts, certainly of music, was in America. It was not a lack of technical virtuosos that impeded the country's musical progress. Institutions like the American Academy in Rome and Mrs. Bok's newly founded Curtis Institute of Music trained such virtuosos. Nor would America ever lack superior symphonic orchestras conducted and heavily staffed by Euopeans. His wealthy countrymen would go on supporting staid musical institutions— schools, orchestras, and a few opera houses and concert halls—all of them devoted to the music of European masters. The future of music in America was threatened by the very institutions of which the country was proudest. Proficiently and perfunctorily these institutions perpetuated the past and they would never produce what the nation needed most: a great native composer. In July George broke a six-month silence with Mrs. Bok to open a campaign that he hoped would address this national deficiency.

In the hail of letters that he loosed on Mrs. Bok, (four letters in as many days), George asserted that America had only one significant composer, George Antheil. Except for the non-Americans Schönberg and Stravinsky, George claimed to be "the most broadly and seriously reviewed composer . . . of all countries." No American composer could make this claim, and no one could produce reviews like his. Also, he was the only American ever "discovered" by that "discoverer of genius," Ezra Pound. Finally, George broached the delicate matter of financial support. The embarrassing fact was that for nearly two years, Europeans had voluntarily supported him. He named Lady Ellerman, Hans von Wedderkop (Paris representative of *Der Querschnitt*), and Natalie Clifford Barney (George ignored the fact that she had grown up in Cincinnati). Another, the Duchesse de Clermont-Tonnerre, had paid out 10,000 francs for the *Ballet Mécanique* piano rolls. Lest mentioning European patronage might make him appear ungrateful for Mrs. Bok's help, he acknowledged that her allowance adequately covered living expenses (1,400 francs a month) but that little remained for music. Finally, in a conclusion that combined praise and a direct challenge, he congratulated Mrs. Bok on recognizing and acting on her great responsibility to the arts. ("You have the finest orchestra in the world and now the finest music school.") Although these were important, the time had come for her to seek a third triumph: the sponsorship of "one of the most promising composers in the world," who was already writing "America's music" and doing it without waving the flag. Beside such an opportunity, the Philadelphia Orchestra and the Curtis School of Music might someday seem unimportant.

Scant hours after finishing the first letter, George, brimming with afterthoughts, composed a second. This time his point was that Mrs. Bok should show the same courage and intelligence that had distinguished princesses and princes of the past who supported those artists whose work promised to benefit mankind. "I am asking for cooperation in the benefiting of humanity. . . . I am only just now collecting my forces. Here I am . . . an American problem. What is to be done about it?"

On the third day George screwed up enough courage to answer the question himself. To impress on Mrs. Bok the difficulty of living in Paris on 1,400 francs a month, he cited the case of Berenice Abbott, who barely survived on the 1,000 francs she earned as Man Ray's apprentice. If Mrs. Bok believed that backing him was at least as important as sending the Philadelphia Orchestra to Europe (in his opinion just another futile display of American wealth), then she would have to be prepared to pay (George estimated $5,600) to have all his scores copied as well as for another European tour. He closed with an either/or ultimatum reminiscent of his childhood demand for a big piano: "Either something must be done, or nothing must be done: there is no middle course."

George's final letter on July 9 brought to nearly thirty the number of pages posted to Mrs. Bok. Its theme was Penrodian (Penrod was, of course, Booth Tarkington's "all-American" hero). Since he had been in every way "a typical American fellow, normal in every last respect, except in [his] passion for music," it followed that no one was better fitted to express the essence of America. As long as the country lacked a great composer, it was like a bell without a clapper. Only he could activate the "silent" bell. "America has one solitary, single chance . . . to have a composer. I believe, honestly, that this composer is myself."

Mrs. Bok's reply reached Paris in August. It contained welcome news. She would determine whether or not he was "a great talent" when she heard his music. Meanwhile, she would send $1,000 for copying, a gratuity George called "very fair" and one he requested she send directly to Sylvia Beach, who would be in Paris in August. At that time he, in all probability, would be taking his annual vacation in Tunis and Sidi-bou-Said, places he favored for their cheap accommodations, romantic ruins, wild Arabic music, and, best of all, the torrid heat that baked the cold of Paris out of his bones. Preparations for this third trip were more elaborate than usual, and they included drawing Sylvia Beach into a zany publicity stunt that George had dreamed up to help launch the composition he had written for Léger's film *Ballet Mécanique*. In July technicians at Pleyel's had cut three pianola rolls for the *Ballet*, which would be played in a single player piano to which an unspecified number of player pianos would be attached and synchronized. Hearing the rolls for the first time on his birthday, July 8, George could hardly contain himself. Here at last was the "real germ of revolution," he shouted to friends gathered for the event. "Here is the beginning of space and time in music." He sent word to Mrs. Bok that soon she too would hear the "sincerest expression of America" ever to come out of the country—"the rhythm of machinery, presented beautifully."

To make sure that the premiere of so revolutionary a work made the largest possible impression, particularly on American conductors, the right amount of "sauce," as George put it, would have to be added. Why, after all, should he undersell something so sensational when with a little publicity it might fetch as much as $10,000? The "sauce" George concocted to launch *Ballet Mécanique* consisted of two components: first, he would not appear at the premiere, a private affair at Pleyel's that he had inveigled Natalie Barney to underwrite; second, it would be reported, immediately after the concert, that he was "lost" in Africa. Sylvia's assignment was to circulate the news of his disappearance. To a second accomplice, an accommodating *Tribune* reporter named Bravig Imbs, George entrusted a more difficult task. Imbs would plant the story in the *Tribune* and add that the composer was in danger of losing his life. To make sure the report had the proper verisimilitude, George promised to supply Imbs with photographs and letters from places along his route, from which he could manufacture whatever he needed.

One day in mid-August, George, as planned, vanished from the Quarter. With him was a dance student called Olga who, on learning that Boski preferred a mineral cure in the south of France to the heat and sand in Africa, had agreed to accompany George as far as Tunis. A week later a postcard from Marseilles reached Sylvia, bearing a single line: "Good-bye for just a little while." Once in Africa the messages and their length increased and told of restored health, excursions among the ruins, concerts of strange primitive music, and other exotic pleasures. Of urgent importance, but not for Imbs's use, was the news that after three years he and Boski had decided to marry.

Meanwhile, Imbs informed Pleyel's that Antheil would not attend the premiere, a truancy that surprised the Joyces, Hemingways, Miss Barney, Elliot Paul, Jacques Benoist-Méchin, and the other invited guests who crowded into one of the smaller salons on September 16 to hear what was, in fact, an incomplete performance of the composer's revolutionary work. Missing were both drums and propellers. One section reminded Joyce of Mozart. Janet Flanner wrote that it sounded like three people doing different things at once—"one pounding an old boiler, one grinding a model 1890 coffee grinder, and one blowing the usual seven o'clock factory whistle and ringing the bell that starts the New York Fire Department going in the morning." It was "good but awful," she concluded. Clarence Lucas (*Musical Courier*) confessed that he had heard only "clashes and unrelated notes" and nerve-racking rhythms. Surfeited after five minutes of such "chromatic harmonies," he could only offer something unoriginal, such as "the composer is now ready for the madhouse." Sylvia Beach and Adrienne Monnier, who had overheard parts of the *Ballet*, glowed with pride and pleasure. Irving Schwerke surprised everyone by holding his tongue, but Benoist-Méchin, who knew the *Ballet* almost as well as George, wrote an ecstatic review for *La Revue European*.

Soon after the performance, Imbs, by now in possession of a dozen colorful messages from Africa, composed the "report" of Antheil's disappearance and slipped it past an innocent copy editor. Under the headline "Friends of Composer Antheil Fear He Is Lost in African Desert," unsuspecting readers discovered that Antheil had last been seen with an Arab guide heading toward Senoussi country and Central Africa, presumably hunting down the rudiments of the Arabian music played in the bazaars of Tunis. That quest, Imbs reported, had taken Antheil to Gafsa

Mary Louise Curtis Bok (Zimbalist)

and on to Gabes, without the assistance of his guide, and then south into the hinterland, where (in Antheil's words) the "real stuff is" and where "the music is absolutely all sticks and as angular as the knockkneed Negroes." Following four days of silence, Antheil's last communique arrived: he had come to an "awfully hot" place "further south." If Antheil was trying to reach the Congo by going south from Gabes, Imbs speculated, it was "a very foolhardy proceeding, especially for a lone man," since part of the desert he would have to cross was "one of the worst in Africa" and had been crossed with success only once, and then only "by a well-equipped and well-armed caravan."

As George had hoped, rival newsmen besieged Imbs and Sylvia for more information about the "missing man." The *Paris Herald* reporter added the lurid touch that the "district through which Antheil started [was believed] to be infested by the wildest and most fanatical tribes of the Senoussi Federation." The English dailies, the *Morning Post* and the *Daily Mail*, widely circulated throughout Europe, carried toned-down versions of the story, but several American newspapers reported that Antheil was not only lost but probably dead. In Trenton, a shocked Wilhelmina and Henry telegraphed Sylvia pleading for information. Back came the consoling news that Antheil was all right and that the escapade was only a "publicity story," which they must keep "absolutely secret." Maintaining the appearance of distress rapidly became a burden, however, and both Sylvia and Imbs agreed that the "little wave of excitement" they had created for their friend would have to end.

What his two accomplices were doing in Paris while he languished in Africa George did not know. But several weeks of basking in the Tunisian sun, even with the voluptuous Olga, made him restless to see Europe and Boski again. One warm afternoon they sailed to Djerba, reputedly the island of the lotus-eaters, and catching the spirit of the legendary hedonists, Olga advised George to marry Boski *at once* and then to ignore the vows so that they could always remain "true lovers." George, delighted with a proposal so "eminently reasonable," promptly wired Boski to meet him in Marseilles, where a few days later, in a performance of amorous acrobatics certain to leave a lasting impression on the jaded hoteliers of that seaport city, he put Olga on a Paris-bound train just one hour before Boski arrived at the same terminal. Together they returned to the hotel where Olga and he had spent the previous night.

From Marseilles the betrothed couple traveled to Trieste, where George, by now desperate for news from Paris, sent Sylvia a two-word telegram:

"Awaiting instructions." Remaining out of sight until Imbs contrived a way to "find" him was harder than getting "lost," and when another week passed without a word from Paris, George informed Sylvia that he had come out of hiding and that he and Boski were going incognito to Budapest to be married. Imbs, too, was finding that "rescuing" George was more difficult than making him disappear. When he finally reported that George had been found by the Foreign Legion, a suspicious editor quashed the story. Had it not been for a drastically condensed version of Imbs's report that Antheil smuggled into the *Paris Times*, he might have had to use the "wild but plausible" invention—he had been held captive by fanatical tribes—he was prepared to tell the press in the event of sudden discovery. Imbs had barely enough time to enjoy his role in the hoax before his boss, more irritated than amused, dismissed him.

After an on-and-off courtship of three years, George and Boski were married on October 4. What effect his marriage might have on Mrs. Bok— and on his allowance—was something Antheil immediately tried to control. It was not an intemperate act, he assured her. On the contrary, marrying Boski would reduce expenses, for besides being a spiritual force that motivated him to work "so tirelessly to make something" of himself, she was an indispensable helpmate who arranged concerts, wrote criticism, and ran hundreds of errands. For example, she had remained behind in Budapest to obtain a Hungarian marriage certificate while George, eager to return to the scene of his triumph now that he had been "rescued" from oblivion, sped back to Paris.

On New Year's Day 1925, Antheil performed his *First String Quartet* at Miss Barney's salon. Few other composers had ever enjoyed a second appearance in such a sacrosanct surrounding; only one other, Virgil Thomson, ever performed for Natalie and her guests. Antheil, like Thomson, made the most of the opportunity. Natalie Barney's interest in modern music was always secondary to her passion for literature, a preference that explains her support of one but rarely of the other. Among the fashionable and titled guests were three who were prepared to emulate, if not exceed, their host's hospitality. One, Elisabeth de Gramont, Duchesse de Clermont-Tonnerre, a talented, strong-willed woman who alone wore a hat indoors at Natalie's, engaged the composer to repeat his program at her residence the following week for a fee of 1,500 francs. A second admirer, not to be outdone, invited Antheil to play the next month at her salon where Ravel, Schönberg, and Bartok had all performed. A third guest outclassed both by commissioning Antheil to complete his second symphony.

With the new year also came encouragement from old and new friends. George Antheil is "a genius," Adrienne Monnier announced in *Le Navire d'Argent*, a review of her own making designed to keep the French informed of developments in American art. Benoist-Méchin informed readers of the *Revue European* that *"il est un fait certain, c'est qu'Antheil est un grand musicien."* And from Nadia Boulanger, the much venerated teacher with whom several promising American composers were studying, came the surprising admission that he was incontestably "a great composer." Although the handicap of his being an American composer in Paris was often used by George to explain hostile reviews as well as the coolness of the French toward his work, he had gradually begun to meet his French counterparts, notably Darius Mihaud and Vladimir Golschmann, the brilliant young head of an outstanding concert organization, whose conducting of Stravinsky's music George greatly admired. Golschmann, in George's opinion, had the temperament and understanding to conduct his nearly finished second symphony (*Symphony in F*), but persuading Golschmann to read and then direct it would require more than diplomacy. George's solution—a sumptuous dinner at Fouquet's, the smartest and most expensive café on the Champs-Élysées—was a gastronomic extravagance neither ever forgot. All went as planned until the bill arrived and George reached for his wallet. He had forgotten to bring it. Tremblingly, he confessed to his guest. Golschmann, to George's immense relief, burst into laughter, paid the bill, and asked to see the score of the unfinished symphony.

With Golschmann's services virtually assured, George stepped up his campaign for renewed funding from Mrs. Bok. He had decided to increase the amount he had already requested to $5,000 and to ask for $2,000 as soon as possible, or barring that, $1,000 immediately. How he would use the money to make a "gigantic impression," first in Europe and later in America, he explained in a second barrage of meticulously detailed letters. Of overriding importance was a prompt performance of *Ballet Mécanique*, for it had come to his notice that Stravinsky had obtained duplicates of his pianola rolls and had announced that his next work would be for "more pianos." Since receiving such a large sum of money was contingent upon satisfying Mrs. Bok's musical tastes and demands, George suffered another agonizing crisis of uncertainty. To prevent her from dismissing his music as "sheer madness," he drew up a nine-page document, whimsically titled "Many Thoughts for M.L.B. and a Key to My Music to Be Remembered While Listening to It." This, although intended to enlarge her understanding of his work, came nearer to being an apologia than a useful explanation. Again he invoked the names of his defenders, Ezra Pound and Richard Aldington, although he knew that both had previously irritated Mrs. Bok. Pound, she had once warned George, praised too much and too indiscreetly; Aldington, in her opinion, was a cheap critic and should be avoided. In defense of his "new music" George cited the antecedents of Beethoven, Debussy, and Stravinsky, composers whose original musical "forms" had once made a sensation.

By March, with still no news from his patron, George began showing signs of paranoia. Worried that Mrs. Bok might have found his instructional document patronizing, he requested that she disregard everything he had written and wait until she had heard his almost completed *Symphony in F* before making a final decision. In construction, influence, and intention, the new symphony was the opposite of *Ballet Mécanique*, even though one, as George said, could not have been written without the other. As neoclassic as Stravinsky's *Piano Concerto*, this symphony would be the first, and fatal, indication that George had followed his mentor more closely than many realized and that the *Ballet* was really the climax and his final experiment in "mechanical music." At the time, however, he was convinced that this somber, tender, and pitiless work would impress "modern and traditional" audiences, including Mrs. Bok.

Money from Philadelphia always acted on George like a whirlwind. Without having heard a single note of his music, Mrs. Bok sent $2,500. It was a gift deserving of a benediction. "To you, kindest of people and most gracious," intoned George, "may God bless you and make your life happy daily. May music bless you, which you love, and I love also, with all my soul." Every penny, he vowed, would go into publishing, copying, and performing his music. Already, thanks to her earlier payment, he had begun having his scores copied (copyists, baffled by the seemingly erratic music, frequently repaired what they assumed were obvious errors, thus forcing George to correct their corrections), and with the latest stipend, he would do the same with both *Symphony in F* and the piano concerto.

What the African hoax had failed to win for *Ballet Mécanique*—the few offers for the work fell dismally short of Antheil's expectations—perhaps a lavishly publicized performance could accomplish. With enough money to cover concert expenses, including a small guarantee, Antheil's dreams became his guide. He reserved the largest (2,500 seats), most magnificent, most chic theater in Paris, the Théâtre des Champs-Élysées, where three years before he had made his controversial debut. To conduct, he hired Vladimir Golschmann, who in turn hired eighty-five musicians. The only serious problem was a score that called for sixteen mechanical pianos, all to be operated by cables attached to a master keyboard. It is doubtful if that many pianos existed in all of France, and even if they did, bringing them together on one stage would have been a daunting task. Antheil assembled eight grand pianos, engaged eight players, and wired up an amplifier to the master piano he would operate. As for the nonmusical instruments the score required, local hardware stores supplied saws, hammers, and electric bells; and from a flea market came two airplane propellers that would help bring the *Ballet* to a noisy and windy climax.

The announcement of the concert Sylvia Beach posted at Shakespeare and Company spread over the entire side of the lending library, covering all books from M to Z. Local papers reported that two of Antheil's works would be performed for the first time and reminded readers that his music had created riots all over Europe. Elliot Paul advised concertgoers to carry umbrellas, presumably as a protection against flying objects. A few days before the event Ezra Pound arrived from Italy and began rounding up friends who, under his command, would pack the galleries. George rejoiced that all Montparnasse seemed to be behind him.

On June 19, ticket holders were barely able to penetrate the thick crowds of latecomers unable to get inside the Théâtre des Champs-Élysées. All 2,500 seats had been sold. Sylvia Beach and Adrienne Monnier, detained by the throng, watched an elegantly dressed couple step from a limousine and join the crowd. The woman looked like a character in a Henry James novel; the man, tall and handsome, wore a top hat. A whisper of names produced positive identification: the woman was the Princess de Bassiano; her escort, who drew more attention, was T.S. Eliot. Inside, comfortably lodged, sat James and Nora Joyce, flanked by their children, Natalie Barney and her entourage, Sergei Diaghilev, Constantin Brancusi, Serge Koussevitzky, and Antheil's concierge, Madame Tisserand, who had vacated her post for the first time in forty years. Attired in a black silk dress, her face powdered a snowy white (it was flour, she later told George), looking very majestic and distinguished, she sat smiling next to the Duchesse de Clermont-Tonnerre. Up in the top gallery clumped Ezra Pound and his band of well-primed cohorts.

Golschmann and Antheil had arranged the program so that each piece would provide a distinct step in a sequence of ascending tempo, rhythm, and complexity. After Weber's *Freischutz Overture*, came the familiar *Concerto Grosso* of Handel; then, after intermission, the two Antheil compositions—*Symphony in F* and *Ballet Mécanique*—followed. For two-thirds of the concert, the audience listened patiently and politely. *Symphony in F* reassured conservatives that the composer's bark was much worse than his bite. Only Pound's gallery mates uttered a few growls. By the time the pianists had seated themselves at the grand pianos positioned in midstage, the audience was ready for excitement. The hubbub subsided when George appeared and installed himself at the mechanical piano from which he would control a collection of fans, propellers, xylophones, and other pieces of sonorous hardware. Suddenly, tremblingly, the opening thunderclap of sound exploded—a terrific boom of percussion—followed by a tangle of jagged discordant rhythms. Since many in attendance fully expected to be deafened by the tremendous reaches of sound, the noisiest parts were the most popular. Whenever the dynamics dipped to mezzo forte and the principal interest switched to rhythm, the crowd whistled, clapped, and stamped their feet. Halfway through the piece, the audience broke into opposing camps. One, leaderless, feared that its aural sense was about to be permanently impaired; the other, organized, trained, and commanded by Ezra Pound, answered every shriek of complaint, every hiss, boo, hoot, and catcall with resounding cheers, wild applause, gibes and taunts; and from Ezra poured "awful French words." "Get out if you don't like it," shouted an agitated Antheil supporter, and according to Elliot Paul the suggestion met with some favor. Meanwhile, the *Ballet* rolled on, although determining which sounds were emanating from the musicians and which from the audience was impossible. Fights erupted in the orchestra; the combatants jumped to their feet, removed their coats, and spilled into the aisles. Pound, roused to action, made a rapid although ungracious descent from gallery to gallery, stepping on hands and heads en route, landing in the midst of the fracas, uttering the "simple language of resentment," and shouting in a mixed French and American accent, "Silence, imbeciles!" Anything else he said was inaudible, for once started, *Ballet Mécanique*, like a runaway Chaplinesque machine, could not be stopped. Golschmann signaled to activate the propellers. A great whirring noise filled the theater. Up went coat collars and umbrellas. William L. Shirer and Stuart Gilbert (reliable men not known to indulge in fantasy) watched with alarm as the violent currents of wind lifted a periwig off the head of a portly man in the front row and deposited it, gently and undamaged, at the rear of the theater. Here was music one could feel as well as hear. Then suddenly it ended, as shudderingly as it had begun. Applause drowned out the lingering traces of opposition and continued long and loud enough to summon Antheil back to the stage for numerous bows. "The combatants filed out peacefully," reported Elliot Paul. The "atmosphere about the theater" had been "most welcome for the art of music. Everyone knew they had been somewhere."

While few would ever forget where they had been, many neither comprehended nor enjoyed what they had heard. Antheil's "noisemaking," Shirer confessed, did not fit his conception of music. Although disappointed with the concert, Harry Crosby congratulated Antheil on the verve of his performance. Elliot Paul complained that, because of the lack of proper instruments, the *Ballet* had not been well presented, although enough of it had come through "to give an idea of its contents and spirit." For Sylvia Beach the performance possessed the powers of strong drink: it "simply picks you up and drops you down with a bang." Of the reactions from serious students of Antheil's music, Benoist-Méchin's were the most disturbing: Certainly *Symphony in F* did not lack intelligence; it was a splendid work but not an "important piece of creation." While he approved of the atmosphere and the *"éclairage"* of the whole thing, he liked less the elements built into it. The problem was both simple and complicated: *Symphony in F* was a neoclassic composition, a mode which Benoist-Méchin did not prefer but to which he admitted being sometimes drawn. Despite a poor performance, which had given a false view of the composer's personality, the *Ballet* remained, in his opinion, Antheil's most advanced work.

With the afterglow of triumph still bright, George reported to Mrs. Bok that he had given the most successful and profitable concert of his life. This time he had. He challenged her to name another composer who had attracted 2,500 people to hear "a new unproved modern thing." Two months earlier the same theater had been only half full for a Satie memorial festival. And on the evening following his triumph, a performance of the latest Stravinsky composition had failed to fill the much smaller Salle Gaveau. Of course after so sensational a concert there had been more than the usual realignment of supporters and detractors. The former now urged him to remain abroad for the rest of the year so as to increase his chances of taking up the "leadership of modern music" where Stravinsky had left off. Their recommendation made sense for, after all, at twenty-five George was

George Antheil, Paris, mid-Twenties

George and Boski Antheil, wedding photo

too young to be classified as "arrived" or "accepted." Then, too, additional European concerts would doubtlessly strengthen the impression he would eventually make in America. The prospect of returning home famous was now an almost certain reality.

With so much accomplished and with so many projects planned (Pleyel's was to record his works and several publishing firms would print his music; in addition, he had made arrangements to give more chamber music concerts as well as another performance of *Ballet Mécanique*— "entirely his own"—during the summer), George unabashedly renewed his petition to Mrs. Bok for more money. Another grant of $3,000 would cover guarantees for two orchestral concerts in the fall, and since both would "unquestionably" pay for themselves, he would use the $3,000 refunded to him for a European tour. If she doubted his ability to make large sums produce results, he reminded her that with the $2,500 she had given him, he had accomplished what he had intended to do with a sum twice that size. "I managed to do everything I promised for $6,000 on $2,500." Just one more installment would make him, by autumn, "the most prominent young musician in Europe." The "MOMENT HAS COME TO STRIKE AND STRIKE HARD. Will you still be with me?" Mrs. Bok would wait a month before replying to that question.

Before returning to Rapallo, Ezra Pound arranged for a performance of his opera *Le Testament*, which he and George had finally finished after working intermittently on it for over a year. At the Salle Pleyel, before a stylish audience that included many who had attended George's concert two weeks before, Ezra (at the drums), George (at the piano), Olga Rudge (at the violin), and a few other musicians (one of whom played a five-foot *corne*, an animal's horn on which he could blow only two notes) accompanied a group of singers in a performance that Virgil Thomson described as "not quite a musician's music" but perhaps the "finest poet's music since Thomas Campion."

A few weeks before the June 19 concert, George had accepted an invitation to participate in a special program devoted to new work by Nadia Boulanger's American pupil-composers Virgil Thomson, Herbert Elwell, Aaron Copland, Walter Piston, and Theodore Chanler. For the first and only time, George joined his countrymen in a concert of American music, a misnomer, according to reviewer Schwerke, who complained that what he had suffered through was a parade of immaturities so lacking in American qualities that it might better have been called a "concert of music by American composers." Thomson retorted that all the selections represented the "newest in American talent" as well as the latest Parisian fads; that is, all "applied old-master layouts to contemporary melodic inspirations and harmonic concepts." Having endured a concert he dismissed as a "chaos of incredibilities," devoid of "genuine experimentation in design, decoration, sonority, or the subtle things of spirit that distinguish the musician-composer from the composer who is not a musician," Schwerke surprisingly eked out a few words of praise for Antheil's contribution. "One may not have liked what Mr. Antheil says in his quartet, but he certainly knows how to say what he wants. There was apparent in this music a gratifying technical mastery of means, some harmonic passages full of flushed and melting color." George, flabbergasted and delighted, sent the review to Mrs. Bok and informed her that Schwerke had been "systematically" against him for three years and that this was "the *worst* not the *best* criticism" of George's new string quartet.

The friendship that blossomed between the Harvard-educated, Boulanger-trained composer Virgil Thomson and the academic dropout from south Trenton was the "chief event" of Thomson's first winter in Paris. "For the first time in history," he told a friend, "another musician liked my music . . . and said 'hello.' Somebody recognized what I was all about. . . . Imagine my gratitude." That welcome recognition, moreover, came from the man Thomson considered the "first composer of our generation (of this there isn't any doubt) and was supported by deeds." The admiration was mutual. George proclaimed Thomson the "most talented" American composer in Paris, venturesome, innovative, and almost "Satie-like in [his] complete cut away from the prevailing Debussy-Ravel plus early Stravinsky mode of the day."

Both men shared an interest in the arts allied to music. They often read the same books and "discussed them in relation to the progress of musical art." George showed Virgil the plans Joyce and he had drawn up for *Cyclops* and explained how he had developed a "technique of setting words to music, off-accent to the normal procedure." To illustrate the idea he composed two little songs set to poems from *Alice in Wonderland*. Virgil found them enchanting, and years afterward George intimated that they might have been the genesis of Thomson's operatic work. Stravinsky, they agreed, had entered a seemingly permanent neoclassic period. Whereas at one time new Stravinsky compositions had been entirely novel "revolutions," they now seemed repetitive. Virgil's pungent summation of the situation thrilled George: "From this point onwards, Stravinsky will continue to give a great many people pleasure." If by that he meant the Russian composer had ceased being a revolutionary and that he had achieved "his ultimate ambition or direction," then overtaking the master, George surmised, would be all the easier.

With George, Thomson "talked, walked, and drank by the hour." From time to time, George even lodged, fed, and gave him money. When George urged him to stop writing critical articles for *Vanity Fair* and devote all his time to composing, Thomson concurred. And when Gertrude Stein invited George to the rue Fleurus (she had heard about him from Sylvia Beach), George, perhaps certain that his friend would provide some intellectual ballast, asked Virgil to accompany him. The rewarding consequences of Thomson's meeting with Miss Stein are well documented. It was not George, but Virgil, whom Gertrude asked back to her salon. George, by revealing that he had thrown in his lot with her adversary James Joyce, had inadvertently barred himself permanently from the company of Miss Stein and her friends.

The most pressing common concern George and Virgil shared, however, was the practical necessity of getting their music performed as often as possible. Shortly after the Boulanger musicale, Virgil met Mrs. Virginia Gross, the wife of the First Secretary of the American Embassy, a woman of wealth (a Crocker of the California banking family), charm, breeding, and intelligence, who longed for the one thing that would make her life in Paris complete: admission to international society. Once Virgil and George understood that Virginia Gross would support almost any scheme that promised to open to her the portals of the more exclusive Paris salons, they promptly organized a series of concerts in her palatial flat on the Champ-de-Mars, close by the Eiffel Tower. The music would be entirely their own. There would be four concerts, all scheduled in July immediately following Grand Prix week, and the guests, they assured her, would include prominent Parisians as well as every title-holder they had ever met. George hired Vladimir Golschmann to conduct and rounded up supporting musicians. Virgil sent invitations to all the acceptable writers, artists, and composers still in Paris in midsummer. Together they consulted William Bullitt, former ambassador to the U.S.S.R., on how best to solicit the attendance of diplomats. Finally, they sat down and drew up a program.

Each afternoon began with tea and ended with champagne and a sumptuous buffet served by white-gloved butlers. All five of Mrs. Gross's salons had to be opened wide to accommodate several hundred distinguished guests as well as Golschmann and the musicians with their instruments.

Except for Pound's *Quatre Chansons du "Testament,"* the programs, as announced, all featured the compositions of Antheil and Thomson. Among these pieces were Thomson's *Five Phrases from the Song of Solomon*, scored for a soprano and a versatile percussionist who played the cymbals, a tom-tom, a gong, and a wood block; Thomson's bewildering *Sonata da Chiesa*, this one scored for trombone, horn, violin, trumpet, and clarinet; and Antheil's *Symphony for Five Instruments* and his seldom performed *Piano Fugue, 1913*. To experience the pièce de résistance—*Ballet Mécanique*—more than the usual complement of guests squeezed into the jammed confines of Mrs. Gross's flat. With eight grand pianos filling the entire living room and xylophones and percussion instruments spread out in an adjacent room and on the staircase, Golschmann was forced to conduct standing on the centermost piano. Guests recoiled from the crashing opening chord, some appearing to fall over from the gigantic concussion. Others writhed as they absorbed the pounding of the strange synchronization issuing from neighboring instruments. With the restoration of silence, shaken and thirsty spectators rushed for refreshments and champagne. After overindulging, they released their pent-up energies in some acrobatic exercises of their own. According to Antheil, when he and Thomson last saw their hostess that day "she was being thrown up and down in a blanket by two princesses, a duchess, and three Italian marchesas." With her entry into fashionable circles presumably a fait accompli, a grateful Mrs. Gross bestowed bonuses of $500 on each composer-impresario.

Months of intense activity brought an exhausted George to the midpoint of the year. As he would write in his book, *Bad Boy of Music* (New York, Doubleday, Duran & Co., Inc., 1945), he had attained all the fame he was ever to have in Paris. In the summer he traveled alone to Tunis, and as usual the place proved restorative. But back in Paris he fell ill, this time seriously. For six months he battled pneumonia. The enforced inactivity, after so much industry, was hard to bear, partly because the collapse might have been avoided. The first half of the year with its "too abundant music, writing, its countless sleepless nights, its bewildering kaleidoscope of friends and acquaintances, each one to be properly estimated, cultivated, or discounted; its concerts, musicales, salons, dinners, manipulation of incessant musical politics, its complete Machiavellianism" had drained all his reserves, and he had allowed it to happen. Resuming work on the still-unfinished piano concerto wore him out. Regaining the lost momentum seemed beyond his power. When doctors recommended a

long vacation from the damp climes of Paris, Golschmann suggested
Chamonix as an ideal place to rest, regain his health, and finish the concerto. Sylvia assured him and Boski that all would be the same at 12 rue de
l'Odéon when they returned. With the decision to leave Paris practically a
certainty, a communique from Mrs. Bok in response to his petition for
additional funds virtually decreed it. Instead of the $3,000 he had asked
for, Mrs. Bok had sent $5,000. George delayed his departure no longer.
Golschmann agreed to make final arrangements for the October concert;
George surmised the conductor enjoyed this opportunity, for without him
Vladimir could "take his own tempi."

The Antheils sojourned first in Tunis. George's health steadily improved, but he lost a battle in his campaign to usurp Stravinsky's leadership. Perhaps it was a premonition that Parisians would not like *Symphony in F* any more the second time than they had the first that made him
decide to remain away and enjoy the beauty of Chamonix, where he and
Boski settled in mid-October. Being away from Paris at least spared him
what would have been an uncomfortable evening. The symphony, which
he called cubistic, neoclassic, of enormous line, as much a gigantic work as
Ballet Mécanique, and deeply indebted to his new "hero" Beethoven,
drew only a lukewarm response from an audience that expected "new
contortions of the old classic sounds" instead of a composition preoccupied with "style, chic, pretty new sound, quick musical wit, everything
but new expression of form, of greater abstract meaning of music." The
rebuff was the first sign that Antheil's popularity might be waning. Elliot
Paul's predictably enthusiastic review provided some comfort, but if he
and other reporters had been well paid for their kind words, as Thomson
later revealed, it could be no real solace. It is possible Paul did not even
attend the concert, since he wrote that Antheil acknowledged the applause
of "an appreciative" audience by repeatedly risingg and bowingg. Nearly as
inventive as this phantom composer was Paul's fanciful description of a
luminary-studded audience that included Honegger, Milhaud, members
of "Les Six," and, filling the front row, couturier Paul Poiret and a string
of his mannequins.

But it was not Paul's roseate review that the absentee composer pored
over so intently in remote Chamonix. It was instead a notice by a French
critic named Guy de la Pierre, who, although he had somehow missed the
point of the symphony, had described it as an example of "super neoclassicism" and the fruition of all that Stravinsky and "Les Six" had so well
started. Moreover, the critic had appointed the creator of this revolutionary

George Antheil returning to his Paris apartment
as Sylvia Beach looks on

work leader of a new movement called "formalism," which he predicted would "super-classicize" neoclassicism. *Symphony in F*, therefore, was the prototype of the new formula. Whether because of his recent illness or because of his impressionability, George found more in the notice than welcome adulation. It indicated a direction that might yield higher artistic and glory-filled rewards. Therefore, his work-in-progress, the piano concerto, became increasingly neoclassic in style and principle, and eventually he began to consider it as typically Parisian, perhaps even a synthesis of his tumultuous years in the city.

Chamonix, with its attractions of cycling, walking, skiing, and mountain climbing, proved remarkably rejuvenating for George. Going back to Paris seemed increasingly less attractive, and in November the Antheils traveled to Salzburg, then to Vienna, where the music was dreadful, and on to Budapest, where they settled near Boski's mother. George, much improved, turned to his piano concerto in earnest, and soon reported to Sylvia that two-thirds of the work was finished. He was especially pleased with the middle movement. "It is the best slow music I have written since the string quartet." The first movement had swelled to at least five times its original size, and the third was "a brilliant and fast finale." Since each movement lasted about ten minutes, the composition would be one of his longest.

While George composed and dallied in Budapest, his future was being decided at a party in New York. Among the guests that Donald Friede, a vice-president of the book publishing firm of Boni and Liveright, had invited to his midtown apartment were Lewis Galantière and Aaron Copland. Some time during the evening Copland played an excerpt from the *Sonata Sauvage*. The guests were delighted. So was Friede. Galantière, who had witnessed George's concerts in Paris, predicted that if George were to perform at Carnegie Hall, he could fill the place. Why not bring him to New York? Friede promptly drafted an invitation, offering George travel expenses and a share of the profits of an all-Antheil concert. It could hardly have come at a more propitious moment. Because American concert managers had shown so little interest in the *Ballet*, George was in a vengeful mood, and with a sort of "I'll show 'em" gesture, he accepted Friede's offer at once, requesting only that no members of the League of Composers (which had rejected the *Ballet*) be hired.

The invitation catapulted Antheil into a frenzy of planning and practicing. Besides Carnegie Hall (Friede set a date in April), there were two other concerts to prepare for, one in Budapest in January and the other in

Paris in March. Performing with him in Budapest, at his request and gratis (Pound paid her expenses), was Olga Rudge, who "for once," Antheil reported to Pound, "played beautifully as she rarely does, and got good criticisms." Since the concert might enhance Antheil's chances of being invited to the mid-European festival later in the year, an honor bound to make a "great impression" on "American financial circles," he was pleased that Béla Bartók, one of the festival organizers, had been "very impressed." At the March concert in Paris, Golschmann would conduct the premiere of the recently completed *Suite for Orchestra* and the piano concerto.

It can hardly be determined now what George Antheil's reputation might have been had he not appeared at Carnegie Hall. That concert, if it did nothing else, reinforced a legend that would forever be a burden. Nothing he did or said afterward could alter the image he had begun crafting years before and which, by 1927, was unshakable: that he was the clown prince of the avant-garde, an *enfant terrible*, a master of mechanical music, combative and iconoclastic, capable of inciting riots. He could transform music into sensational spectacle, and such spectacle, he had discovered, made him notorious and famous.

What he had perfected abroad, he could repeat at home. Every stratagem Friede devised to make the New York performance another sensational triumph—perhaps the composer's greatest—was supported by George. While vacationing in Italy in January, George had even gained Friede's approval for a repeat of the semi-successful "misadventure" in Africa. A recital with Olga Rudge in Rome provided the setting. Again he prevailed on Sylvia Beach to tell obliging journalists that he was lost— this time for five days and with a cat called Crazy—somewhere in central Europe. Then after languishing in Florence until February 18, the day of the recital, he departed for Rome by train. Reporters, using George's inventions and a few of their own, turned an orderly and ordinary concert into a publicist's dream. Reports carried in New York newspapers (with help from Friede) said that George, having trudged all the way from Budapest with a rucksack and Crazy, had arrived in Rome on the evening of the concert and without a pause had gone directly to the stage, still wearing his hiking outfit, and played the violin sonata from memory, a feat that brought tumultuous cheers from the crowd.

The morning that the small White Star liner *Ascania* dropped anchor in New York harbor, Donald Friede and eight reporters boarded a tugboat and went out to meet her. Aboard was the man Friede had christened "America's sensational modernist composer." Antheil looked even more like a boy than in his pictures. Friede too was a surprise, being younger than Antheil had expected; decked out in a bright kimono and blue Cossack boots, Friede looked more like a circus barker than a concert manager. The reporters, annoyingly, asked none of the questions for which he had rehearsed answers, but Antheil managed to repeat that the *Ballet* expressed in "a dignified way the essence of America." When they asked to hear him play, he struggled to wring from a much-abused ship's piano some semblance of his music, an effort that only increased their bewilderment. Antheil was a ready-made for cartoonists. One depicted him as a weary-looking composer dragging a car filled with bells, horns, and assorted musical instruments. The caption read: "That's my *Ballet.*" When a columnist (*World*) complained that George's music lacked melody, Friede invited him to his apartment to hear George play. The columnist—James M. Cain—came, listened for an hour, and in his next column retracted all criticism.

Despite Cain's favorable reassessment and a long review in *New Masses* of Pound's book on Antheil, which Friede's firm published shortly before the concert, and an article in *Vanity Fair* in which Ford Madox Ford identified Antheil as a respected composer in Europe, the tenor of the publicity campaign remained unaltered. New Yorkers had been promised a different kind of spring festival, a musical circus, and no amount of serious discussion of the composer's music could convince them that this would be anything but a titillating spectacle. Friede's tactics had also antagonized the critics. Marketing the concert as though it were a book, he later admitted, had ruffled their tempers and challenged their vanity and thus had virtually invited a critical disaster.

For a week Friede escorted Antheil on unending rounds of interviews, parties, and late nights in Harlem speakeasies and Broadway clubs that left him dazzled and confused and exhausted. For fifteen anxious minutes at the first rehearsal, Antheil labored to convince incredulous musicians that the music before them was serious and playable. Fortunately the *Second Violin Sonata* and the *String Quartet* required only a few rehearsals. The untried *Jazz Symphony*, however, proved more troublesome. Friede had found a musical legend, W.C. Handy, to conduct it, but after three painful rehearsals, Handy had failed to produce anything resembling the composition Antheil had written. For all his musical accomplishments he seemed totally bemused by the intricate score. It made no sense to him at all. Concealing their disappointment, Friede and Antheil asked the hapless Handy to step down. His replacement, Allie Ross, forced to pull the piece together quickly, demanded and received, besides a very high fee, permission to schedule all the rehearsals necessary.

On the evening of the concert, the crowd waiting for standing-room tickets outside Carnegie Hall was unusually large and once inside flowed far down into the aisles. As Galantière had predicted, the concert was a sellout. Pictures of Antheil adorned the program. One photograph showed the serious artist, deep in concentration, his hands lightly folded; a caricature by Miguel Covarrubias depicted Antheil in a contorted position at the keyboard. The composer's pretentious and sometimes cryptic notes filled two pages: the *String Quartet*, he announced, eliminated the objectionable feature of quartets—orchestra writing. The *Sonata for Violin, Piano and Drum*, a composition "somewhat related" to Picasso's 1918 cubist period, treated the piano percussively and "as a many toothed and pointed instrument against the banal violin." Antheil considered his *Jazz Sonata* to be a musical comment on the American Negro, specifically a "reaction toward Negro jazz as apart from sweet jazz." *Ballet Mécanique* purported to express "America, Africa, and steel" in three movements— allegro, allegro, and allegro. As an example of pure music, it found its "aesthetic" analogy in the mechanically beautiful automobile rather than in the Venus de Milo.

What Friede had touted as the "biggest musical event of the year" turned out to be a financial disaster for the ambitious manager and a critical catastrophe for the composer. The first ominous signs appeared during the *String Quartet*, when a "deadening house curtain" made the music scarcely audible in parts of the hall. The same acoustical deficiency also vitiated the impact of the *Sonata*, but Antheil's dextrous playing of the piano and drum joggled the sullen audience into the first outburst of laughter. The backdrop for the *Jazz Sonata*, showing a gigantic, big-buttocked Negro couple ecstatically dancing the Charleston, provoked even more mirth. Friede withered when he realized for the first time how incongruous the backdrop looked in staid Carnegie Hall. The musicians (Antheil at the piano) played perfectly, however, and the audience responded with the first genuine applause of the evening. By the time Friede raced backstage to order an encore, the curtain had already dropped and stagehands were rolling in the grand pianos and props for the finale. The second backdrop, displaying a huge spark plug rising up between crossed elevated structures and skyscrapers toward a painted sky crowded with steam-shovel buckets, was run down with ease. But installing a large cyclorama, designed to give added depth to the semicircle of grand pianos, necessitated raising the curtain and this prematurely exposed to view the backdrop that Friede had counted on to make a dramatic impression at the start of the performance. The sight of the workmen jockeying ten pianos into place, while electricians scurried about hooking up bells, a siren, and a full-sized airplane propeller, was too amusing to miss, and as word of the stage proceedings spread, scores of people hurried back to their seats to watch the show. Finally, the pianists—Aaron Copland, Max Ewing, George Herzog, and Carol Robinson among them—sat down at their instruments, now arranged in a huge semicircle; behind were eight xylophonists, four bass drummers, and George O'Neill, a former student of Antheil's in Paris who had volunteered to operate the various mechanical devices. Last of all came Antheil. Without a glance at the audience, he seated himself at the controlling piano.

Eugene Goossens, hired especially to conduct the *Ballet*, raised his baton, and the first fierce notes of the composition all New York had been reading about for weeks resounded through Carnegie Hall. For several minutes all listened attentively, but when the wind machine was turned on part way through the first movement, their attention dissolved into amusement. Instead of aiming the propeller upward, away from the audience, O'Neill had pointed it directly at the eleventh row of the audience. With a breeze of mounting velocity bearing down on them, those buffeted by the strongest currents clutched their programs, women grasped their hats, and one resourceful gentleman tied a white handkerchief to his cane and waved it as a token of surrender. Reducing the speed of the machine to a bearable level hardly diminished the mirth. Everyone knew, after all, that *Ballet Mécanique* was supposed to incite some kind of demonstration, and those who had come intending to foment America's first musical riot made their move. Starting with the opening of the second movement and continuing sporadically during its duration, a band of inexperienced and poorly organized rioters, mostly young Greenwich Villagers who had congregated in the rear of the hall, whistled, wound rattles, meowed, and stamped their feet in what turned out to be a fruitless effort to stampede the audience into something resembling a riot. Goossens silenced them with a single glance. After that, there were no more contrived disturbances, only departures of audience members. The final movement, employing every instrument and device, moved steadily to the shattering climax. But so unexpectedly did it arrive that the audience, unsure wheth-

Sylvia Beach and James Joyce

George Antheil, Paris, mid-Twenties

er the piece was over or not, sat stunned and silent. Then, as though from a great distance, came the unmistakable wail of a slowly accelerating siren. In the closing minutes of the *Ballet*, O'Neill had furiously wound the device up, but its delayed action had not sounded at the right moment. Now in the hushed confines of the hall the "infernal thing" erupted with full force, nearly drowning out the weak applause of loyal supporters.

Reaction was monotonously and predictably negative. All save one reviewer panned the concert, and seven reviewers succumbed to using the same bad pun, remarking that the performance had "tried to make a mountain out of an Antheil." A slightly more imaginative punster described it as "infantheilism." Critics took a vindictive delight in documenting their disappointment, although Ben Hecht, reporting the event for the *Chicago Daily News*, tweaked his New York colleagues for professing a boredom their actions and words belied. The few who mentioned the music drew invidious comparisons between Stravinsky and Antheil. W.J. Henderson (*New York Sun*) out-hyperbolized his colleagues: *Ballet Mécanique* was a "whooping piffle, mere noise and pretense . . . not worthy of a single word of comment or line of description." The whole thing amounted to "an explosion of harmless gas." Pitts Sanborn (*New York Telegram*) commended the audience on being too good-natured to riot and for using the cruelest of weapons—gentle apathy—to show disapproval. Nunnally Johnson (*New York Evening Post*) called it an unabashed put-on. Antheil's *String Quartet* gave four violinists the chance "to play hell" out of a single note; the *Sonata* provided Antheil and his violinist the same opportunity, with only the note changing; in half an hour, Johnson estimated, they struck the note 5,280 times, or if laid end to end, a mile's worth. Antheil's drum playing (he attacked the instrument from the rear while playing the piano with one hand) was a rare feat, indeed. The *Jazz Sonata* sounded too much like Stravinsky, and the *Ballet* demonstrated every known form of noise except hiccups. Sam Chotzinoff (the *New York World*) sampled audience opinion: George Gershwin said he detected no resemblance between Antheil's and his own music. From Gilbert Seldes (one of Antheil's "enemies") came the unexpected admission that the *Jazz Symphony* was better jazz than Gershwin and better music than Stravinsky. Paul Robeson admired the percussive effects. "Prodigious and wonderful," ejaculated Lewis Galantière, adding that "Antheil and Stravinsky are the two greatest masters of rhythm we have ever had." Apart from Nunnally Johnson's sardonic commentary, reprinted in the *Paris Tribune* shortly before Antheil returned to Paris, only the *Paris Comet*, a small English-language magazine, reported what had happened in New York. As sympathetic as Johnson was sarcastic, the reviewer ("Billy") concluded that Americans had obviously misunderstood Antheil and that the concert was his "greatest success."

In Trenton the next day George repeated at the local Kiwanis Club, whose members had given him a standing ovation, that the concert had elated him. Their response duplicated the one Paris had given him the first time he performed there. Kiwanis members could thus conclude that musical history was being repeated in America. Privately, however, George was far from certain that history had repeated or would repeat itself. Among other disturbing developments, a second performance was canceled. When poor reviews ruled out a successful repeat program, Friede had hastily canceled the second performance and told reporters that George had sprained his wrist and could not play.

For Wilhelmina, history had indeed repeated itself. "What kind of a boy do I have?" his mother sobbed after the concert. Neither his father nor George's old nanny, Anna Newman, had an answer. The tongue-lashing that Wilhelmina gave her errant son was far more harrowing than the critics' attacks. Once more he had been a "bad boy," a thoughtless son who had deliberately forsaken the lessons and models provided by devoted parents. Stubbornness, pigheadedness, and willful disobedience had brought him what he deserved: catastrophe.

More worrisome than the reviewers' or Wilhelmina's chastisement, Friede's colossal blunders, or even the total loss of the concert was what effect the performance might have on Mrs. Bok. Annoyed by the advance ballyhoo, she had not attended, sending in her place Josef Hofmann, who, ostensibly struck mute by the whole affair, preferred to let the critics tell the "tale of Hofmann." To counteract his silent condemnation, George posted Mrs. Bok a detailed account.

His principal complaint was that while Friede had realized "$50,000 worth of publicity out of the thing," he had been subjected to the "unheard-of viciousness of the critical press." "Spiritually, the long-awaited advent of *Ballet Mécanique* . . . was a great blow." But it was also a great blow to America, for it had floored the critics and would remain forever the best expression of mechanical music, at once the apex and the end of a period, as were *Sacre du Printemps* and *Tristan und Isolde*. George would leave America with an abiding loathing for the critics who resented his hard-won and sincerely bestowed European reputation and with an acute sense of the irony of leaving his native land, nearly penniless and in dishonor, for a foreign continent where he was esteemed and loved. The trip had ravaged his savings. Only $400 of the $5,000 he had had a few months before remained. Unless he could depend on Mrs. Bok for comparable amounts, the future looked grim. Despite the "unheard-of audacity" he had suffered under, however, he would return to Europe to fight his cause rather than to sulk.

George's brave petition failed to move Mrs. Bok. Although she could make no pronouncement herself, she had abhorred the manner in which the Carnegie Hall concert had been presented ("It was blatant, sensational, and screaming"), and on the advice of trusted friends, she decided to withhold any more large outlays of money. Her letter reached George in Paris where, with Friede and Boski, he had arrived at the end of April. On his return he was saddened by more than the Carnegie Hall fiasco. Contrary to reports he had received while in America, the premiere of his piano concerto had failed to win anything close to general approval in Paris. At best it had been only politely received. Old friends and admirers of his mechanical music, he learned, had been stunned by the derivative themes of the concerto and even more so by the blatant neoclassical influence of Stravinsky. Antheil, the pathfinder who had challenged and then ventured beyond Stravinsky, seemed to have become a mere imitator and, what was worse, a heretic. The rejection, coming so swiftly and immediately after the American disaster, staggered George. A hostile, skeptical, and disenchanted band of one-time friends and supporters was the last thing he had expected to find on his return. From "one of the most talked about, most feted" people in Paris, he was in danger of becoming one of the "most abused."

For comfort and advice, George turned to Ezra Pound. Ignore all the "yawps" of the New York press, Ezra urged. "Nothing is to be expected of that country and least of all any sort of comprehension of anything." Additional worry, he warned, would only make the concert a total loss. The publicity remained an asset. Make use of it. And as for Paris, escape if possible the "tittle-tattle" of the rue de l'Odéon. Perhaps like Joyce, George had already had too much of the place. Ezra described a similar "bad patch" in his own life as "a damn bad quarter of an hour" when one "is no longer the white hope of boy prodigism and not yet the *homme fait*." Above all, it was necessary to forget what happened in New York and to use Mrs. Bok's allowance to get on with life.

In Antheil's estimation, he was a man without a country and without a hometown if, like Gertrude Stein, he still considered Paris his hometown. Like a toppled potentate, he would soon drift to the nearest hospitable shelter (in this case Germany) where there were admirers and where his reputation had survived his years of absence in France. By coincidence, an old German friend, Hans Stuckenschmidt, reentered Antheil's life at this crucial moment. A year in Paris had left Stuckenschmidt thoroughly fed up with both French music and the oppressive influence of Stravinsky and eager to return to Germany to take part in a burgeoning opera movement then sweeping the country. State-supported opera houses (eighty-five of them), he told Antheil, regularly presented works by Weinberger, Weill, Berg, Krenek, and Milhaud, and although all of their music was popular, no more fascinating subject existed for his countrymen than contemporary America. An opera about the United States, perhaps one that would focus on New York, would satisfy an obvious demand and was bound to be a great success.

Despite his friend's assurances, Antheil procrastinated. Would plunging into a relatively unknown musical form lead to another disaster? Would an opera based on New York evoke too many unpleasant memories? For a while he tinkered with an opera (*Ivan*) that he had begun in the spring, but the libretto seemed wrong, and when he detected overtones of neoclassicism, he abandoned it and made a start on the opera that Stuckenschmidt had suggested. Soon afterward, Ernest Krenek, author of the immensely popular opera *Jonny Spielt Auf*, unexpectedly turned up at 12 rue de l'Odéon and for four days showed Antheil how to construct an opera and "corrected" the work he had done. Impressed with the results, Krenek sent a glowing report to his publisher, Universal Editions in Vienna. In December Antheil received a second guest, Hans Heinsheimer, Universal's theater division director, who, finding the opera libretto "good book" and the score promising, offered Antheil a contract (also an advance of $425) and conjectured that if he finished soon, his opera could be produced as early as May 1928.

Antheil did not finish soon. *Glare*, or *Transatlantic* as he later renamed it, was not performed until May 1930, and long before that he had decided to make it an avenging angel that would demolish the clique responsible for a monumental crime—the destruction of an American composer—and obliterate the "double flops" of New York and Paris. Conceived during the "darkest period" of his life, the winter of 1927–1928, it would expose an America contemptuous of talent and guilty of condemning its artists to "lifelong exile." That it might transcend his own dark dilemma and reveal things about America less sinister seemed a remote possibility to the embittered composer, who worked alone and ill in Paris.

Since his return to Paris, Sylvia Beach and Robert McAlmon had watched their friend's descent into depression with growing anxiety, and when they learned that he again had pneumonia, they regarded this latest and most serious sickness as a sign that George might succumb to tuberculosis. Keeping their fears a secret from George, they took up a collection to send him to Amelie-les-Bains, a "consumptive resort" in southwestern France. In a tearful "farewell-to-Paris" letter to Mrs. Bok, George exaggerated his condition by saying that doctors had discovered an "elementary but nevertheless serious tuberculosis," and then played on her sympathy by saying that poverty might prevent him from ever returning to the city he loved. Where he would go after his "cure," he had no idea. While he stopped short of holding her responsible for his wretched situation, he hazarded that unless something changed soon, she might one day be accused of denying help to "America's first composer of an American opera in Europe" at a time when he was close to "perishing of overwork, tuberculosis, and even hunger."

George's premonition that he might expire if Mrs. Bok did not act promptly proved wrong. Amelie-les-Bains was just what he needed. Relaxation and exercise erased the fatigue and anxiety brought on by frustration and fitful sleep during the "dark days" in Paris. In response to a flattering letter George had written just before leaving Paris, Otto Kahn sent a friendly reply. After assuring George that the mismanaged Carnegie Hall concert had in no way prejudiced him against his latest work, Kahn asked if George could provide an "opernmassig opera" on an American theme, something "dealing with the present day and in the idiom of our country." *Transatlantic*, George assured Kahn, would satisfy all his wishes. Set in contemporary New York, it was "of the purest lyric order" and the first opera "to put America in a grand simple melodic line," and although he admitted it was not the first to use jazz, it was "certainly the first to use a typical American jazz in an American way." The election day choruses (*Transatlantic* was a political work like *Boris Godunov*, from which George had learned much) would certainly create considerable excitement, but as a whole his opera contained "none of the 'modern elements'" that might annoy New York audiences, and while "it [had] elements to compel the interest of the left wing as well as the right," it possessed above all the "element of a real success." As much as George would have liked to place his opera with Kahn, he realized that the odds were against it. In May Heinsheimer summoned him to Universal for a contract-signing ceremony, and George, by now fully cured, left at once for Vienna, the "soft-speaking" city where he would pass the autumn.

Wamby Bald, George Antheil, Hilaire Hiler, Paris, mid-Twenties

Hilaire Hiler, George Antheil, Wambly Bald, Paris, mid-Twenties

After the pleasant interlude in Vienna, going to Berlin to assist with the production of *Transatlantic* was a shock. It was more wildly expensive than ever, and remaining there long would be ruinous. Writing music for the Stadtstheater production of *Oedipus Rex* brought in barely enough to cover the rent of a cold-water flat that the Antheils reluctantly shared with the American poet Walter Lowenfels and his wife, whom George had enticed to Berlin with the prospect that the Stadtstheater might accept his satiric play *USA with Music*. Although Kurt Weill offered to set it to music, Lowenfels chose George to do the score. Then when the directors of the Berlin opera requested extensive revisions in *Transatlantic*, Lowenfels (with George's approval and help) rewrote the libretto and changed George's original romantic characters to "demi-caricatures" and his melodramatic story into a satire of political corruption. George pronounced the revision "beyond reproach," but the directors disagreed and again refused it. Only its politically sensitive content, George concluded, could explain the second rejection. Dejected, he turned for help to Heinsheimer, who responded with the welcome news that the director of the Frankfurt opera had read *Transatlantic* and would produce it. Best of all, only a few "special changes" would be necessary. With no reason to remain in Berlin and with an unexpected check for $1,000 (for printing) from Mrs. Bok, as well as her promise to increase George's allowance to $100 a month, the Antheils departed for Rapallo to visit Ezra Pound.

Also residing in Rapallo, the Mediterranean town Pound had adopted several years earlier, were W.B. Yeats, Gerhart Hauptmann, Franz Werfel, and Emil Ludwig. Pound received the new arrivals (rather coolly, George thought), installed them in a small apartment, and escorted them to the Hotel Rapallo café to meet his literary friends. Although George had agreed several months before to write some incidental music for Yeats's play *Fighting the Waves*, he had been too busy with *Transatlantic* and other projects to do it. Now George agreed to take on the task immediately. The "short musical setting" he produced delighted the poet, who besides paying him twenty-five pounds complimented George on creating just the kind of music he had always wanted for his play. Later the same year the play had a popular run at the Abbey Theater in Dublin. George soon observed that Pound and the other literary notables were inveterate readers of detective stories. So voracious was their demand that they had exhausted the local lending library. It was a situation George set out to rectify with a detective story of his own making.

Perhaps as powerful an incentive to George's fictional creativity as the dearth of detective novels was the second anniversary of the deathless Carnegie Hall concert. In a letter to Stanley Hart, George once more tried to explain its significance. *Ballet Mécanique* had been a necessary development in his career. Both the mechanical music and the now expunged neoclassical compositions that followed had been stages leading to the clear and completely different music of the present. He reviewed for Hart his past mistakes, the critics' shameful conduct, the terrible consequences that resulted from miscalculation, and the tremendous willpower that had enabled him to survive. Primarily responsible for all his misery, however, was that "blue-bellied bastard Friede." The "damned New York concert" had changed everything. Nothing was "quite the same as before" and the struggle to regain momentum and reshape his career had been "super hard." Only now, after two years, were things coming out all right and in fact "infinitely better" than if he had tied up his "hopes and fortunes in Paris." To be sure, he was far from being finished with the place. Some day he would return, speaking French, working with the French, but shunning the crowd that had left him cold. Above all, he was finished with Montparnasse.

Whatever cathartic benefits confessional messages like these brought George, they were not enough. The detective story he vowed to write would not only supply his friends with another mystery to solve, it would provide an opportunity for the author to purge, perhaps forever, the incubus of a stubbornly noxious event. *The Denny Murder Case* (Antheil's original title) is a roman à clef. It recounts what happened in New York from the time Antheil arrived to the time he and Friede sailed for France two months later. The familiar notice that "none of the characters in this book is a living person" is almost playfully ironic, since, except for a few survivors, all the characters die, and one, David Denny (unmistakably Donald Friede) is already dead (of knife wounds in the back) when the novel opens. Equally easy to identify are: Gertrude, Denny's (Friede's) wife; Denny's (Friede's) mother, a "business-like old millionairess"; Aaron, Denny's (Friede's) elder half-brother; John Alvinson (George Antheil), a young musician; his Russian wife, Frieda (Boski Antheil); and Dr. Stein (Dr. Berman), the gland expert Antheil knew in Berlin in 1922. The mystery of who murdered David Denny and four others is eventually solved by Stephan Bayard, the head criminologist, and Stacey Bishop (which was also the author's nom de plume).

Alvinson and his wife are guests of the Dennys when David Denny dies. Small, blond, and possessed of an international reputation, Alvinson has not yet attained his rightful position in the music world because he has devoted himself too much to "music of the modern school." The widely known fact that Denny, spoiled by a rich mother and spurred on by a socially ambitious wife, tried to make his reputation as a concert manager at Alvinson's expense makes Denny a prime suspect. "You [Alvinson] were cheated, defamed, and betrayed by David Denny two years ago," Bayard contends. Alvinson agrees. And Denny, the investigator continues, "did absolutely nothing to right himself with you . . . he promised you money when you reached Paris . . . and then never sent it." Again Alvinson agrees. "Denny did [the concert] for publicity . . . not for you. . . . He did not hesitate to ruin your reputation through a concert that could not fail to place himself in the limelight." And why did he do this? Bayard explains: Denny "had to do something to keep himself" in his newly acquired class. But in the process he ruined "one of America's greatest promises for some years." A prejudiced public dismissed the performance as an "arranged affair." The critics unanimously condemned it. From the shambles, Alvinson emerged penniless and disgraced. Only through "superhuman effort" did he overcome sickness and depression and repair his broken career. But why, Bayard asks, has he come back to Denny's home? Alvinson's reply is quiet and confident: with new success he forgave Denny and came to New York to tell him so.

One other reason exists for suspecting Alvinson. He is, according to Dr. Stein, a "pituitary thymocentric," a disorder common to potential criminals as well as to eccentric men of genius (such as Stravinsky, Joyce, Wilde, da Vinci, and Napoleon). Though Alvinson may seem closer to being a genius than a criminal, Bayard is taking no chances. In rapid succession, Denny's mother and half-brother, Aaron, are shot to death, both killed by a single bullet in the forehead. Next it is Dr. Stein's turn. He barely survives a temple wound. And suddenly the real killer, fearing detection, destroys herself. It is Denny's wife, Gertrude, a pure thymocentric (more criminal than creative), who killed David Denny because he was a "heartless, spoiled idiot" and Aaron because he rejected her love and then nearly killed Stein because he was about to identify her as the murderess.

In a postscript, Antheil rewards Alvinson (a true pituitary thymocentric) with the hard-earned success so long denied him. In the final scene, Alvinson sits spellbound, watching the premiere of his first opera at the Metropolitan Opera House—a rich compensation for one who starved for years in foreign countries, who suffered the obloquy of anti-American critics, and who in his own country endured the barbs of xenophobic reviewers and the snobbery of wealthy patrons who passed him by in favor of "poor creative" artists from Bulgaria. "Simple, melodic, and new in technique, but not too difficult for the general public," the opera raises a "storm of approval" and discloses what almost no one recognized before, that the "long-sought-after musician" and leader of the "musical destinies of America" is John Alvinson.

Antheil sent the manuscript to the London firm of Faber and Faber. T.S. Eliot, the first reader, called it "a by-product of an important coming musical composer," and "a very good detective story." The faults—prolixity, stylistic crudities, and a too-obvious patterning on the work of S. S. Van Dine—could be repaired. Less offensive were an overuse of scientific patter and a shallow indulgence in the topics of literature and art. Other readers concurred, and in August Faber offered Antheil a contract and requested only minor revisions, among them the permission to substitute a nom de plume that was a little less frightening to English readers than Antheil's selection—Miguel Queires. Antheil agreed to everything and even suggested that George Stacey Trent (Stacey Trent was the name of a popular Trenton hotel) might be a suitable pen name. Faber retitled the book *Death in the Dark* and published it in 1930.

In May the Antheils wended their way south to Rome, then on to Capri, and eventually to Tunis. In July they moved again, going north to Chamonix, where George found a letter awaiting him from John Erskine, an English professor at Columbia University and president of the Juilliard Fund for American Music. Erskine related that he had taken a keen interest in George's career ever since a student (Stanley Hart) had called his attention to the "genius" who had nearly vanished in the "wilderness of Trenton." The Carnegie Hall concert had fully convinced him that Hart had spoken the truth. Although Erskine refused George's request to turn his recent "bestseller," *The Private Life of Helen of Troy*, over to him for operatic dramatization, he had unearthed a little-known and delightful legend about the Greek beauty that just might be appropriate. It was the story of Helen's last love affair with the virile ghost of Achilles, which ended only because Helen, having agreeably exhausted the ecstasies of the sybaritic life, persuaded her partner to resume being a "happy ghost" so that she could die contented. Erskine suggested that it might be called *Helen Retires*. Delighted with the proposal, George suggested that they begin working as soon as *Transatlantic* was launched.

"Opera," Antheil explained to a reporter after the premiere of *Transatlantic*, "has to be the best show you can put on; it must be the quintessence of all that the stage and modern life have to offer." At the time of its conception in the gloomy aftermath of the Carnegie Hall debacle, *Transatlantic* hardly promised to be the quintessence of modern life. Dispirited and shattered by events in New York and Paris, George had lapsed into prolonged despondency; it was during this time, with Heinsheimer's help, that he had begun the opera. Set in New York, from which emanated the "horrendous glare" that had momentarily blinded him to the consequences of his actions, the opera would expose the corrupt institutions and the meretricious individuals who had conspired to destroy him. There is no doubt that the opera was intended to be another effort at self-exculpation, like *Death in the Dark*.

Between the conception and the performance, Antheil reworked the opera at least five times, the most extensive revisions being done with Lowenfels. The early plot summaries that he sent to Mrs. Bok contain no hint of the satirical treatment the two men eventually gave the material. The opera began as a "romantic tragedy."

> *Glare* takes place in the New York City of today. The background is the unnamed party's selection of their candidate for the forthcoming presidential elections. The characters are Helen, a very beautiful woman who is the mistress of old Ajax, a very rich man and a political boss. He is the financier of the political career of Hector, a nation's "favorite son," beloved of his people. Other characters are Hector's trusted friend, Leo, and Leo's fiancée, Gladys. Jason is the former husband of Helen. Like *Boris Godunov* . . . *Glare* develops its tragedy in a semi-political atmosphere, only its victim in this case is a woman, and not a man.

The climax conveyed the despair that overwhelmed Antheil following the New York disaster.

> Act Three, Scene One, opens in Hector's apartment, overlooking New York City. But the curtains of the gigantic windows are closed when the curtain goes up. Hector comes back discouraged, tired, sick at heart. He meditates on Helen, is jealous of her past and everything and everybody about her. At last he can stand his thoughts no longer. He rushes to the gigantic windows and tears them open with the intention of throwing himself out into the street far below. But he is stopped by the vast night panorama of New York, the electric signs, the lights, the truly magnificent city! "New York—is here!" he

cries. "Heartless city of steel! I was too weak to conquer you—only hearts of steel can do that, while my heart was made of flesh only! False Glare! Glare! Heartless Glare! Ah! let me only have the truth of night, everlasting night!"

Mrs. Bok's reactions were unencouraging. She objected to an American opera constructed on such "sordid subject matters," even though the music was far more important than the content. Also, the story seemed confused. Too much happened. She would prefer a simpler plot, much less action, and a "keener line leading to the dramatic high points."

Mrs. Bok's advice notwithstanding, the version of *Transatlantic* that went into production at the Frankfurt Opera House was a multimedia extravaganza in three acts that lasted over three hours. The technique was cinematic, Antheil explained: "Rapid action, lots of things happening all the time." Act Three contained some thirty scenes played out on a "constructivist stage," parts of which could be darkened and lighted as required; at the beginning of the act, for example, while the hero attempted to strangle the heroine, a "revue dancer" on another part of the stage expounded the hero's thoughts and provided election returns. Just as startling were the sets and props. The first thing the audience saw was an ocean liner, majestically moving across the stage and bearing the lead tenor (a stagehand's error nearly caused the ship to sink at the premiere). Other scenes took place in a Childs restaurant, in a bathroom (the scene of one of the most popular arias), on the Brooklyn Bridge, in a cabaret, and at election night headquarters. There were moving elevators, revolving doors, jingling telephones, and newspaper bulletins. The score included parts for two flutes, two oboes, three clarinets, two bassoons, four horns, three trumpets, three trombones, tuba, celesta, strings, two saxophones, and two pianos. The melodies followed the accents of the speaking voice, the libretto being in prose. The music acted as a commentary (usually satiric) on the words, as in the opening love passage where the music burlesqued the overly romantic language.

Except for the technical slip-up at the start that nearly sank the ship, *Transatlantic* unfolded without a serious mishap. Antheil paled slightly when the gangsters in the Bowery scene appeared in turtleneck sweaters rather than in the jackets actually worn by underworld characters in the twenties, but that scarcely marred a production that captured the American atmosphere. The singers performed superbly. Four curtain calls followed the first act, three the second, and at the conclusion, Antheil took numerous bows with the director, the conductor, the singers, and then again with the director.

Transatlantic, boasted Antheil with customary hyperbole, earned him "90 percent of the musical respect of Germany." Nonetheless, it would not be an easy opera to sell. Opera house directors, some "scared away by the gigantic cost," showed no interest in booking it. Antheil reconciled himself to the inevitable: following a short engagement, *Transatlantic* would close. It was a "white elephant," so overloaded with complicated staging and technical devices that only the largest and most modern theater could produce it, and even there costs would make production unlikely. The experience had taught him what to avoid next time. His second opera would go beyond *Transatlantic*: it would be simpler, purer, linear, and free of complicated effects and devices; perhaps, he quipped, it would even be something that could be whistled.

To his astonishment, Irving Schwerke, who along with Sylvia Beach, Adrienne Monnier, Bill Bird, Nancy Cunard, Ezra Pound, and his father Homer had attended the Frankfurt opening, called *Transatlantic* "one of the most exciting spectacles on the operatic stage," a work of an "outstanding talent," and an opera of which "America should be proud." The latter observation echoed Pound's pronouncement that it was the first important milestone along the "American musical road." Moreover, Schwerke described the "present day rhythm and idioms" as theatrically and emotionally intriguing. The "amazing variety of rhythmic invention, harmonic puissance, and melodic flow" contributed to an accomplishment only a composer with technique and insight could manage. The critic's volte-face could hardly have come at a better time. Antheil, moved to repair the damage wrought by years of internecine war, lost no time assuring Schwerke that, despite stories to the contrary, he had read "every word" of Schwerke's criticism constructively and in his own way had profited from his "always deep and instinctively right advice."

Mrs. Bok learned enough about the Frankfurt production of *Transatlantic* to decide she did not like it any more than she had when George first began sending her resumes. Why had he emphasized "some of the worst elements of American life"? Did he not realize that an opera in which the president telephoned a lady in a bathtub was offensive and that the "dubious politics" could only leave Europeans with a distorted and cheap impression of America? George, ever deferential, answered her Howellsian reproof by promising to write an opera that would show "the better and more idealistic side of America." The point, however, that ev-

George Antheil, John Erskine, Leopold Stokowski, New York, 1933

Vladimir Golschmann and George Antheil, Paris, 1926

eryone (at least in America) had missed was that his opera ended with an optimistic plea "to all people to stop fussing with small things and to turn their minds to idealism and big things." It demonstrated that a "new era" had arrived in which the United States would show that "the only way to cure the evils of the world and its countless . . . riddles" was through "WORK and through work alone."

George's apologia made little impression on Mrs. Bok, and when he sent her a copy of *Ulysses* and said that he and Joyce would soon resume work on *Cyclops*, she dismissed it as an example of "bad taste." For Mrs. Bok it was time for a showdown. To begin with, she and George had different points of view, and George's was one she shunned. His protracted pleas for understanding and his insistence that her continued belief in him was essential to his work needed clarification. If he thought she went on supporting him because she had always believed in him, he was mistaken; in fact, she would no longer wait to see her "original belief" in him vindicated. She did not want him to "conquer the world," as he put it, to demonstrate that she was right. She had gone along with him only to give him a chance, and, sadly, thus far nothing he had done deserved her endorsement. Their musical views were simply too divergent. "I want you to face this," she demanded, "and simply accept it and try to get on your feet financially apart from me as soon as possible."

With *Transatlantic* a rapidly fading hope and a rupture with Mrs. Bok a virtual certainty, and a "gift" of $500 from Otto Kahn their only nest egg, George and Boski passed the summer in Antibes, the grateful guests of Hans Heinsheimer. When Heinsheimer returned to Vienna, they moved along the coast to Cagnes-sur-Mer, a picturesque village that served as a playground for celebrities, artists, and writers seeking relief from Paris, and installed themselves in a roomy, wall-enclosed, and inexpensive villa, La Planestel. Nearby lived Jean and Claude Renoir, sons of the artist; Peggy Hopkins Joyce, a voluptuous and eccentric millionairess; old Paris companions and artists Hilaire Hiler, Francis Picabia, and Tsuguhara Foujita; and Abraham Lincoln Gillespie, George's one time Philadelphia roommate, who was now energetically creating his own legend as a Joycean poet. Few had come to Cagnes to work, and those who had quickly abandoned their good intentions. George, shuttling between his study and the Novelty Bar in the village, uttered mock complaints about his waning powers of concentration and fretted over *Helen Retires*. In his opinion, Erskine's libretto had burgeoned into several hundred pages of "very fancy poetry" completely alien to the original idea and scope of the opera.

When he had had enough of it, he turned to other projects that at least provided pleasant interludes, if few promising results. He composed songs and a duet for violin and cello, a folio of South American and Antilles music called *Archipelago*, the preludes that Martha Graham later used in her surrealist-psychoanalytical ballet *Dance in Four Parts*. He maintained a desultory correspondence with Jean Cocteau, who had agreed to collaborate on a ballet based on his *Les Enfants Terribles*. But Cocteau, alternately ill and preoccupied with other projects, gradually slipped out of contact. George tinkered with the ballet, intrigued by the possibility of dramatizing it in French, German, and English, the latter translation to be done by Sam Putnam, editor of a new little magazine called *New Review*, who had appointed George music editor (without salary) and asked him to contribute an article to the first number. And, finally, there was the unfinished *Cyclops*.

That Antheil had never actually written a score for *Ulysses* never bothered Joyce. What did annoy him was Antheil's abandonment of their proposed joint effort, *Cyclops*. Miss Beach was annoyed too, and perhaps at Joyce's instigation, scolded Antheil for neglecting a good thing. He composed one of his oracular defenses to account for his dilatoriness. *Ulysses* and even the *Cyclops* episode, he explained, had presented such enormous technical difficulties that years of hard work would have been needed to solve them. Far too much time would have been lost at the start of his career in Paris, when he was busily building a reputation based on *Ballet Mécanique*, the piano concerto, and *Symphony in F*, the last two of which, he claimed to have predicted then, would stand him in good stead if his mechanical music (*Ballet Mécanique*) someday brought him to catastrophe. That day of course came, just as he had believed it would, in April 1927; but fortunately he had the other compositions on which to rebuild his career ready. *Cyclops*, had he devoted his time to it rather than to the piano concerto and *Symphony in F*, would have contributed little or nothing to his stature. Furthermore, the problem with *Cyclops* remained; opera was simply "not developed enough to stand the stress and strain of the real Joycean technic." *Cyclops* was far too radical. He reminded Sylvia that "its simultaneous stages, slow motion picture camera technique, [and] rapidity of scene change . . . would have prevented it from ever seeing the front lights." And without the support of a strong publisher, it would have little chance of success. Before the performance of *Transatlantic*, a work only half as radical as *Cyclops*, he hazarded that he might have sold it to Heinsheimer, but even that possibility now seemed remote.

As it turned out, Joyce had found another musical interest: Byron's iconoclastic play *Cain*. The drama in which Byron anticipated "Joyce's interpretation of Cain and Abel as light-bringing Shem and conforming Shaun" would make a fine libretto and, more important, an ideal work for added, predicted that the combination *Cain*-Byron, Antheil-Sullivan, with Joyce functioning as scissors-man, "would be the greatest event in the artistic future." For Antheil, the play offered "the great opportunity of [his] career as a composer." Despite Joyce's optimism, Antheil demurred. *Cain*, he insisted, would be acceptable to the German stage only if Joyce wrote the libretto. Would he be willing to rewrite the play? Now it was Joyce's turn to hold back. "I would never have the bad manners to rewrite the text of a great English poet," he answered. He agreed, however, that "somebody must curtain the text of the first and third acts, and if it is to the advantage of the scheme in general, my name may be used. I am quite content to go down to posterity as a scissors and paste man, for that seems to me a harsh but not unjust description."

When it was obvious that Antheil's interest in the project was tepid, Joyce provided him with an opportunity to bow out. "If you feel that you cannot write this opera at once with enthusiasm and with spiritual profit to yourself and your art, without any consideration for the veering tastes of impresarios, please say so without hesitation and allow me to offer poor Byron and poorer Sullivan elsewhere." When for reasons he never disclosed, Antheil failed to attend Sullivan's concerts in nearby Toulon and Marseilles, after receiving urgent invitations from both Joyce and his daughter, Joyce asked Antheil to return his copy of *Cain*. Disappointed with the way matters had gone and aware that he had frustrated Joyce's plans for Sullivan, Antheil cited the great amount of work demanded by *Helen Retires* as the reason he had neglected *Cain*. Nevertheless, he promised to return to it as soon as the opera was over, and he reaffirmed that working with Joyce remained the "most idealistic and sympathetic idea for [his] talent" he knew of, and if Joyce could finish a full version of the script and send it to him in America where he would soon go to work with John Erskine, he would gladly prepare himself for the resumption of their common task. Joyce sent no script to America, and eventually the project was dropped. When a reporter asked why his collaboration with Joyce had ended so quickly, Antheil replied, "I dared not. The impossibility of getting Joyce to delete even a word scared me off. He didn't ask me about it at all. The first thing I knew a package arrived containing the first two acts. I read them and shuddered."

When the Antheils sailed for America in April 1931, they intended to stay only until George finished *Helen Retires*, but in fact they remained nearly a year. From time to time, George visited Mrs. Bok, on one memorable occasion playing selections from *Helen Retires* before a gathering of "blue-stockings" at the Art Alliance, which was adjacent to the Curtis Institute. And in Trenton he conducted the local symphony orchestra through the more difficult passages of his works with "no furrowing of the forehead, no stamping of the feet, no wild gesticulations," much to the satisfaction of a large audience that lustily applauded his efforts. *Helen Retires*, however, absorbed most of his time. Afternoons and evenings (mornings were for sleeping, walking, and driving in the country) he spent bent over the little desk on which he had once done his homework, tearing down and rebuilding the score.

In the spring the Guggenheim Foundation awarded him a study grant, the only requirement being that the stipend ($2,500) had to be used in Europe. Returning to France was now a necessity. Resettled in their "incredible house" at Cagnes, George luxuriated in the "good life." Below him on the "glittering synthetic beaches" romped synthetically happy people. One day somebody pulled a grand piano down to the beach and everyone danced. The open immorality of the place reminded him of Berlin. The "lovely nudes" languishing everywhere seemed to belong to nobody, yet he "knew them to be the wives, mistresses, and lone wolverines of the Cagnois." One evening the vacationing Berlin Opera Company came to his villa, and after dancing in the garden till dawn, fell asleep in rows, in the shade, some in the nude. The times were "distinctly Hellenic." With Ross Sanders, a lanky, mild-mannered American painter who had been an ace with the Royal Flying Corps, George assembled a telescope out of stove pipe, odd pieces of wood, and cheap powerful lenses. Evenings they gazed at Mars and Jupiter and the great nebulae 100 million light years away. After a day of composing, contemplating the "strange mathematics of infinity" could be an inspiring experience, and George expressed some of the strange feelings of time and space in a series of one hundred piano preludes, a project suggested by a volume of Max Ernst's paintings titled *The Woman with 100 Heads*.

Eventually George discovered that maintaining the "good life" required more money than a foundation grant provided. And at the start of 1933, he gloomily predicted that Boski and he would soon face the leanest time of their lives. In July Mrs. Bok had cut off his allowance, but since his Guggenheim stipend had begun the same month he had not petitioned her to renew it. Now that he had been guaranteed a second Guggenheim award of $1,200, only half as much as the first, he missed that "soothing" monthly check that made his "creative life certain." The reduction had come at a bad time, too, since the dollar value had plunged from twenty-five to nineteen francs.

George's final letter to Mrs. Bok from Europe filled thirty-seven pages. It began with an apology. It had just occurred to him that he had hardly ever written to her without asking for money to remedy or offset some impending calamity. In his defense he could offer only the counter truth that his life had been "deeply troubled and tragic." He reassured her, however, that any dollar signs in his letter would have nothing to do with her. Although the future, like much of the past, would probably bring more trouble, he had much to look forward to. Besides *Helen Retires*, the successful performance of *Capriccio* (under Goossens' direction) in St. Louis would most certainly open up America to his music. For him, a composer unfortunately ahead of his time by five or ten years, the way had not been easy. With rare candor, he admitted that money—thinking of it, worrying about it, and living with the bad decisions he frequently made because of fretting over it—had nearly destroyed his career and even himself. Money had influenced his decision to appear at Carnegie Hall. Now, as he approached his thirty-third birthday (the age of Christ, he reminded her), he could say that he had twice been crucified but saved each time by the music to which he had sacrificed himself. Unlike others who luxuriated in passion and pride, he had rededicated himself to the music of the future, music forged out of suffering and disillusionment and therefore enduring and living. He would triumph "over everything," like Jean Christophe, and compose his "beloved music." Ahead lay his "best creative years" when he would be less gullible, less ingenuous, more circumspect, and more realistic. Many had taken advantage of his "incurable idealism." He had often been betrayed and exploited. Ezra Pound, for one, had capitalized on his early notoriety to put himself in the limelight. Georgette Leblanc and Donald Friede had done the same. Such faithlessness notwithstanding, he remained an idealist. Never had he sought revenge. There had been no time for that. He had forgiven the miscreants and being too busy with his music, he had no doubt invited "new catastrophes." What else, he wondered, could be expected of the scion of "an honest God-fearing family"? He, the son of an "ultra-honest man," abhorred the bogus, the lie, the charlatan; but, admittedly, he shared his father's weakness: a tendency to exaggerate and paint "fine pictures." Nonetheless, it was a weakness that could be traced to self-hypnosis rather than to deliberate lying. He had gradually controlled this flabby side of his character.

George closed with a peroration swelling with promise and confidence: "I want to write a very great music . . . a music that will burn up the world . . . a music that is dependent on no great conductor's opinions nor those of the critics . . . a music that shall sweep all before it. I shall yet do it. I am better fitted now . . . cleaner in my soul and mind . . . and I am filled with a deeper fury . . . a deeper love for music than I have been before. I have gone through a crucifixion and a clarification! Everything that I might amount to in this world, I owe to you. Please accept my undying gratitude!"

Except for an allusion to the reduced Guggenheim grant, George remained true to his word: he had written Mrs. Bok a letter without dollar signs. If he thought that reversing the usual procedure would bring a blessed check from her, he was disappointed. Nor did she answer his epistle. A month later, in August 1933, George sailed for America alone. Boski remained behind in Cagnes to dispose of their villa and rejoined him a few days before the premiere of *Helen Retires*, which opened at the Juilliard School of Music on March 1, 1934.

Three days later it retired forever. Antheil pronounced it a "flop." Erskine preferred to say it was "damned and praised." Critics generally liked Erskine's libretto, but Antheil's score was another matter. Most agreed there was too much of it. Henderson (the *New York Sun*) objected to the long solos, the wavering orchestration, the "devious and uncertain" recitative; he made the point that the jazz and frivolous waltz pieces seldom interpreted character and that the vocal line was "distorted to the fashions of modernists."

Erskine paid Antheil $400 ($100 for each performance), adding that he had enjoyed their collaboration and assuring him that the opera would doubtlessly bring him the recognition he longed for in America. At least he hoped so, for he now admitted that Antheil's music had not shown sufficient "respect" for what he had tried to say in the libretto. He had not spoken earlier, because getting a fair hearing for Antheil's music in America seemed more important than protecting his own text. Now however he could say that Antheil had "pretty thoroughly missed the point of the opera." Erskine had to agree with the critics that the music "had very little connection with the words and practically none with the spirit of the words." Antheil, using jazz where a lyric treatment would have been more appropriate, had tried to turn the work into a burlesque, which it was not.

Helen Retires, above all, was an ironic poem. Should it ever be revived, significant changes would have to be made in the score. But Antheil had had enough of the opera, and in the unlikeliness of a revival, the chances of its bringing in any money seemed almost nonexistent.

Suddenly at loose ends, Antheil joined Ben Hecht and Charles Mac-Arthur, who had started making motion pictures at the old Paramount Picture Studios in Astoria, New York. Antheil furnished the scores, but the one film in which his music was actually used, *Once in a Blue Moon*, flopped. To augment his income, he composed "Parisian" ballet music for George Balanchine, who had made the discovery that ballets that were sufficiently Parisian brought New Yorkers to the theater in droves. It was strange after being recognized for years as an American in Paris to find that he was now looked upon as a European, if not always a Parisian, in New York. Alas, however, New York was not Paris. The old Paris salons, presided over by sophisticated and at least semi-intelligent people whose judgments on all the arts shaped the cultural life of Europe as well as America, had no counterpart in America. At best, New York supported only "would-be snob groups" that perpetuated outdated opinions.

Balanchine's efforts to involve Antheil in what might have turned out to be a parody of his former life in Paris actually was pivotal in his leaving New York. Long before the disappointing performances of *Helen Retires*, Antheil had written to Sylvia Beach of his intention to return to Paris and to his old apartment in the rue de l'Odéon. He confessed that for the little money they had eked out the United States, heavy demands had been made on both Boski and him. Paris was different. In spite of poverty, Paris always remained herself; money was not essential to her development. For him, Paris would forever be "the only spiritual place in the world." Someday he would return and remake it his home. But leaving Paris and staying away had been good for him, too. Performances in Germany and America had given him the courage to stand up to any challenge, something that had been difficult for him to do in Paris, where he had been shamefully dependent on false supporters. Although Sylvia Beach was not one of the unfaithful, her respect for Antheil had gradually fallen, and by 1930 she confided privately that he was "a regular little cad . . . an ungrateful *arriviste*."

George never saw Europe again, and Paris perforce would forever remain a spiritual home. Perhaps that was what he really wanted it to be—a place where he had received more acclaim than any of his American colleagues had ever had, even if it was not quite the unanimous recognition he had so often reported. America, as he intimated to Sylvia, had become a bigger challenge. "I am through with Europe," he told a reporter in December 1933. "Since 1927 I have been, in a sense, a man without a country. I am still a nobody here. But here I will become somebody or remain a nobody." The location of his new battlefield had at least been established.

On leaving Cagnes for the last time, he had admitted to Mrs. Bok that he was tired and worn out by wandering everywhere in search of quietude, health, or success. Now he longed for some place to call home. While still in New York and still uncertain of where he would go and what he would do, George tried once more to persuade Mrs. Bok to restore his monthly stipend. Again she refused, explaining that he would misconstrue any help as a sign that she had renewed her faith in his musical gifts. The truth was she had none whatsoever. She still objected to his habit of placing the blame for his lack of success on others. It showed how far his egoism had transcended his rational self-confidence. The time had come to be self-supporting, for it would be the height of self-delusion to expect any more assistance from someone who could no longer honestly endorse his music. George wryly noted in his reply that nothing had changed between them and added that it would be his last letter to the one who had always been "more than generous" and whom he had never betrayed.

Six months later George changed his mind. He had just had an exciting idea for another opera. With a little "leisure time," he could compose a score that would excel anything he had ever done. Would Mrs. Bok reconsider his case in the light of this unexpected development and perhaps grant him a "last chance" to demonstrate his talent and establish himself in America? Days passed. Then Mrs. Bok replied. "If you feel you can do a new opera well," she wrote, "I will give you the amount. . . . I do not like to refuse you the chance to do it." Unbeknownst to her, the book on which George intended to base the new work was Erskine Caldwell's recently published novel *Tobacco Road*. Fortunately, perhaps, nothing ever came of the project.

In 1937 the Antheils migrated westward. They moved leisurely, making long stopovers in New Orleans, El Paso, and Santa Fe. Eventually, they reached Hollywood and took rooms at the Hollywood-Franklin Hotel. George thought the place had some of the atmosphere of the old Paris Latin Quarter. It was a little like being back in the rue de l'Odéon.

In California Antheil orchestrated film scores for several major studios. He also became a journalist. To the *Chicago Sun* syndicate he supplied a daily advice-to-the-lovelorn column called "Boy Meets Girl." To *Esquire* magazine, he contributed articles on fidelity and endocrinology. The latter topic, which he claimed had so impressed the Paris police (they used his theories for typing criminals) that they made him an honorary member, also became the subject of his book *Every Man His Own Detective* (1937). Into an impressively accurate prediction of the outcome of World War II, named *The Shape of Things to Come* (1940), Antheil put the collective prophecies of several longtime friends, including William Bullitt, former American ambassador to France, and his brother, Henry Antheil, then a member of the United States State Department.

Among Antheil's Hollywood friends was the movie queen Hedy Lamarr, who had once summoned him to her Benedict Canyon retreat to ask his advice on which glandular extract might increase the size of her bosom. What interested her more in 1941, however, was finishing an invention she believed would help the Allies win the war: a radio-directed torpedo. With Antheil's help (he had a knowledge of electronics) she did, and together they patented the device the following year. In 1945 Antheil published his autobiography *Bad Boy of Music*, a joyous mixture of fiction and fact that became a bestseller.

What Antheil earned writing occasional movie scores supported his serious music endeavors in the 1940s and later. Compositions such as *Serenade No. 1 for Strings,* the *Fourth Piano Sonata*, the *Songs of Experience*, and the *Eight Fragments from Shelley*, according to the critic Charles Amirkanian, are "cast in classical forms, incorporating a very individual mixture of bittersweet lyricism, satirical paraphrases of military marches, American folk tune quotations, and rambunctious boogie-woogie rhythms, often tempered with the metallic dissonance of his early style." During the 1950s Antheil returned to the operatic form, completing four operas, the most notable being *Volpone*, in just five years. In 1953 he wrote the music for a ballet based on Ernest Hemingway's short story "The Capital of the World."

Although aware that he had a heart condition, Antheil refused to slow down. "I want to die in the saddle," he told friends. On February 12, 1959, in New York City, he died of heart failure. He was fifty-eight.

HAROLD STEARNS

I found out I was an American after
all. And when I had lost my own country,
as I thought—I really found it.
(from *Rediscovering America*)

In his seminal account of the expatriate movement, *Exile's Return* (New York, W. W. Norton, 1934), Malcolm Cowley describes how Harold Stearns, on Independence Day 1921, traveled by taxicab from his Greenwich Village apartment to the Cunard Line piers along the Hudson River, paused at the gangplank to explain to reporters why he was going to Europe, and then, doubtlessly buoyed by the project he had just completed and the journey before him, boarded the *Berengaria* and sailed away, not for a short summer trip as he had envisaged, but for a stay that lasted over a decade. In the early thirties, when Cowley began writing *Exile's Return*, Stearns was still in Paris, without money, jobless, and in poor health. To his rescue came an old friend named Evan Shipman and the American Aid Society, an organization that sometimes raised passage money for destitute Americans stranded abroad. On January 20, 1932, Harold Stearns, bearing a one-way ticket, left Le Havre on an American-bound freighter. Two weeks later, customs officials in Hoboken passed him through without a glance. No reporters were waiting at the dock to interview him.

What captured Cowley's attention and stimulated his imagination was

Harold Stearns's sensational departure, not his unceremonious home-coming. In *Exile's Return*, Cowley presents Stearns as an "Alexander marching into Persia," a "Byron shaking the dust of England from his feet," a charismatic figure whom young men everywhere were preparing to follow "eastward into new prairies of the mind." The extravagance of Cowley's accolade, while guaranteeing Stearns a secure, if minor, place in literary history, partly obscured the reasons why Stearns deserved to occupy such a place.

Although Stearns's well-publicized withdrawal from the United States has been seen as a symbolic act that inspired other disaffected Americans to follow his example, only a few of those who left the country at that time said they were pursuing the pathfinder into exile; they had independently reached their own reasons for going abroad. At most Stearns was a catalyst for those whose experiences led them to the same dismal discoveries about America that Stearns had made.

If the picture of Stearns as a Moses of the Lost Generation seems somewhat exaggerated, it is nonetheless true that his position as an incisive critic of life in America as well as an advocate of exile was firmly established before he left for Europe, and after the publication of the project he completed on the morning of his departure, this reputation was fixed forever. On that day he had risen before dawn to complete the preface for the massive symposium, *Civilization in the United States* (New York, Harcourt Brace & Co., 1922). As editor, Stearns had gathered essays from thirty contributors, many of them his friends, on topics that ranged from politics, law, education, intellectual life, music, art, and sex, to radicalism, family, nervousness, sport and play, and racial minorities; all of these topics, Stearns noted, had been chosen to assist "like-minded men and women to see the problem of modern American civilization as a whole." What they saw had been seen by others, by Sinclair Lewis for example, but never before had so many writers reached identical conclusions at the same time. Lest they be accused of creating a false impression of unity or of deriding America's weaknesses while ignoring its strengths, Stearns claimed that all had vowed "to speak the truth of American civilization" as they saw it "in order to . . . share in making a real civilization possible." Since these group judgments had emerged from a disinterested investigation, they were all the more noteworthy for being so similar.

Three basic contentions, Stearns explained, formed this "strong impression of unity": first, American life suffered from a "sharp dichotomy between preaching and practice"; second, because of the power of "cer-

tain financial and social minorities," American civilization was still regarded as Anglo-Saxon, an illusion certain to thwart efforts to achieve
"any genuine nationalistic self-consciousness"; and third, the social life of
America was emotionally and aesthetically starved, a pathetic fact amply
supported by the "mania for petty regulation; the driving, regimenting,
and drilling; the secret society and its grotesque regalia; [and] the firm
grasp on the unessentials of material organization of our pleasures and
gaieties." The maggots of hypocrisy, elitism, conformity, and bigotry had
reduced life in America to this sorry state of cultural impoverishment.
Civilization in the United States was uncivilized. The investigators, in a
spirit of intellectual cooperation and investigation and with a desire to
restore "civilization" to the country at a time when a potential for enrich-
ment and disaster existed, recommended that Americans, "without sentimentality and without fear," take a "first step in growing up" and examine
themselves without self-consciousness.

The widespread belief that Stearns had the courage of his convictions
contributed to his acclaim in the early twenties. For him and others disenchanted with America, exile seemed a logical if not easy step; but Stearns
alone among the contributors to *Civilization in the United States* had
acted on his principles. It was a decision that he had apparently been
contemplating for close to a year, for in an article describing the alternatives open to a bored, restless, troubled American youth entitled "What
Can a Young Man Do?" (published in *The Freeman* in August 1920) he
had answered his own question with the blunt command: "Get out!"
America offered no challenge for "imaginative and adventurous and artistically creative young men." Instead of providing flexibility, color, the possibility of adventure, and a chance to shape events, the institutional life of
the country blackjacked youth into accepting the "status quo *not* of 1920
but of the early eighteenth century in government, of the early nineteenth
century in morals and culture, and of the stone age in business." Conditions were even worse for writers, artists, and actors, for whom the choice
was between compromise and sycophancy or neglect and starvation. Was it
any wonder then that young men, impatient with fakery and in search of
the genuine, were leaving on every boat for Europe where, as Stearns
promised, "life can still be lived" and where nearly a year after writing
those words, he himself traveled in quest of the "real thing."

Stearns had visited Europe briefly in 1914, and like all first trips, as his
account written twenty years later revealed, it left an indelible impression.
In the spring of that year—he had just celebrated his twenty-third birth-

day—he felt a longing to go to sea. One of the sustaining joys of life in New York was hearing the ships' whistles coming from the river, a reminder that the sea, which he had loved as a child in New England, was close by. Its nearness conjured up visions of romance, the unknown, and faraway enchanted lands. The first of the faraway places he reached was London, where dazed by English manners and confused almost to the point of paralysis by his efforts to do the "right thing," he wandered about, alone and self-conscious, until he was mercifully "put on his feet" by Somerset Maugham, with whom he had struck up an acquaintance in New York two years before. Maugham, noting that the young visitor lacked proper clothing as well as money, supplied both, and then personally escorted him around the city. A week later, Stearns set out for Paris, traveling as far as Ostende with Harvard classmate Walter Lippmann.

Bursting with "life and color and stridency," Paris exceeded all his expectations. A few hours after his arrival, he had blended into the crowds of the socialists who were protesting the assassination of their leader Jean Léon Jaurès. Everywhere he saw portents of war. On August 4, once more in London, he joined the throngs milling at the base of a booming "Big Ben" to celebrate the declaration of war. The mood of hilarity stiffened his nationalistic pride. America, he would write later, "would never be dragged into any such mass murder as the European war . . . might well turn out to be."

That fall Stearns settled in Greenwich Village and took up what he called in retrospect a "typically Bohemian existence." He also began examining the subject that would increasingly absorb his energies, test his liberal views, and eventually make him one of the country's preeminent intellectuals. His abiding topic became America, or rather, the America that ought to be. The previous year, the year he graduated from Harvard and moved to New York, he had begun examining the nation's cultural shortcomings, a task complicated by the need to squeeze his observations into the book and drama reviews he contributed to the *Chicago Sun*, the New York *Dramatic Mirror*, and the *New York Press*. In 1915 he joined *The New Republic* as a "salaried contributor." Launched the year before by Walter Lippmann and Herbert Croly to achieve a liaison with an older generation of pragmatists and to encourage a national revival of the arts, politics, and education, the journal gave Stearns an ideological base on which to establish his position as a critic of outmoded standards and an advocate of liberal correctives.

As vital as the reformation of the country's dismal institutional life was to Stearns and to his colleagues, their responsibility was hardly so pressing that it demanded all their time. Chroniclers of Greenwich Village say that its heyday began in 1913, when an anarchist from Illinois named Polly Halliday opened a restaurant below the Liberal Club, at 14 MacDougal Street, which rapidly became the gathering place for Village intellectuals. It was there, Van Wyck Brooks remembered, that Harold used to pass his days, talking with anyone who happened along about "anything at all." If there was no one to talk with, he wandered around the Village, sometimes playing poker, browsing in bookstores like Boni's, or stopping in at bars. At night he went off with any one of his girlfriends, most of whom gladly bore more than their share of expenses. Beneath the mask of indifference Harold wore, some had discovered a small, mischievous boy who was scared and in need of help. "Keeping" Harold, whether for maternal or other reasons, was a rescue operation that brought his guardians abiding satisfaction.

Brooks, who knew Stearns as long and as well as anybody, also recalled that, despite being well-known in the Village, Harold "never seemed to have any close friends." He almost never smiled, and he "lacked a sense of humor." Curiously, though, these un-American traits increased his appeal. Although he "could be devastatingly brilliant," it was a charm he could also turn on and off at will. Harold's inscrutability, however, made him truly glamorous. The man was an enigma. No one, not even Brooks, could ever be sure what he was thinking or whether he was thinking at all.

There was nothing equivocal, however, about Stearns's position on the European war. Watching the crowds in London cheer the declaration of hostilities reinforced his opposition to the war. The prospect of American involvement and the enforcement of conscription was even more abhorrent to him. He determinedly adhered to the principles of pacifism and isolationism, although it appeared that everywhere the "deep wish for peace" that gripped the majority of men had come close to losing "all connection with reality." It was dismaying to see that the war was growing into "something so all absorbing and gigantic and awful" and that even anger was irrelevant. When the worst happened and Congress granted President Wilson's request for a declaration of war against Germany in April 1917, Stearns assumed "a monastic stance," refusing to review books concerned with the conflict and refraining even from discussing it.

Had it not been for an unexpected and attractive offer as associate editor of *The Dial* magazine, he might have maintained his antiwar posture indefinitely. The position offered a weekly salary of $50 and a favorable draft

Harold Stearns

status; the only drawback was moving to Chicago, where *The Dial* was then being published. Stearns would later call the Middle West "self-complacent, intolerant, priggish, successful, . . . and infernally dull." The positive aspects were that he was required to adhere to something close to a regular writing schedule, and his work brought him into an active literary world that included Lewis Mumford, Thorstein Veblen, Robert Morss Lovett, Conrad Aiken, and Clarence Britten, the last of whom Stearns hired as his assistant.

As the casualty lists lengthened, Stearns's opposition to the war weakened. Other liberals, too, he noticed, had either muted or modified their views. His editorials for *The Dial* focused on the need to end hostilities rather than on the war itself. If the war was being fought to preserve democracy and to make future wars impossible, as Wilson had said, then the nation, Stearns argued, must pledge itself to forging a democratic peace treaty. Above all, America should transcend nationalistic interests. Although he did not condone "Wilson's war," Stearns did ally himself with the president's "liberal crusade" for an honorable peace. As for conscription, opposition to which marked the true liberal, Stearns said nothing, presumably because supporting Wilsonian principles presupposed that one must condone, however antithetical to liberal beliefs, this violation of individual rights.

The defeat of Wilson's peace proposals, which reputedly broke the president's heart, also shattered Stearns's spirit. His final editorials termed Allied intervention in Soviet Russia a violation of Wilson's Fourteen Points, specifically Point Six, which called for the evacuation of Russian territory and international cooperation with the Bolshevik government. Also, Stearns predicted that the temper of the nation as well as that of England and France would remain vengeful and strongly nationalistic. The League of Nations, which he had cautiously supported, would be powerless without American support, and the chances of ever having a truly comprehensive and democratic peace appeared unlikely.

Stearns made these and other objectionable results of the war the subject of *Liberalism in America* (New York, Boni and Liveright, Inc., 1919). Writing with unaccustomed concentration soon after resigning from *The Dial* in April 1919, he produced an epitaph of the liberal movement. According to Stearns, liberals had succumbed too readily to the president's idealism and promises of a just peace. By quietly condoning Wilson's war as something that would produce noble ends, they had "stooped to conquer." Furthermore, they had ignored immediate problems, and when the war ended and Wilson failed to persuade the Allies to support the Fourteen Points, liberals suffered a disgrace as great as his. "The plain truth of our war to make the world safe for democracy," Stearns concluded, "is that today there is less freedom and right of assemblage, less tolerance, more governmental control over political and economic opinion, less liberty for teachers and college professors, more reaction and militarism than was the case the day we declared war on Germany." Their credibility damaged by the outcome of events and discredited by their own weaknesses, liberals in postwar America could hardly hope to restrain an increasingly rigid, isolationist federal government. As a political and philosophical force, liberalism was virtually spent.

From the pyre of defunct liberalism emerged a changed Harold Stearns—bitter where he had been forgiving, impatient where he had been tolerant, pessimistic where he had been optimistic. A pall of disenchantment hangs over his twenty essays printed in *The Freeman*, the progressive weekly founded in 1920 by Albert Jay Nock, Van Wyck Brooks, and Lewis Mumford. Stearns denounced, with a free-for-all abandon that exemplified *The Freeman*'s motto "Do as you like," every development responsible for reducing postwar America to a cultural wasteland, whether it was the damaging effects of too much industrialization on man's well-being, the glorification of the average in all areas of American life, the resurgence of a rigid puritan heritage that threatened to suppress what little vitality still remained alive in the country, the hypocritical surface morality that Americans blandly practiced, the paralyzing presence of censorship (mostly in literature), the noisome invasion of Prohibition into the lives of Americans, the contaminating commercialism of professional sports that resulted in the fixing of the 1919 World Series, or the partisanship of American intellectuals that obstructed the steady pursuit of truth. The country had become a battleground between "young intellectuals," progressives like himself dedicated to bringing "the national life a little nearer to greatness," and "America" (Stearns's designation for an older, conservative, effete generation of theorists who were wanting in true moral idealism and whose support of America's vapid institutional life made it less and less inhabitable for both the disinterested critic and the aspiring artist). Although Stearns may have been addressing an audience much smaller than he imagined and one that was already convinced that society "could never be changed by an effort of the will," he nonetheless believed that he spoke for many. There was no doubt in his mind that he was the exemplar of young American intellectuals and their most vituperative and outspoken spokesman.

The twenty articles of indictment against America that Harold Stearns wrote for *The Freeman*, along with two he contributed to other journals, were published in November 1921 under the title *America and the Young Intellectual* (New York, George Doran Co., 1921). All had been written between June 1920 and the time he went abroad in July 1921. Stearns left America at the urging of Brooks and Mumford, both of whom believed (wrongly as it turned out) that the work would take Harold's mind off a personal calamity they feared might have long and devastating consequences. Although Stearns was able to bring a lucid and cogent intelligence to the work and although there must have been times, however short, when it mitigated the pain of his loss, Harold Stearns carried the grief caused by the death of his wife, Alice Macdougal, with him long after she died, suddenly, on January 11, 1920.

Stearns had met Alice Macdougal in New York about the time *The Dial* moved to New York from Chicago. Alice, a book editor for Boni and Liveright Publishing Company, was, Brooks recalled, "attractive, intelligent, and stable." Harold found her "irresistible." She was very likely the first woman with whom he had had more than a transitory relationship and possibly the first he had ever loved. On Armistice Day—he waited until then so as not "to exploit any possible feeling of sympathy"—he proposed, and the following February they married. Theirs was a modern marriage. On their nuptial night, Alice kept a business engagement and Harold played poker. They agreed to postpone their "trip" (really their honeymoon, a word neither liked to use) indefinitely and to go on living in their own apartments. Alice, it was understood, would continue to use her own name. Clearly, Stearns's bride was a redoubtable woman; she also had great expectations for her husband. Harold later revealed that Alice had persuaded him to write *Liberalism in America* because she believed he must do something to distinguish himself. When he explained that he had already done something distinguished by marrying her, she replied that she would have refused to marry him if she had thought that that was the most important thing he could do. The bonding elements in their marriage were Alice's devotion to Harold and Harold's humility towards his wife. ("Everybody has to have some weakness," Stearns wrote in retrospect, "and I was hers.")

In September 1919, Alice, having informed her husband she was pregnant, returned to her parents' home in San Francisco to have the child. While she was away, he would finish his book, and when she returned, they would decide where to live. But Harold, alone once more and feeling like a "spiritual orphan," wondered whether the vagabond life might soon start

W. Somerset Maugham

Sinclair Lewis

again. He hardly had enough time to find out, for Alice, after giving birth to a boy named Philip on January 4, 1920, died of complications resulting from a Caesarian operation. Stearns was plunged into grief. "There was just emptiness, blank, loss of all feeling." For three months he stayed drunk and did no work. He spoke only of Alice and the son he might never see, for Alice's parents had taken custody of the child. "He didn't have any idea of what he wanted to do," Brooks remembered, "and he didn't want any help except for occasional loans to buy liquor." Everything seemed meaningless.

Although Stearns would say in his autobiography that the only antidote for loss or pain was work, the critical investigations he had undertaken at his friends' urging, while they led to accomplishments that consolidated his position as a critic with a bright future, did not bring the improvement in Stearns's spirits that Brooks and Mumford had hoped for. The depression into which he had fallen after Alice's death lightened, but he had not been able to reconcile himself to the loss of both a wife and a son. "They meant too much to him." The convincing air of indifference that he normally assumed about personal problems had vanished, and he spoke of his double loss with uncustomary sentimentality. At a farewell dinner a few days before his departure, Stearns told a Harvard classmate named Harry Wolfson that he was going abroad "to regain his emotional stability." Getting away might help him sever ties with the past. Perhaps in France he could relax and calm down, and when he felt capable, he would return to America and resume his career.

Although it is true that the war, the collapse of liberalism, the shattered peace treaty, and the festering ills that plagued America had all embittered Stearns, it is also true that Stearns's basic reasons for going abroad were primarily personal. The advice he gave young struggling American artists was to get out before it was too late; this was an extreme solution to a cultural problem that could only worsen. When he himself left, many believed that he was following a course consistent with his views. It was instead personal loss and disenchantment with life itself rather than dissatisfaction with America that was the main, if not the sole, reason that Harold Stearns left the United States.

A month passed before Harold Stearns, in the company of Sinclair Lewis, made a clamorous and memorably boozy entry into Paris. Instead of disembarking at Cherbourg, Stearns left the *Berengaria* in England and spent several weeks revising his contribution to *Civilization in the*

United States and trying unsuccessfully to persuade English writers to contribute to a second symposium on American civilization. Somerset Maugham, Stearns was disappointed to discover, no longer lived in London. Sinclair Lewis, however, had just moved to a cottage in Kent, and early in August he invited Harold to visit him. Stearns had hardly settled in when Lewis began complaining that he was working too hard on his new novel, *Babbitt*, and that he needed a rest. Why not stop for a few days, suggested Harold, and "take me" to Paris? He would introduce Lewis to "some nice people," and the trip would be good for Lewis's work.

On the boat train, on the Channel ferry, and on the *rapide* that delivered them to Paris, "whenever and wherever [they] could lay hands on a brandy or a whisky," Stearns remembered, they did. Groggy and scarcely sober, they rolled into the city, vowing to lay siege to "gay Paree." The inebriated two-man assault lasted five days. Lewis's vitality was inexhaustible, and at one point Harold called on Lewis Galantière to help pilot them around. Sinclair wanted to see everything at once—the Latin Quarter, the cafés, any convenient historical monument, and above all, Montparnasse by night. At the Dôme they shared a table with Malcolm Cowley, who had been in Paris for several months. Lewis, obviously drunk, Cowley remembered, brought round after round of drinks, summoning waiters by pounding on the table with his silver-headed cane and shouting "Garcong, garcong. Come here, you bloody garcong!" When a reporter tried to interview him, Lewis fended him off by pretending that Babbitt was a novelist. How much of that boisterous evening, indeed, how much of their sojourn in Paris, they remembered, Harold estimated, might be made to fit "into a very small page of a very small notebook." It was an impressively accurate observation when one considers the synopsis of the trip they confined to a very small postcard to Sherwood Anderson. It read: "Propositions: We love you. We miss you. We have seen nothing of Paris. We do not expect to, but if we missed Paris, Venus was there." In parentheses, Harold added: "Also Bacchus."

Back in Kent, sober if not refreshed, Lewis wrote to his publisher Harcourt that the truant trip to Paris had been "great . . . pure but wet" and that Stearns, whom he had "watched with care," was not "half so shaky and drunken" as many thought. "He's a curious, solid, enduring person, for all his dissipating, and I think he will have an ever widening future. I'm for him." Over a year later Stearns remembered the escapade as "more amusing, more profitable . . . [and] more veracious than a trip back home in the flesh." Profitable it certainly had been in more ways than one, for besides paying his companion's expenses, Lewis, on departing, had left an undisclosed amount of money with Stearns, enough to last him more than a month.

Why Stearns did not return to England, neither man ever said, but perhaps it was because Lewis suggested that since Stearns had no reason to go back, he might as well stay in Paris and have his things sent over. Whatever the explanation, Stearns remained and was comfortable enough with Lewis's money and the modest payments he received from the *Baltimore Sun* for occasional articles he sent the paper in care of his friend H. L. Mencken. He knew too that the local "newspaper boys," especially Sam Dashill and Roscoe Ashworth, would always slip him a few francs and that he could depend on Galantière's largess as well. His move from the downtown hotel where he and Lewis had registered to a tiny hotel in the rue Delambre made life not only cheaper but a good deal livelier. He had relocated in the very epicenter of Montparnasse, just around the corner from the Dôme (then "an old fashioned bistro") and the Rotonde ("small and dirty"). Nearby were the Dingo, still a "tiny workmen's café," and soon to appear, the Coupole, and what would become his favorite haunt, the Sélect.

Living again among students, journalists, writers, and artists, as well as "plain serious drinkers" was like being back in Greenwich Village, but there was one important difference: in Paris one could drink in public without fear of arrest. When asked why they lived in Paris, Americans would sometimes say it was because they liked being able to drink without the risk of going to jail. As trite as the explanation may seem, Prohibition was an oft-cited and, for many like Stearns, the most odious example of governmental restriction of one's freedom. Prohibition for Stearns was a sign of the decline, if not the decadence, of American life. Stearns, outraged by the moral implications as well as the soaring price of contraband liquor, had, according to Gilbert Seldes, devised a one-man bootlegging operation in New York that delighted everybody. Harold's scheme was to befriend every steward on every French ship that tied up along the Hudson River; from them he obtained supplies of wines and spirits that, at no profit to himself, he sold to his friends. He thereby avoided the taint of profiteering and provided them with genuine French products and the satisfaction of being part of a stratagem to outwit a practice as objectionable to him as conscription.

Stearns's opposition to Prohibition also had deep personal roots that were "intimately connected," as Brooks noted, "with his own need for drink." In dry America Stearns would often drink to excess to assert his independence; in Paris, where one was not compelled by edict to stay sober, there was no such reason for intoxication. When, mainly for financial reasons, Stearns switched from spirits to wine, beer, and champagne, he asserted that "at heart" he was "a moderate drinker." But the availability of alcohol as well as unlimited credit encouraged less than moderate consumption, as those who gazed with alarm or admiration at the *soucoupes* piled before Stearns knew.

If Greenwich Village had lost one of its leading intellectuals, Montparnasse had gained its only one, at least for a while. Stearns was an anomaly. His promising career, his reputation, his books and articles, his Harvard education, even his age, thirty-one, set him apart from others. No one in Montparnasse could produce credentials as impressive as his, but like the professor whose kudos intimidate his students, Stearns sometimes felt set apart by the achievements that were partly responsible for his being in Paris. The longer he remained in Montparnasse the larger became his reputation as a cerebral solitary. But in the fall of 1921, he had not yet withdrawn into himself, satisfied to have the bustle and stir of humanity all around him but not touching him. He had come to Paris, after all, to regain his emotional stability and to enjoy the tantalizing pastimes the city so abundantly provided, one of the most enjoyable of which was talking.

Stearns often said that when he arrived in Montparnasse, talking was at its best. Whatever form it assumed—conversation, gossip, *blague*—it was the Quarter's principal claim to distinction. Certainly it was one that Stearns honored and perpetuated and practiced among serious-minded students and a few artists who became his friends—George Biddle from Philadelphia; Nina Hamnett, a former Slade School student who had taken over Modigliani's studio; Man Ray; and the sculptor Jo Davidson. Also living in the Quarter at the time were Florence Gilliam and Arthur Moss, founders of *Gargoyle*, the first English-language magazine of the arts on the Continent; Maria and Eugene Jolas, who later in the decade started *transition*; Ezra and Dorothy Pound and their neighbor, poet Cheever Dunning; novelist and publisher Robert McAlmon; Sylvia Beach, proprietor of Shakespeare and Company bookstore; James Joyce; Stearns's former colleague on the *New York Press*, Djuna Barnes; Alfred and Dorothy Kreymborg; Gertrude Stein and Alice B. Toklas; the composer George Antheil; and Ernest Hemingway.

Stearns probably never knew when he decided to extend his summer holiday into an indefinite sojourn but he made clear why he had in his autobiography. Time, he explained, simply went by magically, and life in Paris, as countless Frenchmen had noted, passed like a dream. Weeks became months and months turned into years, and America, although fortunately not Americans, receded. Paris was indeed a place where one could forget. But as the first year drew to a close and his always meager bank account dwindled, the dream life was harder to sustain. Then suddenly it ended. Even in inexpensive Paris, one could not live without money, or at least not without the reputation of having it. Avoiding the proprietor of his hotel because of an unpaid bill, Stearns became furtive. Sneaking out of his room before dawn and returning late at night succeeded for a while, but eventually he was caught. Instead of an eviction order, however, the proprietor produced three letters: one contained a royalty check from the publisher of *Civilization in the United States*, another an appointment to the staff of the *Paris Herald*, and the last an invitation from a "nice American girl" named Jessica to a Christmas Eve fete. With money, a new job, and a girl, Harold's moribund dream life was spectacularly revived.

Grateful though Stearns was to Jo Davidson for finding him the job with the *Herald*, what the job brought him in salary hardly compensated for what it took out of a man whose chief weaknesses, by Stearns's own admission, were procrastination and indolence. Not only were the hours long and depressingly regular, but his first assignment as a roving reporter demanded too much legwork, and his second, as a rewrite editor, was tedious and boring. After a year he had had enough. Just before Christmas 1922, he walked out and never returned. About the same time, he lost touch with his Baltimore employers and the dispatches he had desultorily supplied to Mencken stopped. Had it not been for the help of the resourceful Davidson, Stearns might have remained unemployed indefinitely. Shortly after joining the *Herald*, Stearns, thanks to Davidson's intercession, had taken a position as Paris correspondent for the society, sporting, and country life magazine *Town and Country*.

For Jessica, however, Harold did not have to thank Davidson or anyone else. She may not have been his first American woman companion in Paris, but regardless of her position in the sequence of women who entertained and were entertained by Harold, Jessica was a talented artist and knowledgeable art historian. Although their time together was brief, a perverse joy permeated their last meetings and final farewell. Jessica had barely left Gare Saint-Lazare bound for Le Havre and America when Harold began thinking about Agatha, Jessica's friend, a divorcée who,

H. L. Mencken

Jimmy Charters (left foreground), Leigh Hoffman (right), Paris, 1928

although she lacked the brains and the artistic ability of her predecessor, had "attractive looks and great personal charm." Harold took her to the Quatz Arts ball, the art students' annual pagan frolic that was renowned for its nudity and unrestrained behavior. Nothing he had seen in Paris more completely defied everything Americans cherished or exposed what they lacked. Agatha invited Harold to Brittany, where they visited Dinard and Deauville, resorts that he would see again with another companion and as horse-racing reporter for the *Paris Tribune*. When Agatha asked Harold to show her how to write "practically for a newspaper" and divulged that the only topic that interested her was "women's clothes," he condescended, although the subject could hardly have been more "repugnant and uninteresting." Gradually, his association with the aspiring Agatha intensified and created so much "emotional bewilderment and uneasiness" that he was forced to find relief in the company of an American girl he had known in Greenwich Village. When Harold and his new companion returned from a trip to Lyon, Agatha had disappeared. Again unattached, Harold met still another American divorcée, named Josephine Bennett. She became his ideal of what a woman should be. She was older, "attractive, intelligent, witty, and a good sport." She had a considered view of life and of her economic and social position. She also had more money than either Jessica or Agatha, a handsome apartment, and her own car, which she expertly piloted to destinations Harold selected, including St. Malo, where while watching the spectacle of horse racing on the beaches, he rejoiced to see a robed country priest boldly place his bet at the pari-mutuel. That amusing observation, however, he omitted from the account of the excursion he sent to *Town and Country*.

Reporting the priest's aberrant behavior would hardly have surprised *Town and Country* subscribers, for after reading a few of the fortnightly letters Stearns had begun supplying the magazine in May 1922, they would have recognized the episode of the worldly priest as another of the correspondent's gibes at American prudery. Despite whatever misgivings he had about his qualifications for the job (he admitted later that he thought he was the last person anyone would have selected), it paid well and, most important, it provided a new and steady outlet for his criticism. Typically, Stearns's letters combined thoughtful if rather ponderous reporting, travel information, and commentary on world events affecting France; they were similar in content but not in spirit to Janet Flanner's biweekly "Letter from Paris," which began in The *New Yorker* the same spring (1925) as

Stearns's letters ended. Although Miss Flanner scrupulously obeyed the command of editor Harold Ross to report only what the French thought, Stearns was free to write whatever he pleased. With the contrasting patterns of French life all around him and the fresh perspective that distance from America provided, he resumed his examination of American civilization.

Harold's epistles were really paeans to his adopted country. What America lacked, he insisted, France usually possessed in abundance. What he had promised his countrymen they would find abroad, he claimed to be discovering daily, although reiterating the superiority of French civilization, he professed, sometimes made him melancholy. Stearns did not understand, however, the French reaction to Prohibition, which he could only attribute to complete befuddlement; either the French failed to understand Prohibition, or they refused to believe it existed. At this time the French government was sponsoring a National Wine Week in order to increase consumption, so it is likely that their mystification about Prohibition deepened. The French attitude toward literary censorship was also enlightened. At the same time that an American gentleman had been arrested for sending a copy of Rabelais through the mail, the president of France was unveiling a statue of the "indecent rogue"; and while Joyce's masterpiece *Ulysses* was being published in Paris by an American woman, the book was being banned in her homeland. Even American authors visiting Paris talked more openly than they did at home. Away from the pressure of social opinion and custom, they spoke their true minds honestly and forthrightly. Paris, far from being out of contact with American literary life, was often the place where literary Americans flourished.

A problem that worried Stearns more than either censorship or Prohibition was the increasing Americanization of the French. More industrialism, more efficiency, more mechanical invention, faster communication and travel—the shibboleths of American progress—had already created a conflict between "New World intensity for getting on" and "Old World charm." If the French were ever sold on American efficiency, he warned, they might go so far as to abandon such endearing customs as the three-hour lunch and the two-hour aperitif. Worse, they might adopt American attitudes toward work and money. The trouble with Americans, Harold argued, was that they spent the best part of their lives performing "meaningless activities" they called work in order to obtain "meaningless possessions," or simply more money. The French, on the other hand, labored to earn money so that as soon as possible they could live without working. Possessions had nothing to do with contentment and happiness, as those who had worked to live knew. Like obligations they could become burdens. The American system ignored what the French traditionally cared most about: the satisfaction of human needs and comfort. Like the French, Stearns contended that as long as he had money "to eat well, sleep comfortably, buy a book or two, and be able to move about," he was content. Anything more, while welcome, would have little value; anyway, to earn anything even close to a real wage in Paris, he had to confess, was nearly impossible for him. Harold hoped that the conflict between the cultivated life of France and the raw, pulsating aggressive "New World" would be resolved by employing the vitality of the new to make life easier and to satisfy man's quest for beauty. His hopes reveal a desire to leave undisturbed a way of life in which he found it possible to work and be happy, neither of which, he insisted, had ever been possible at home.

Harold claimed that the same desire to satisfy human needs was responsible for the oft-discussed but much misunderstood Gallic views on love, sex, and marriage. Romance for the French began where it ended for Americans—in marriage. Love for the French had a broader and finer meaning than it had for Americans: it was an amalgam of physical, spiritual, and intellectual attraction, the "real motive force and dignity of life." As for sex, the French attitude was cleaner and healthier than ours. The French, unlike Americans, spoke gaily and openly about it, never to the point of satiety but with an insouciance that encouraged a familiarity and frankness about the facts of life. The result—something Americans and the English often most needed—was both a psychological and spiritual release.

Harold Stearns's need for psychological and spiritual release had been obvious for some time. In New York he had been worried about sex. But as he had discovered, what was readily available to the French as part of their heritage often eluded the Anglo-Saxon. Ever since the summer of 1921 when he appeared on the terrace of the Dôme and shyly confided to Malcolm Cowley that he wanted to sleep with a *poule* named Lucette, his amours had been either short encounters with prostitutes or affairs with American women, usually vagabond divorcées from whose company he regularly and ceremoniously fled. For Stearns, the much-vaunted French examples of sexual behavior remained unrealized, not because they were beyond realization but because Harold was neither capable nor willing to act on them. It was enough to talk about love, sex, and marriage, to have affairs, and to indulge oneself occasionally with prostitutes. Titillating forms of rebellion, they provided all the tangy satisfaction of reveling in the forbidden. Paris offered too many temptations, too many opportunities, too much variety ever to make the French models of love and marriage any more than ideals and prosaic alternatives for the unattached American in Paris. And for the puritan New Englander, there would always be an alluring hint of the lascivious in the Gallic attitude toward sex. Harold's expanded amatory life in Paris, stimulated by a sexual freedom that condoned the pleasures it allowed, differed only in degree from the one he had pursued in Greenwich Village.

Paris, he was learning, was like the Village or any other Bohemia in another respect, too: it could be a testing ground as well as a playground. Although that observation appeared in a *Town and Country* letter addressed to parents of young Americans determined to migrate to the city as he had, Stearns might have been posting the message to himself. In answer to his own question, "What makes Paris the greatest testing ground of character in the world?", he drew on his experiences of the previous year and a half. For the first time in his life, the young American was free from social pressure. Family, associates, friends—all were far away. Alone, he lived in a deceptively "soft and mellow" environment that glorified enjoyment, induced languor, and pardoned irresponsibility. With no position to maintain as at home, he could do what he liked—dress shabbily, get drunk, carouse, vanish for a week with a friend, mix with whomever he pleased. The whole rhythm of life encouraged experimentation, adventure for its own sake, indulgence, and all in a city where reproach was virtually unknown. He was free to go to the devil on his own terms.

Paris would either make or break the young American. It would not shield the weak from his weaknesses. Away from a society that routinely imposed protection in the form of restrictions and exhortations, away from external disciplines, he was on his own. No one would tie moral reminder strings around his fingers. No one would make him feel dependent. If he lacked self-control, personal strength, or self-sufficiency, he would go to pieces fast. If, on the other hand, he possessed strength of character, if by some good fortune he had withstood the pressures at home that robbed so many of their individuality and dignity, he would not only grow in Paris but he would thrive in "the ground of individual volition and individual desire."

In a place where the customary moral rules were absent, the risks were high but worth taking. The alternative—keeping inquisitive youth at home where ignorance is bliss—would never provide answers to the question of the spiritual mettle of American youth.

When Harold Stearns advised young Americans to get out of their country and go to Paris, he could not have known exactly what awaited them. Three years later the possible consequences of following that injunction must have seemed to him to be complex and even perilous. Paris could be a Babylon. Exile could destroy as well as liberate. Even Harold was making the unexpected discovery that being in Paris had strengthened his weaknesses and eroded his strengths. Following another year of even less activity than the previous one, he admitted that with so many temptations to leisure available, one had to agree with Oscar Wilde that the "only absurd thing [was] not to yield to them." That he had frequently done so some had already begun to notice.

Under the poetic headline "Owl, Like Poe's Immortal Raven, Breaks into a Writer's Haven," a reporter for the *Paris Tribune* recounted how Stearns had been seen wandering around the Quarter carrying a live owl wrapped in a checkered napkin. The bird, according to its new owner, had flown into his apartment at midnight and, "not finding a bust of Pallas" anywhere, had alighted on a dusty copy of *The Dial*. That Harold and his nocturnal visitor were "birds of a feather" was the point of the spoof. Like its protector, the wise bird was "not in the best of health" and showed a strong aversion to "politics, race problems, psychology, complexes," and other "intellectual diversions" popular in the Quarter. That the bird would eventually recover from its decrepit state, however, seemed certain, for as Stearns supposedly reminded the reporter, had not other wise birds been known to lose some discretion when they first came to Paris?

A second reminder that Stearns was guilty of allowing temptations to sully his reputation appeared a few months later in the same newspaper. The "doyen of Montparnasse" (Stearns), an anonymous reporter revealed, had written sketches of twelve well-known Americans in the Quarter. The author, continued the reporter, admitted that he had been almost forced to write the book because persistent friends, once they heard about it, had annoyingly and repeatedly inquired about his progress. As for its content and spirit, the only clue resided in the titles he had considered. The first, *Why Boys Leave Home*, he had discarded as too serious; the second, *Studies in Stupidity*, implied among other things that Americans—and

Quat'z arts Ball, 1922

Dingo Bar, 1922, Jimmy Charters (far right)

perhaps Stearns himself—were in Paris for the wrong reasons. Since neither *Studies in Stupidity* nor any other book about Montparnasse characters ever appeared, the effort to embarrass Harold into writing a book failed.

The same phantom book reappeared in an attack Sinclair Lewis made on the whole colony of Left Bank "geniuses and their disciples" in *Scribner's* (May 1925). Motivated as much by spite as conviction, Lewis charged that "standardized rebels" in "flight from the crushing standardization of America" had turned the Café Dôme into a "cathedral of American sophistication and standardization." Ministering to the congregation of loafers and sycophants was the "very father and seer of the Dôme," the "king of kings . . . ex-cathedra authority on literature, painting, music, economics, and living without laboring"—Harold Stearns. Four years after having praised Harold as a "solid, enduring person" with "an ever widening future," Lewis had concluded that his erstwhile friend no longer had a future. Even if his long-promised "assassinatory book" (*Studies in Stupidity*) ever appeared, Lewis predicted that it would be nothing more than a denunciation of those "false idols of the intelligentsia . . . [that had] become tired of lending him . . . money." The imputation that Stearns measured the intellectual development of people by the amount of money he could borrow from them and that if they refused him, he made them the objects of scorn brought a stinging retort from Stearns. Lewis, besides being a cad and a bounder, had missed both the good and bad points of the Montparnasse colony, the former because he could not understand them, the latter because he exemplified them. Even the most insensitive Americans living there had felt the spiritual forces of French life. That Lewis had not, Stearns concluded, was the reason he had scurried back to America.

The spiritual vigor of France had nothing to do with the hasty journey Harold himself made back to the United States the same year. Jo Bennett had one day identified what he was missing. "You want to go back to America," she observed, "not to live [but] to see your son." Impressed by her perspicacity, Harold had agreed, and she had given him travel money to Carmel, California, where the boy, now five, lived with his grandparents. It is possible that Jo hoped never to see Harold again in Paris and that behind her generous act was the same concern that had bothered Lewis and Cowley, namely that Harold Stearns was going to pieces fast and that unless something was done to arrest his decline, he would sink deeper and perhaps permanently into a mental and spiritual morass. Maybe seeing his son would give him something to live for, a sense of responsibility, even of parenthood; and perhaps returning to America would also provide the incentive to resume the career he had interrupted four years before and had only desultorily pursued in Paris.

But being with his son produced the "keenest sense of loss" Harold had ever experienced. What held them together at first, he wrote later, was a bond of common solitariness before alien things. From it came a feeling of warmth and comradeship. He soon saw, however, that Philip was really Alice's son, not his. He had her physical attributes. His gestures, sense of humor, and generous impulses were all hers too. The boy obviously belonged to his grandparents, the Macdougals. There were even disconcerting signs that Philip was not aware of his paternity. What legal barriers Stearns would have had to overcome to gain possession of his son were no doubt less formidable than the psychological ones his in-laws had erected. With these kind and obliging people he had little in common except Alice, once the strongest reality in his life, and his son, now a stranger who had been taught to call him Harold. Being with them made him feel like an interloper, and Carmel, for all its scenic splendor, only made him realize how much he already missed even "a slight, derivative, and unsatisfactory reality like Paris."

In Baltimore Harold broke the homeward journey to call on H. L. Mencken, who provided his old friend with quantities of synthetic gin, the latest gossip, and a selection of choice absurdities. In New York Malcolm Cowley, wearing a large sunflower and carrying a banner reading "Welcome to Our City," greeted him in Pennsylvania Station, served more synthetic gin, and accompanied him to Frances Gifford's Greenwich Village apartment, where the drinking went on and where Harold nearly expired from gas seeping out of Thorne Smith's apartment on the floor above. So frenzied were his friends' efforts to recapture the old days that Stearns took refuge, in an uncustomary state of exhaustion, in the Lafayette hotel, to await his ship back to France.

New York, Harold informed the curious in "modest" and "respectable" Paris, was, contrary to myth, all of America concentrated and intensified in one place. The entire population, it seemed, was hysterically making money, "working at the game of pretending to work," shamelessly engaging in heterogeneous lovemaking, and joining clubs and fraternal orders to stave off loneliness. The patterned life that he had rejected, with its restraints and controls, was still being rigidly enforced. In America, it was still virtually impossible to develop an individual way of living or any real sense of happiness. Nonetheless, he had to admit, there were a few encouraging signs that the country was becoming more civilized. There was less bigotry, less repression, and fewer examples of excesses of virtue (due probably to the fear among those responsible that they were fighting a losing battle). Also, he was pleased to see there were more aesthetic controversies, an increased artistic appreciation, and a vastly improved theater. To the question of whether he would ever live permanently again in America, however, there was only one answer: an "unqualified negative."

Although in California Stearns had called Paris an "unsatisfactory reality," it nonetheless provided what his native land could not—a home, however ephemeral. And yet, leaving the United States for a second time had given him a sense of uneasiness. Was he running away without good and sufficient reason? Never before had he felt quite so much like "an uprooted aimless wanderer," and although it was good to be in Paris again, he could not entirely eradicate the feeling of displacement the trip had produced. As usual, he was broke, without a job (his last letter to *Town and Country* appeared September 1, 1925), and without a friend or a woman to support him. While waiting for something to turn up, he passed the time strolling around the Quarter, cadging drinks and a meal if possible, or a few francs from obliging friends or gullible strangers. Things might have been easier if Jo Bennett had not gone off mountain climbing in Switzerland with the Hemingways. Fortunately, his room had not been rented, but if he were without funds for long, he would lose that too. Eventually, he figured out a way to make money from his typewriter without using it. He would sell the machine for a few dollars, and then after a week or so, he would ask to "borrow" it from the new owner, saying he needed it to write an article. He would then resell it to someone else, being careful to avoid the first buyer. How many times Harold successfully sold his typewriter is beyond reckoning, but the enterprise stopped when Malcolm Cowley bought it and took the machine out of the country. What additional ruses he devised or indecencies he suffered during the summer of his "discontent" Stearns excluded from his autobiography, but Gilbert Seldes reported in 1925 that Harold had become a "scarecrow, silently telling his countrymen 'Go home, or you'll end up like me'"; and Van Wyck Brooks was disturbed to learn that Stearns had taken to sleeping on park benches.

If Harold's dream life was ever to be revived, acts of extraordinary beneficence, acts only a few of his acquaintances were capable or willing to perform, were needed and needed promptly.

Kiki, Paris, 1924

This time, in order of appearance, two women and three men rallied to Harold's rescue. From Switzerland came Jo Bennett. If she was surprised or disappointed to find Stearns back in Paris and in his usual penurious state, she concealed it. She showed that she was still a good sport (Stearns's highest compliment) by entertaining Harold's latest companion, a new-found friend from New York named Belinda, who arrived brimming with money and aspirations to take in Paris and environs on her two-week vacation. Harold escorted her to Longchamp to see the races, to Fontainebleau for a weekend, to his favorite Quarter cafés, and all too soon, to the Gare Saint-Lazare, where the customary affectionate farewell kisses renewed familiar ruminations on the transience of seemingly durable relationships. Like her predecessors, Belinda made Harold a parting gift of unspent francs. Life in Paris, he was happy to see, was slowly returning to normal.

What had brought Harold and Belinda together in New York was his projected book about Americans in Paris. Understandably, her confidence in it exceeded his, and after Harold returned to France, she promised to use her influence to keep the project alive, especially with the publisher Horace Liveright, for whom Stearns had acted as Paris agent since 1923, when he had tried to interest him in Gertrude Stein's *The Making of Americans*. Now Harold had another recommendation. It was a collection of stories with short interchapters entitled *In Our Time*. Only the interchapters had been published in Paris. The author, Ernest Hemingway, wanted an American publisher to bring out the enlarged version. Liveright was indeed interested and Stearns had carried the good news back to the author in Paris.

Hemingway had lived in Paris almost as long as Stearns. To the still-unpublished aspiring writer, Stearns's literary standing must have seemed imposing; but the man was more impressive than his reputation. What he had not learned about Stearns from Stearns himself, Hemingway had gathered from Harold Loeb, Jo Bennett, and the local newsmen. By the time he started writing *The Sun Also Rises* in 1925, Hemingway had reached certain conclusions about Harold Stearns and about what had happened to him in Paris. His profile of Stearns as Harvey Stone in *The Sun Also Rises* is astute, sympathetic, revealing, and accurate.

When Jake Barnes, the protagonist of *The Sun Also Rises*, comes upon an unshaven Harvey Stone sitting alone on the terrace of the Sélect with a pile of saucers in front of him and asks if he has heard anything from the States, Stone replies, "Absolutely nothing." It hardly matters though, for he adds he is through with "them" anyway. But since he is waiting for money from home, it does matter. Stone has not eaten for five days. Only three days earlier, however, he had won two hundred francs from Jake, but Jake says nothing about his winnings and gives him one hundred francs. Stone complains that begging for money is humiliating. When he is out of money, he just wants to stay in his room, "like a cat." The two men go on drinking and talking. Stone has just remarked that Mencken has written about all the things he knows and now is on to the things he does not know when Robert Cohn, an obnoxious young American writer, joins them. "Hello, Robert," Harvey says. "I was telling Jake here that you're a moron." Before Cohn can react, Stone asks what Cohn would rather do if he could do anything he wanted. When Cohn answers that he would play football again, Harvey revises his opinion. Robert Cohn is not a moron, he is "only a case of arrested development." Harvey ignores the young man's threat to push his face in and leaves. Robert expresses his distaste for the man, but Jake has a different opinion. "I like him," he says. "I'm fond of him."

What is missing from the novel are the reasons why Jake Barnes likes Harvey Stone and Robert Cohn does not. The qualities that endear Stone to Barnes have the opposite effect on Cohn. Stone fuels the latent antagonism between Barnes and Cohn, and since Cohn is the least sympathetic character in the novel and Barnes the most, Barnes's reactions to Stone weigh heavily in his favor. But why does Barnes rush to defend Harvey Stone?

The answer is contained in a few pages of manuscript that Hemingway withheld, perhaps on Fitzgerald's recommendation, from the published novel. In the excised pages (a continuation of the above scene), Jake reveals that there is "something nice and simple" about Harvey, a quality his detractors invariably overlook. It is true that the rotten stories that circulate about Harvey come from those who are offended by his habit of borrowing money and then telling grand stories to justify it. For someone without any fixed income, however, there is nothing else to do. When people find out his stories are untrue, they are angry. But, explains Jake, Harvey is only making use of his "fine imagination," and besides, he has always repaid whatever he has borrowed. Jake answers Robert's charge that Harvey is "an awful liar" by reminding him that "every good man [is] in some way or other." Still convinced that Harvey is only a bum, Robert mutters, "But he gets on my nerves."

Similarly, Stearns could get on Hemingway's nerves. Stearns had told F. Scott Fitzgerald that Sinclair Lewis's attack on him in *Scribner's* had created "a sort of universal blackball against him" in New York. When

Fitzgerald, concerned that Harold was "going to pieces" in Paris possibly because of "a series of accidents and coincidences," asked Alexander Woollcott to help Stearns publish in New York any articles he might write, Hemingway wrote to Fitzgerald that it was useless to try to reform a has-been who had done nothing for almost two years. Any softness toward the down-and-out Stearns was misplaced, Hemingway advised. Except for giving Stearns money (Fitzgerald had already done so) and being nice to him, there was nothing anyone could do. The "poor old bastard lives altogether in his imagination," Hemingway explained. "I always get awfully sorry for people and especially for liars, drunks, homely whores, etc. . . . After all, panhandling is no damned fun. A gent who's drinking himself to death ought not to be constantly having to raise the funds to do it with. I do think Harold had a pretty damned good head. Also think he destroyed it or completely coated it with fuzz by drinking."

Having given Fitzgerald the lowdown on Stearns, Hemingway asked him to keep it confidential. It would only make life tougher if Harold were to think Hemingway did not believe in him. Watching the man decline was "pretty sad," but nothing could be done about it.

The third man to come to Harold's rescue was a fellow Harvard graduate named Alex Small, who after abandoning a brief academic career in France, had become one of the *Tribune*'s most popular and acerbic columnists. Small's biweekly column, "Of Fleeting Things" (Stearns had suggested the title), bristled with denunciations of America as harsh as Stearns's; but his favorite target was the pretentious, do-nothing American expatriates, with the exception, of course, of Harold. Small's caustic writing was as intriguing as Stearns's silence, and a colleague described Small as "an indefinable blend of Samuel Johnson, Henry Brooks Adams, Rabelais, and Xenophon, with traces of Thomas Hardy and perhaps Ambrose Bierce." Small proposed an unusual solution to Harold's chronic problems of unemployment and penury: a job with the *Paris Tribune*. The only requirement was that Stearns surrender his identity and reappear as "Peter Pickem," the sobriquet of the paper's horse racing tout.

Mid-life career changes must often seem either comic or pathetic to those who do not experience them. Harold's slide from a position of intellectual preeminence to that of local tipster had elements of both. Abandoning a career that had challenged and invigorated his critical powers and had made him the spokesman for a disenchanted generation to take a twenty-dollar-a-month job as racetrack reporter seemed to verify that he was determined to ruin not only himself but also his career. However, as more than a few had noticed, Harold had increasingly taken on the look of a hobo. A newcomer to Paris, William L. Shirer, was thunderstruck the first time he saw Stearns shuffling around the *Tribune* office, a shabby, unwashed, unshaved, melancholy figure, a specter of the Greenwich Village intellectual he had once admired. To another journalist, A. J. Liebling, Stearns was one of the most remarkable sights in Paris: a "nonwriting writer [permanently] hanging on the bar like a crook-handled cane." Others, remembering Stearns's anthology, snickered: "There goes American civilization—in the gutter." To those less faultfinding, he was simply a "picturesque ruin." If anyone fit the common (and basically incorrect) conception of the "lost generation," it was Harold Stearns.

What few seemed to realize was that Harold, despite his disheveled appearance, actually liked his new assignment and performed it with verve and devotion. He loved the horses, the races, the gamblers, the touts, the crowds. Horse racing, he was soon fond of repeating, could be more stimulating than a walk through the Louvre. Mastering the intricacies of the sport came easily. With pardonable caution, he urged readers to bet to place rather than to win; that was the only way to make any money out of the French racetracks. Several among his *Tribune* staffers, hoping to parlay savings from low wages into substantial winnings, regularly gave Harold money to bet for them and agreed to share any winnings and not hold him responsible for losses. On winning days Harold showed up at the office with more money than he had had in years. But if his hunches had been wrong, he had only his meager salary, an even smaller expense account, and credit at a neighborhood restaurant to keep him going.

After a few months as Peter Pickem, Stearns had established a routine that remained unchanged for the next three years. Racing in France was year-round, and for most of that time (except in winter) there were races daily, and Harold attended all of them. After half a day at one of the tracks near Paris, he would return to the *Tribune*, usually late in the afternoon, and file a story about the races he had just seen as well as a forecast of and his tips on the next day's races. It was an assignment that required "two different and opposed attitudes of mind—one retrospective of what had happened, the other prophetic of the next day." At times when his tips had gone astray or ended "in the cabbages," as the French put it, the necessity to switch from apologies to confident predictions required "something very like moral courage." Almost as daunting was having to face the winners and losers among his newspaper colleagues and friends; the winners were sometimes too proud to admit they had taken Stearns's tips, the losers were only too ready to blame him for their losses. Being a tipster demanded more than a knowledge of horses and tracks, intuition, and luck, it also required fortitude and resilience.

Although Stearns scarcely blanched at being called Peter Pickem (he was also known as "Filibert," after the winner of the 1923 Grand Prix de Deauville on which he had placed a large bet), he was delighted when his French *confreres* began addressing him respectfully as "Monsieur Stearns de Chicago." Among them he had authority and position. It was pleasantly diverting to join them in the press box, exchange familiarities and tips, and watch the preliminary race activities. Below, the jockeys mounted their horses and received final instructions; then came the slow parade through the gate and the defile and then the gallop back to the starters. Spectators numbered 50 to 60,000 at the Grand Prix events in the summer and packed the grandstands. They had sharp eyes, quick speech, and an exuberant sense of humor. Harold estimated there were more racetrack devotees in Paris than in any other city in the world. Their prevailing good nature, he explained, was the result of their sensible practice of betting only a little more than twice what they could afford to lose.

As arresting as the colorful crowds were the racetracks and their settings: Chantilly was surrounded by woods and spacious lawns, and close by was the castle. The formal gardens of Longchamps in the Bois were magnificent in May and June, as were the bare, bleak slopes of Vincennes in the winter. Maisons-Laffitte was set in a small wooded park beside the Seine. Beside the trim paddock and the noisy field at Le Tremblay on the Marne crowded small shops selling fried river fish. There was a splendid view of Paris from the high hill on which St. Cloud perched, little summer country tracks at Rambouillet and Fontainebleau, and jumping and trotting circuits, one inside the other, at Enghien. Soberly dressed, Stearns traveled from one racetrack to the next, each with its own flavor, crowds, and setting. He was a stolid, placid man who pursued a routine that excluded nearly every activity that had once been important to him.

If anyone had asked Harold what he was doing besides attending races and writing his *Tribune* column and lounging in cafés, he would have answered: nothing. With enough money to live on, credit at a few cafés and restaurants, the diversion of the tracks, and the prospect of a winning day every so often, his dream life in Paris had expanded spectacularly. Existing in a "kind of soft haze of pleasant unreality" and unperturbed by past regrets and unmindful of future plans, he preferred this way of life. Con-

Ernest and Hadley Hemingway, Schruns, Austria, 1925-26

Harold Stearns, 1930s

tentment consisted of just being alive and enjoying whatever pleasures were at hand. For once, he made no attempt to read anything or do any extra work. Life was most amusing and at its best when not taken too seriously. Yet, as he would write in retrospect, succumbing to a mood of pleasurable quiescence posed some perils, especially for a New Englander of his temperament; the longer this life continued, the weaker became the "tradition of purposefulness and accomplishment and moral integrity" in which he had been raised and to which he owed his professional standing.

Harold was nonetheless determined to sustain that mood or incapable of changing it, and he methodically maintained an unvarying schedule. Following the races, he would put in a two-hour stint writing his column; then came dinner with Alex Small or Dorothy Smith, the *Tribune*'s society editor and Stearns's off-and-on companion, and finally retirement to the Café Sélect, where he would often remain till dawn, quietly drinking champagne, listening to the formidable Madame Sélect recount the day's events, watching the antics of a "shamefaced" dog called Bobby and the "spectacle" of a strange crowd of variegated nationalities and dubious sexes, the loudest being Scandinavians, followed by Americans, English (mostly homosexuals), and then Russians, Germans, and French, the last drawn there by the zany behavior of the clientele.

As one of the Sélect's oldest clients, Harold enjoyed virtually unlimited credit. Except for the occasional drink or two he might win rolling dice with Madame Sélect (which was an honor, since her victories were considered dubious) or cadge from a softhearted acquaintance or friendly stranger (their numbers fell as the decade wore on), Stearns relied on his good-customer standing and his practice of settling up whenever "fortune smiled at the track" to support his drinking needs. But with a single evening's consumption likely to exceed a dozen coupes, Harold's tab often reached two hundred francs, an amount awesomely represented by a tower of saucers that nearly reached the ceiling. "You must come and see Harold's pile of saucers," regulars urged visiting Americans, as though Stearns and his saucers were a tourist attraction. Occasionally, a startled onlooker paid for the whole collection, perhaps, as Bill Cody suggested, so that he could talk about it later.

Customers were accustomed to seeing Stearns sitting solidly on a high stool at the bar, usually alone and looking straight into the mirror on the opposite wall, his expression calm and inscrutable and his figure in repose. In the mirror he could see who came in, who went out, and who occupied the neighboring stools. There he sat like a Buddha (*Tribune* staffers christened him the "Hippique Buddha") presiding over a congregation of novitiates. Curious and courageous questers of wisdom would sidle up to the silent man, buy him a drink, and wait for the "oracle" to speak. To one such seeker, Bill Widney, who made a specialty of entertaining celebrities, Harold spoke: "There's no substitute for straight thinking." Satisfied, Widney slipped silently away. To others, however, notably a *Tribune* colleague named Louis Atlas, he talked of something much dearer to his heart and dreams—a horse.

Many regarded the story of the filly that Stearns had either bought, won, or inherited (no one ever found out exactly how it had come into his possession, if indeed it ever had) as apocryphal. Strangers who heard Harold describe the animal's merits had no reason to suspect that it might be imaginary and gladly contributed to its upkeep. And even the suspicious often found his account of the filly's training so convincing that they convinced themselves that perhaps it really did exist after all.

Forbearance and a respect for the teller's sensitivity forbade requests to see the horse. It was enough, according to Louis Atlas, to listen politely whenever Stearns reported that he had gone to visit the animal, and to perhaps ask when it would make its debut and how much it cost him to keep it. "Got a bill for 7,000 francs today," Stearns would reply. And after a pause, during which the enormity of the figure was allowed to sink in, he would add: "that covers three months food, stable care, and trainer's bill—and it's worth it."

After a while Stearns stopped talking about his horse. Louis Atlas, who had come to believe in the animal's existence almost as much as its owner, tactfully respected Stearns's sudden silence. It never occurred to him to ask Harold what had happened. "It wasn't the kind of thing you could talk about." Others talked, however, and their explanations tended toward hyperbole. Some went so far as to say the horse had committed suicide. But one night in the Sélect, George Seldes and a group of Harold's friends heard the story of the filly's death from the grief-stricken owner himself. He told it brilliantly, Seldes remembered, creating "a little epic of effort and heroics and devotion" that held them spellbound. After describing how he had nursed the ailing animal through her last days, Harold paused, raised his eyes to his listeners, and said softly: "She died in my arms." It was the tragic end of a great dream.

Soliciting contributions for the upkeep of a phantom filly was not the only way Stearns accumulated betting money, covered his losses, or weathered impecunious times. As Peter Pickem, Harold was well known even among tourists, and when they asked for tips, he would often offer to place their bets for them if they were unable to go to the track themselves. Many accepted. Harold did not tell these trusting strangers the horses he had picked for them. Instead, he would give the names of all the horses running in the event. The next day he would return their bets, explaining with apologies that he had been unable to go to the track. Unbeknownst to these gullible gamblers, Harold had in fact gone to the track and had pocketed winnings he had made by betting their money.

As a tout with a better-than-average record of winning horses, Harold attracted a sizable number of followers among his *Tribune* colleagues and a few affluent residents of the Quarter. He also offered them the opportunity of placing their bets with him if they could not go to the track. Just before Harold collected their bets, he would fill his column with the names of almost certain losers; then he would bet their money on his real choices. For a while the scheme went undetected, but one day he forgot to place the $50 bet someone had given him to back a twenty-to-one shot, and the horse won. Mortified, Stearns disappeared for a few days. But as news of the ruse spread, his standing as a bookie slipped precipitately, and with it his always fragile posture of self-sufficiency and resourcefulness gradually crumbled too. It was bad enough to be dependent on others for help so much of the time, but it was humiliating to be found out as a double-dealer. Continuing to balance "his disreputable life like a comic juggler," observed his friend Evan Shipman, would require more ingenuity, stamina, and good fortune than even Harold had a right to expect.

Also threatening his dream life were losses of another kind. Beginning in the midtwenties, the steady invasion of Americans had changed Montparnasse, and not, in Harold's opinion, for the better. From a place that had once provided for almost nothing the simple joys of good conversation, camaraderie, and intimacy, it had become a "Bohemian Coney Island" where money often determined whether one would be able to enjoy what few pleasures remained. Also, only a few were left of the early residents of Montparnasse. The recent arrivals, their numbers increased by the availability of cheap transportation, seldom spoke French and, worse, had come to Paris seeking glamour rather than what Paris symbolized. They, like the unfortunate Sinclair Lewis, missed the opportunities and the creative stimulation and rewards of Paris that others had previously discovered. Only superficially could they experience the fierce challenge to pendantry, dullness, fixed ideas, and the whole of bourgeois morality

Louis B. Atlas, Paris, 1927

that had once animated Montparnasse and united its residents under a banner of defiance. Just being in Montparnasse had symbolized rebellion.

These distressing conclusions were confirmed by his observation that the rich, idle, fashionably attired crowds at Deauville and the impecunious, idle, disheveled crowds in Montparnasse were identical. Any differences were external and factitious. Linking these groups was their desire to be exclusive, to be different—the age-old infantilism of human vanity. Montparnassians, in fancy dress and with money in their pockets, could blend with the Deauville set. Depriving the latter of their wealth and attire and placing them in the Quarter would be even less noticed. Both groups, moreover, had uniformly bad manners—they were inconsiderate, irresponsible, indulged in malicious gossip, and did not comprehend loyalty and friendship. They exhausted themselves trying to avoid dullness and boredom without ever realizing that their self-conscious efforts increased both.

One person who belonged to neither group and who tried to make life easier for Harold after his luck began to run out was Kay Boyle. She found his talk spellbinding and his fantastic stories truthful; his derelict condition elicited her sense of pity. Beneath his carapace of silence and apathy, there was an engaging and complex human being. It was heartrending to see him making the rounds everlastingly attired in soiled, rumpled clothing, much of it in need of repair. That was something she could change. She washed his shirts, mended his socks, and pressed his suit. But her efforts hardly made any difference. Somehow Harold always managed to preserve a shabby appearance. His clothing, Hemingway once quipped, seemed to soil while he dressed. Kay Boyle patterned one of the major figures in her novel *Monday Night*, the book she called her most satisfying, on her acquaintance with Stearns. In the book Stearns is Wiltshire Tobin, a writer who has spent twenty years in Paris (*Monday Night* was published in 1939) working for a newspaper instead of writing the books he came abroad to write. With ringing self-mockery, he explains his seeming dereliction: "Sure, I'm a writer. The only drawback is that I've never written any books. Otherwise I'm one of America's outstanding literary men."

Another who found it impossible to ignore Stearns's decline was F. Scott Fitzgerald. Just before he left Paris in October 1928, Fitzgerald ran into Harold again, and finding him more depressed than he was the last time they had met three years before, and "feeling drunk and Christ-like," Fitzgerald suggested that if Stearns wrote an informal letter explaining why he went on being poor in Paris, Fitzgerald would try to place it in *Scribner's* magazine.

Published under the title "Apologia of an Expatriate," with an explanatory note that the author was "a few years ago . . . prominent among American intellectuals," Stearns's letter repeated the central and by now obsolete message of *Civilization in the United States*: that standardization and the worship of mediocrity made a free, creative, and private life in America impossible. By contrast, voluntary exile in Paris, regardless of the inconveniences—and there were many—was a liberating experience impossible to duplicate at home. For the "joy of being let alone," for the freedom to drink as much or as little as one wanted, for the opportunity to conduct one's sexual life and to organize one's work as desired—for the chance to live one's own life—Harold admitted having paid a high price, so steep, in fact, that anyone without his "oriental fatalistic streak" would have swum back to America long ago rather than have borne what he had. Besides suffering physical discomfort, the chilling loss of vitality from cheap (or sometimes no) food, and the weariness of spirit that comes from hard work with miserably low pay, there were the even more painful spiritual injuries—the humiliation of being avoided by friends because your condition distresses them, the silent pity of those you would ordinarily like to ignore, the necessity of associating with second-rate people until you could scream with impatience, the sense of isolation, and the realization that all sorts of fantastic yarns are being fabricated about you. No one knew better the bitterness of being an expatriate or hated it more than Harold Stearns.

Rather than confess that his life in Paris was hardly his own, that the experiment in self-exile had nearly failed both practically and philosophically, and that the penalties for staying on were more debilitating than those he cited in the letter, Stearns resurrected the moribund defense of expatriation that had once given substance to his life and writing. For truth he had substituted myth. Fitzgerald was right. It "wasn't much of a letter." Furthermore, he complained that the payment of $100 Fitzgerald sent him for the article was not enough and intimated that Scott had probably withheld some of the money. A disappointed Fitzgerald wrote Hemingway that doing favors for people like Harold was risky.

Harold was again momentarily rescued from his latest slide into despondency and physical decay by a stranger, a wealthy young American sportsman named Jim Marty, whose enthusiasm for horse racing exceeded even Harold's. Marty opened his home to him ("it was the nearest thing to a home I had ever known"), fed him, transported him to and from the racetracks, bought him clothes, and put up the money to cover Harold's racing bets. Thanks to Marty, again there were winning days, when because of luck, judgment, or hunches, Harold left the track with money in his pocket, a circumstance always sure to resuscitate Harold's precarious confidence in the future and in himself. Again it was possible to live without worries, to take chances on long shots, and even to make plans to write the oft-delayed book on Rabelais.

Stearns never forgot the day Jim called his attention to a twelve-year-old mare called Belle of Zante, a third-place finisher in a handicap race at Longchamp the previous season. Despite being an "old lady," she had been sold to a new owner who had trained her to run the hurdles at the arduous Auteuil course. It was like asking one's grandmother to compete in a hundred-yard event, Harold remarked, but the very unlikelihood that Belle could even finish the race let alone win it made her beguilingly attractive to the intrepid bettors.

On race day, Belle looked half asleep. She walked haltingly, "almost as if she had a game right hind leg." One glance at her jockey—the picture of despondency—made it obvious that she could not win. "Backing this animal," quipped Jim, "required being a 'Christian' and believing in miracles." But they had made their choice, and Jim placed 5,000 francs on Belle to win, an amount nearly equivalent to the horse's worth. Except for a few anxious moments at the start when Belle lagged behind and for a bunching up of horses that took two of them out of the race, the ancient mare ran easily and smoothly and once clear of the critical jump took the lead and held it. The nearest horse at the finish was five lengths behind. Belle's triumph silenced the crowd. Nobody except Jim and Harold had backed her. For their temerity the rewards were prodigious: 1,285 francs for every franc bet, or slightly more than $50 for every forty cents—well over a hundred to one shot.

"There is no glow like it in the world," Harold rhapsodized. "All the other pleasures, even sensuous ones, are not to be compared with it." Their victory toasted with champagne, Jim, as was his custom, gave Harold half of the winnings, this time, however, in exchange for Harold's promise to be measured for a new wardrobe at Jim's stylish English tailor. Of the dress suit, two "sack" suits, one heavy and one light overcoat that Harold purchased, only the last remained in his possession when he came back to America. The others took up what Harold surmised would be a long residency in a hotel cellar, as partial payments for unpaid bills.

The material and spiritual support Jim and his wife, Dolly, had provided vanished suddenly in the winter of 1929. While traveling in Italy, Jim fell and seriously injured his spine; he died a few days later. Within hours, an inconsolable Dolly committed suicide. Two of the most loyal, attractive, and generous friends Harold had ever had were gone. Their deaths left him devastated and once more alone and homeless. The always tenderhearted Dorothy Smith tried to console him, but their relationship had been waning for some time, and she could not provide any lasting comfort. For a short time, however, Stearns felt closer to her than he ever had before and than he ever would again. For support, companionship, and advice, he relied on his friend Alex Small.

As a longtime *Tribune* staffer, Small had concluded that what his colleagues performed was not a job but a joke, a "happy, good-natured joke" that barely compensated for their low pay and long hours. The job Small had found for Harold had enabled him at times to supplement his meager salary with racetrack winnings, and he had enjoyed this arrangement for four years. He might have remained a fixture at the *Tribune* indefinitely had he not been offered a similar position with the *Paris Daily Mail*. Although he would reveal in his autobiography that the *Tribune* job "had been a one-way ticket to the never-never-land of male irresponsibility, absurdity, and entertainment of which all men in their hearts forever dream," this was an opinion he held only vaguely or refused to admit in 1930. Paris was still a beguiling place. Small's warning that he would be unhappy at the *Daily Mail* notwithstanding (even the pretentious sobriquet "Lutetius" the *Mail* conferred on their horse-racing expert augured an unpleasant formality), Stearns resigned from the *Tribune*, composed a swan song so heavy with regret that he half believed *Tribune* owner Colonel McCormick would outbid the *Mail* to keep him, and went off to toast his departure with his disbelieving colleagues.

Alex Small's prediction that Harold would find the *Mail* uncongenial proved true, but not for the reasons Small had imagined. Being an American among Englishmen, an intimidating position despite the cordiality of most staffers, turned out to be the smallest of Harold's worries. By maintaining his customary silence, working hard, paying for his drinks, and admiring the "girls" his colleagues picked up (even though they were "terrible"), he managed to survive the traumatic transition from the "fantasy" life of the *Tribune* to the "healthy" and staid routine of the *Mail*. The episode that led to some discord and finally to his dismissal a year later was Harold's censure of Mrs. Desmond Harmsworth, the wife of the paper's owner and a horsewoman with a stable in France. The incident that prompted Harold's disapproval occurred at Deauville, where Mrs. Harmsworth's newest purchase, a promising two-year-old filly, lost her maiden race due, in Harold's opinion, to poor riding. He indicated in his column that Mrs. Harmsworth had permitted the wrong jockey to ride her horse. Although only mildly reproved for his indiscretion, Harold became a person to be closely watched.

Compared to the alarming problem that occurred a few months later, his run-in with the Harmsworths was minor. Suddenly, without warning, Stearns began to lose his sight. At St. Cloud, where the first attack occurred, he was shaken to discover he could not distinguish the track from the field or even his colleagues in the stand with him. From gray-black, objects dimmed into darkness. Unsteadily he made his way back to Paris, and for the next several weeks he alternated between almost total loss of sight and brief periods of normal vision. Then one day while crossing a busy boulevard, he was again stricken. Frozen in the middle of a traffic snarl he had caused, he was rescued by an alert policeman who led him to a café. Since it was evident that whatever ailed him required attention, he took a leave from his job, with assurances that it would be held for him, and checked into the American Hospital in Neuilly, where the problem was diagnosed as a blood disease. Helped by a few injections and buoyed by assurances that he was in no immediate danger of going blind, Stearns returned to the *Mail*, but for reasons never fully explained, the position that he presumed would still be his was not. For the first time in five years, he was adrift in Paris without a job, and his health had seriously declined. For immediate help and shelter he turned again to Alex Small.

Small's retreat in Collioure, a fishing village close by the Pyrenees, was a pleasant hostelry presided over by a good-natured but strong-willed woman whose culinary skills had brought her a vast reputation and a loyal clientele. To this colorful scenic "backwater" Harold retired, only too willing to place himself in the care of Madame Cantina and Alex Small. Alex at once rejected the Paris doctor's diagnosis. An "ordinary humdrum case of delirium tremens" was Harold's only trouble, the remedy for which, luckily, was at hand: a strong local port wine (Banyeuls), which, when consumed in mighty portions, unfailingly restored one's good health. Rejuvenated, Harold enjoyed the visual delights that had made Collioure an artist's paradise—sandy beaches spotted with black-garbed women perpetually patching fishing nets and sails, clusters of squat buildings with

Alex Small, leaving Berlin for the Russian front, 1939

Dingo Bar with Lou and Yopi Wilson, owners

soft patinas, snowcapped mountains in the distance, and the dark blue water of the Mediterranean. It was like the setting for an old Balkan operetta. Adding to the charm and providing comic relief was the large canine and feline population of the town. Everywhere, hundreds of dogs and cats, well fed and indolent, languished in the sun and preserved an amiability that Harold concluded could only be explained by the dogs' feigned indifference to the cats and the latter's enormous size. All of them had turned Collioure into an Eden-like haven.

But as the weeks passed in this sunny paradise, Harold began to miss the things that had contributed to his breakdown and to experience again what he had learned five years before in another enchanting paradise: that the charm of such places turns sour, their intrinsic falsity ("picture postcard sentiments") begins to cloy, and the sojourner longs to go back whence he came, seeking the relief of reality, even ugliness. Collioure, like Carmel, was a place to be sampled—briefly. In no way did it provide the "real elation of being alive." That sprang from the process of continuously exploring, of inveighing against "what we know and are accustomed to and can deal with—not what we admire and look at." Collioure, its setting and life redolent of another century, had become an enervating backwater.

What Harold could not have known, although he may have suspected it, was that going back to Paris would be more devitalizing than Collioure. The difficulty, hardly unique, was that he was returning without a job. After being gently refused at the *Tribune*, he discovered there was virtually no possibility of finding work anywhere. Returning to the *Daily Mail* was impossible, and because he had once publicly ridiculed the editor of the *Herald*, it would be pointless to try there. Moreover, the stories of how he had used other people's money to cover his bets had spread, and many had concluded that Stearns, with or without money, would always be able to take care of himself. Paris, a "wonderful place in which to loaf, if you also have a regular job," was rapidly assuming an inhospitable cast. To make matters worse, for the first time the resourceful Dorothy Smith refused to come to his aid, although she gave him the cheery news that a Harvard classmate to whom he had made a request for funds before going to Collioure had sent him money, which she had deposited in the local Morgan bank. Her message delivered, Dorothy never again spoke to Harold, nor he to her. It was a rueful parting, for their friendship had been a steady and a long one, and if his reflections on their separation are sincere, he had allowed his injured pride to come between himself and a woman he may genuinely have loved.

The windfall soon disappeared, the bulk of it going for a champagne splurge at the Sélect with the former mistress of a friend. Except for one fortuitous encounter with a "strange" Texan who staked him to a new wardrobe and a day at the races where he collected several thousand francs and then lost them on bad bets, Harold passed the first six months back in Paris (his *de profundis* period) wandering around the Quarter, borrowing money for food and drinks, and when absolutely penniless, sleeping on benches along the Boulevard Montparnasse near the St. Germain church. Mornings he would sometimes join parishioners attending early mass and would sit in the back pews—"just for the little sense of warmth and change and human contact." Later, he would call those long months when resolution and pride finally collapsed under the strains of daily existence the most terrible of his life. More than ever, he survived by keeping himself well deceived, clinging to the illusion that each new and terrible thing would never be repeated and then, when it was or when something even worse occurred, believing that that was the absolute worst that could happen. A life that had once included security, friends, and interesting activities now revolved around food and drink, a few articles of clothing, a bed in a cheap hotel, and, finally, to the mere anticipation of a glass of water at a friendly café.

Shortly after squandering his winnings on losing horses, Harold ran into Hemingway, who was in Paris on a short visit and who, to Harold's relief, acted the "way you would expect a friend to act." Besides giving him some cash, Hemingway paid his hotel bill and even suggested a few places where he might try and sell his work. Hemingway, Harold later reflected, had never let him down nor had he ever been dishonest. Another who was at least as generous was Evan Shipman, also a friend of Hemingway's and a devotee of horse racing. Shipman's appearance in Paris could not have come at a better time. Harold thankfully accepted Shipman's invitation to join him at the Hotel Montana, in Saint-Germain, a place filled with fantastic people who formed "a sort of big family party" and mitigated his loneliness. He tried to write again, but his efforts were frustrated by forgetfulness and an inability to concentrate. Articles were out of the question, as was the oft-postponed biography of Rabelais. Even writing a straightforward account of Collioure was beyond his power. Weeks stretched into months, and finally his life came to a standstill.

In December 1931, Stearns admitted what Shipman and others at the Montana had known for some time: he was a sick man. With the help of a French friend, who probably paid his expenses, Harold returned to the

American Hospital, depleted physically and mentally. This time the diagnosis was what it should have been previously—decaying teeth had poisoned his system. Accepting the only remedy his doctors recommended —removal of all of his teeth—was not easy, but with a stiffly cheerful countenance he surrendered to necessity.

The ordeal, Harold recalled, "despite the pain, dizziness and fever and the awful feeling of being . . . forever mutilated," released him and set him free. At last "it was over with." But more than his illness was "over with." He was through with Paris, too. Everything about it had turned distasteful, partly because he felt so alien and so alone. "With no teeth, few friends, no job, and no money," he "*naturally* decided that all [he] could do was to return" to America "and try to start all over." An interior voice reverberated: "Go home, go home, that is the place for you. Go home to America."

Repatriation was easier to contemplate than accomplish. Exiling himself to Paris had been done without financial hardship, but now Stearns scarcely possessed enough to buy his next meal, let alone his passage to the United States. But the dream had ended, the reality of impoverishment had descended—this time cruelly and with no relief at hand—and some action was necessary. Evan Shipman, a few other friends, and the American Aid Society raised passage money, and one night late in January 1932, Stearns watched the lights of Le Havre disappear as his America-bound freighter pointed out to sea. It was not exactly the parting from France he had expected.

Nor was the American homecoming quite what he expected. After a dozen years of pursuing the fugitive vicarious life that had deprived him of possessions, security, convictions, and happiness, he was returning home a shadow of his former self, full of fear and an agonizing sense of helplessness. Like Rip Van Winkle, he faced the prospect of reentering a land that time had made strange, where even his old friends might no longer recognize him. It was ironic that in his native country, the "agony of isolation" that Paris had occasionally lifted might again become a fact of existence. It was possible that he was about to exchange more vagabondage for the "home" Paris had provided. Perhaps this time he had exiled himself from an exile that had become his *patria*—an admission he came close to making a year after his return in the material he supplied Harvard for the Class of 1913 Notes. Except for a "bit of writing," he wrote, he lived in "complete isolation and a loneliness enhanced by being in a big city . . . full of

Evan Shipman

only shadowy recollections of happier days"; further, he lived only to return to Paris and to some unimportant routine job "that would take up his time—and there forget."

Although resettling in New York during the Depression was no doubt dismal—Harold Stearns started his repatriated life in a small room in the Marlton Hotel, 8th Street—it was not as bad as his note to Harvard implied. For one thing, old friends not only recognized him but they rallied to his assistance. The novelist Thorne Smith put him up in a hotel, fed, and gave him clothes; the renowned journalist Walter Duranty bought him a set of false teeth and a typewriter; the reporter Louise Bryant, wife of John Reed, staked him to an occasional dinner; Evan Shipman's mother let him use her Beekman Place apartment for writing; Malcolm Cowley loaned him a few dollars; and several publishing people recommended this or that project. Above all, there was his old Paris friend and supporter Evan Shipman, who on visits to New York administered to Harold's needs with the care and solicitude of a nanny. He even took him to the trotting races at Sturbridge and other New England tracks and later, in Greenwich Village, helped him relocate in a large, sun-filled room at 10 Charles Street. That room, the most comfortable he had occupied in years, Harold vowed to make the symbol of his success. Whether the room had talismanic powers or not, in it he would write two books, *Rediscovering America* (New York, Liveright Publishing Co., 1934) and *The Street I Know* (New York, Lee Furman, Inc., 1935), the first an unabashed celebration of repatriation, the second a considered retraction of all he had said in defense of expatriation.

What made America a rediscovery for the prodigal son ("I was almost a ghost . . . walking in this new America and New York of 1932") was not the partial relief it offered a chronically lonely man (America was still no place for the lonely) but the opportunity it provided a perennially dislocated man to discover his origins and reaffirm his identity. During his first year back in America, it became increasingly apparent that his sojourn in Paris had brought him to the verge of "losing his country." To be sure, what he had found congenial in France, particularly psychological and sexual values, made even a more enlightened America seem old-fashioned. The need to absorb and mold American thought to European tradition remained urgent, and Stearns, ever the recorder and interpreter of the time, would always maintain that American civilization would be fulfilled only when it drew closer to its European roots. At the same time, however, America, the land of paradoxes, displayed so many positive signs of cultural maturity that the obsequious attention his countrymen had once paid Europeans had virtually vanished. In architecture, music, art, and literature, America had come of age. And as refreshingly emancipated was the American woman, always Stearns's choice over her French counterpart. American women's femininity, by contrast, gave Gallic women's charm "a certain hard metallic quality." An added indication of American womanhood's new stature and of a return to "sexual normalcy" was the repeal of Prohibition, which American women had once backed with an "emotional driving force" but from which they had withdrawn, realizing that the saloon was not the "dangerous rival" they once thought it was and that Prohibition had cost far more than it was worth.

Fastening on America's bright hopes and muting his disappointment in the "new shibboleth shouters," Stearns ended *Rediscovering America* with a familiar paradox: by losing his country, at least in certain fundamental ways, he had found it; likewise, by trying to assimilate the spirit if not the outward life of France, he had found that despite his unaffected fondness and admiration for the French, he was an American after all. From this discovery he derived little pride, but it was worth making, and it profoundly influenced how he described his "flight from reality" in his autobiography.

The title Stearns chose for his "exile's return," *The Street I Know*, came from a poem by another American who had known hard times in Paris, Cheever Dunning:

> The wind blows cold down every street,
> But coldest down the street I know.

Dunning's plaintive observation aptly describes the experience that Stearns frankly and painfully records in a book that could be subtitled "The Autobiography of a Failure." As a recantation of his once spirited defense of exile, the work reveals the depths of humiliation and disillusionment. He admits that his "revolt" had failed, that the dream existence in Paris had often been useless and silly, and that only the drug of self-deception had made his life there bearable. Meanwhile, his gradual submersion in a spiritual limbo resulted in a malaise that could only end in disaster. The inner maturing of the spirit that he insisted was an important by-product of expatriation occurred with painful slowness. The beguiling surface life of Paris, where he had played the roles of the "great exile," ubiquitous café hanger-on, brilliant talker, romancer, erstwhile intellectual leader going to seed, and tout had been irresistible. Even while he recognized its dangers, he had given himself to it. Here was the apogee of what Cowley and others would call the "lost generation." The "real world" that he had lost (as well as himself) was America. To recover it, all he had to do was go back to it. But because of stubbornness, pride, indolence, and indecision, he had remained abroad despite the increasing recognition that Parnassus lacked, at least intellectually, what it had once contained and would probably never offer again. What shook his complacency and made repatriation a necessity was not a surfeit of ennui or a paralysis of will. Physical collapse brought Stearns back to America. That, he concluded in *Rediscovering America*, was the "normal thing" to do when "affairs go badly with you in a foreign country."

There is a curious mixture of nostalgia and jubilation in *The Street I Know*. Buoyed by the appearance of *Rediscovering America* and the approaching publication of his autobiography as well as by the reviews and articles he had sold to several newspapers and magazines, he viewed the return to America as the event that had reactivated his stagnant career. A changed America and its potentialities had rekindled his critical powers. In words as intense as those he had once used to repudiate his country, he wrote: "Once more I was in the land of mechanical efficiency. I liked that; I revelled in it."

Many things in America deserved praise. Change and progress were real. Gradually, Stearns felt the return of self-esteem; he renewed his career. No doubt, too, homecoming offered at least the promise of stability. Certainly it promised an end to the wandering that was endemic to his young manhood and middle years. New York, at first a formidable obstacle, was turning out to be a congenial place in which to start life anew.

His receptive response to a vigorous, challenging America was the result of a genuine appreciation of important changes in the country and not just the random gushing of a bedazzled vagabond grateful to be among his own again. This is evident in his renewed examination of the country's development, first in *America: A Reappraisal* (New York, Hillman Curl, Inc., 1937), an addendum to *Rediscovering America*, and the next year, in *America Now* (New York, Charles Scribner's Sons, 1938), a sequel to *Civilization in the United States*. Stearns's new views of America resound throughout *America: A Reappraisal*. "At whatever point you touch the complex American life of today, you get a sense of new confidence, new pride, and even new hope. . . . Romance has fled Europe in despair and has found a new home in America. Our literature reflects it; our historians

Harold Stearns

are busy with our own colorful traditions; our music is gayer and brighter than Europe's plaintive folk songs and nostalgic military marches; our theater and our cinema are full of vitality, even if sometimes awkward and none-too-subtle; our art is no longer just derivative and, when we really wish it to be, our architecture is superb; our intellectual and scientific life is freer and more fertile than anything one can find in Europe; our political structure is firmer and healthier; our attitude towards religion is more tolerant and intelligent; our social and family and sexual life has more dignity yet more flexibility; our national feet are much more firmly on the ground of good health and sound physical habits." Despite whatever shortcomings once marred America, it now offered the "ordinary citizen" a better chance for a decent life "than anywhere else in a rather muddled and strife-torn world." Democracy fostered a mood of self-confidence and an incentive to discover the country's infinite possibilities.

Discovering civilization in America in 1938 was the purpose of *America Now*. To join him in that discovery, Stearns called on many of the original contributors to *Civilization in the United States*, six of whom complied, and a large number of others, including Louise Bogan, Joseph Wood Krutch, Evelyn Scott, John Kieran, Jacques Barzun, and Deems Taylor. Besides the editing and his introduction, Stearns contributed an essay on the "intellectual life" (its success, he maintained, depended on cooperation). Not surprisingly, given the editor's restored faith in America, Stearns and his contributors reached conclusions about America that are as optimistic as their predecessors' views were pessimistic. Although the contributors lacked the homogeneity that shaped the attitudes of their forerunners (in his introduction Stearns celebrated this diversity as evidence of the changing patterns of American life), they were united in their optimism about the future of America, in spite of the threats of war, fascism, and expanding nationalism. Science, enhanced communication, and the "prophylaxis of ideas" help achieve international goodwill faster than reactionary forces can operate against it. *America Now* is a searching, generally well documented, and comprehensive (included were two essays on religion, a subject missing from the first symposium) work with an optimistic message (now somewhat naive, given the conditions in 1938) that helped Stearns confirm what he decided America had become: a nation intellectually exciting, truly democratic, sincere in its beliefs, and capable of resisting all forms of internal and external oppression.

Stearns entitled the final chapter of his autobiography, "Can Life Begin at Forty-Four?" The question suggests that the career he started before

going to Paris as well as the dream life he pursued there both fell short of
what he now considered a full-fledged life. The heckling mood in which
his early career had been conducted and the defeat of liberalism that had
undercut the importance of that career doubtlessly vitiated that part of his
past. As for the Paris years, life abroad had indeed been a flight from
reality, an interlude alternately gay and tragic and physically ruinous. It
seemed that Harold had lived his middle years first, his youth in Paris,
and at forty-four, he had the benefit of experience, tolerance, and an understanding of his country and himself that enabled him to live a refreshed life.

The single lack in his life was dramatically filled in 1937 when Harold
married a cultivated and wealthy divorcée named Betty Chapin. Enchanted by Harold's autobiography, she had written a congratulatory letter to
him and asked if they might meet. Stearns agreed, and the friendship that
developed led to marriage. Betty Chapin opened Frost Pond, her palatial
eighteenth-century mansion in Locust Valley, Long Island, to the man
who had grown up on a small farm in Massachusetts and who for years had
occupied a cell-like room in the rue Delambre. Friends could scarcely
believe what had happened. Seeing Harold anywhere except in a room or
a café in Greenwich Village or Paris was inconceivable. A few resented
Mrs. Chapin's intrusion, believing she was merely interested in capturing
a celebrity and spiriting him away for herself. But Harold went willingly,
giving up the familiar (perhaps too familiar) haunts of the city, his drinking companions, the bars, the newly established Overseas Press Club,
and the free-and-easy life of the unattached man. Stearns seldom strayed
from Frost Pond or from his wife and her family, and he maintained a
routine so rigid—a walk before breakfast for newspapers and cigarettes, a
period devoted to reading, writing, and corresponding; evening reserved
for talk and more reading—that any interruption was "psychologically
profoundly disturbing."

When Betty prevailed on Harold to move from Frost Pond to a large
summerhouse just five miles from Locust Valley for a few months, he
recorded in his journal that the three weeks spent moving had recalled his
hatred of this activity, which he had had since childhood when he had "no
permanent home or fixed abode." This very "childhood horror," he concluded, accounted for some of his inertia as an adult, such as his staying
on in Paris for so many years. "I was there," said Stearns, "and I wanted to
identify myself with some place"; doing so "was as much responsible for
my continued expatriation as any explicitly reasoned out justification."

Having always been denied a "real home," he had tried to make Paris his home. Such a need hardly exists for those fortunate enough to have known the comforts and security of a "regular" home. But for those like himself, condemned "to be wanderers and footloose residents during their youth and early manhood," advancing years often brought an overpowering yearning for what they never had—a home. "As your reformed prostitute is often your most strait-laced housewife, so your youthful Bohemian wanderer, in later years, may become your most stick-in-the-mud type of householder and local resident." The examples, he believed, dramatized nature's revenge and balance-wheel. Never before, he said elsewhere in his journal, had his incentive for work "been so great." It was an incentive that sprang from his desire to keep a home, his home, intact. His adventure in exile had provided one great lesson: man was naturally a home-loving animal. Experiments in homelessness like his did not work; at best they granted only minimal amounts of happiness or pride. Men, he wrote in his autobiography, are homeless enough without going to pains to become more so. From his example one can conclude that no matter how hard one works at exile, there will always be feelings of uneasiness and insecurity, that expatriation can never really be achieved and that a "contented" exile is mostly an illusion.

Harold Stearns died of cancer in August 1943. He was fifty-two. His last words, in reply to the news that his wife had won a big bet in the Hamiltonian, were: "What horse?" Shortly after his death, Betty Chapin told Maxwell Perkins that Harold had been disappointed that he had not made more of himself. "Almost no one does," Perkins replied.

As a symbol of expatriation, Harold Stearns holds primarily a literary interest. The progression of his life, however, from denial, to exile, to repatriation, to acceptance and affirmation—from a rejection of American values to a reexamination and acceptance of them—remains part of the social pattern of our time. "For better or worse," Stearns the repatriate confessed, "I am an American after all."

KAY BOYLE

"My life can be known through my work."
(in conversation)

In the spring of 1922, Kay Boyle left her home in Cincinnati and settled in New York. She was just twenty years old, jobless, in love with a French engineering student, and determined to be a writer. In New York she found a job with a wholesale dress manufacturer, signed up for a course in short story writing at Columbia, and after a few months, with help from her sister, Joan, an artist on the staff of *Vogue* magazine, she went to work as secretary to a fashion writer named Marjorie Welles. Nursing her skimpy savings and supplementing her small salary by doing occasional book reviews, she survived until June, when Richard Brault, the French student she had fallen in love with in Cincinnati, arrived. Brault had just received his engineering degree, and the Edison Electric Company graciously honored his education by giving him a job as meter inspector. With the threat of penury removed, the reunited lovers moved into a squalid and bedbug-infested one-room flat on 15th Street, and contemplated what they would do next. Foremost among the possibilities was marriage.

Whenever Kay's father, Howard Boyle asked, "What are you going to do?" she always said, "I want to get married." Growing up in Cincinnati, Kay and her sister, Joan, had competed for the attention of the local boys and suffered torments if a week passed without a date every night and at least two proposals of marriage. Joan suggested that Kay might be more popular if she tried being less serious. What boy, after all, enjoyed talking about poetry and Einstein's theory? Kay's mother, Katherine, had also tried to help. She favored an orthodox Jew for her daughter—a rabbinical student at the local Hebrew Union College, who was nearly ten years her senior and crippled with rheumatism. Katherine thought him intellectually stimulating but pitied him. Kay rejected her mother's choice. He was too old, his mind and body too repellent. She preferred a bright young man whose name—Duane Swift—was "the most beautiful" she had ever known.

Katherine had first met Duane Swift, a labor organizer, when she had been persuaded to run on the Farmer-Labor Party ticket as a candidate for the Cincinnati Board of Education. To her own relief, she lost. It was not the first time her political associations had antagonized her husband and father-in-law. When she invited into the Boyle home the children of jailed conscientious objectors who stopped in Cincinnati on their long march to Washington to protest their fathers' incarceration, Howard and his father, Puss, moved out. And when Katherine entertained Lincoln Steffens, who had come to the city with William Z. Foster for a mass rally at the Labor Temple, Howard and Puss had dined elsewhere. It was during her mother's Farmer-Labor Party campaign in the spring of 1921 that Kay met Duane Swift. Working to persuade labor leaders that the radical labor movement could be an effective third force in American political life, Swift shuttled from meeting to meeting in the Boyle Model-T, which was capably driven by his adoring admirer, Kay. If half of those that Swift addressed had been as predisposed to radicalism as his enthusiastic companion, they could easily have formed a third party. But the workingmen were more interested in baseball, drinking, and sex than in the arguments of agitators like Swift. On his companion, however, Swift had made a deep impression. Although Kay told no one, she had fallen completely in love with Swift, and she was ready to leave home and family if he asked her. Swift did not.

However, Kay did not keep her growing attachment to Richard Brault a secret. As expected, Katherine approved, but Howard and Puss acted like conspirators in schemes to uncover incriminating evidence that would embarrass the couple. Such unremitting scrutiny gave Kay the feeling of "being pressed down upon by sheets of iron." She complained to Joan that she feared she might lose all her "sweetness and good will" toward men.

Fortunately, escape from the "hell-hole" of Cincinnati averted that calamity, and now Richard had come to New York. Being far from the meddlesome Boyle men, the couple decided to marry without delay. But on the day after the ceremony, a message arrived from Howard warning Kay not to marry until Richard could support her. Only Puss, Kay concluded, could be behind this last ditch maneuver to control her life. Then from Richard's home in Brittany came another equally irritating and unexpected command. Richard's father, an ex-army officer, demanded that the marriage ceremony be repeated in a Roman Catholic Church. Parental injunctions notwithstanding, at the end of June Kay and Richard had joined a throng of betrothed couples before a magistrate at New York City Hall and recited their vows. Then, two weeks later they mechanically repeated them before a priest as Richard stared grimly into space, deeply conscious of the hypocrisy of observing a sacrament he had ceased to respect.

In November Kay exchanged the opulent world of fashion in the employ of Marjorie Welles for the ascetic world of literature working for Lola Ridge at *Broom*, an international magazine of the arts. A Dublin-born Australian, Lola Ridge was a revolutionary as formidable as Emma Goldman and considerably prettier. With ties to the Irish Insurgents and the Socialist Party, she was an honest-to-goodness proletarian, quick to defend her radical beliefs whenever she had the opportunity. In 1922, Harold Loeb, who had founded *Broom* the previous year, provided Lola with an opportunity to make her position known by appointing her the American editor of the magazine. Certainly Lola's qualifications were impressive. She was an experienced journalist and was widely traveled, radical, and industrious. Moreover, she had agreed to work for almost no salary. In return, Loeb had gladly granted her veto power over the American submissions. They agreed that she would make the final selections in New York while he traveled in Europe. For more than a year, Loeb had traveled constantly, often with an attractive companion named Kitty Cannell. The ferocious Frances Clyne was patterned on Kitty and Harold was the real-life counterpart of Robert Cohn in Ernest Hemingway's novel *The Sun Also Rises*. From various foreign locations, Loeb published issues of *Broom*, and with surprising regularity, he kept in touch with his New York editor and her new assistant, Kay Boyle.

Of the array of part-time jobs Kay inherited from the departing Laura Benet, the most demanding were business correspondent and advertising manager. Loeb had warned that *Broom* would not last long unless ways were found to reduce its losses. Kay's remedies included swapping subscription lists with other magazines and doubling the advertising, but neither course was as remunerative as peddling the magazine at the Brock Pemberton Theater, where Pirandello's play *Six Characters in Search of an Author*, then running serially in *Broom*, was being performed. At only two performances, she boasted to Loeb, she had collected nearly $50.

But despite such enterprising schemes, losses mounted, and when Loeb's uncles, who had reluctantly agreed to subsidize his expensive hobby, withdrew their support, Harold notified his New York staff that *Broom* would have to close. Lola and Kay, however, had made other plans. They cabled Loeb that with his permission they wanted to take it over and try to keep it going. To their relief, he agreed, but not for long. In a second cable he withdrew permission. The sudden reversal left them no choice but to resign. Lola cryptically blamed the "machine" for the misfortune. Kay complained to Loeb that "this assisting at the burial of a yet living thing is not one of the happiest things in the world." What neither woman knew was that Harold had acted to ensure *Broom*'s continuation. Already enroute to New York to assume control of the magazine was Matthew Josephson who, after consulting with Loeb, had conferred with Malcolm Cowley in Paris about the selection of another person (Slater Brown) to fill the vacancies left by Lola and Kay.

Meanwhile, a desire had been growing in Richard to visit France. A long time had passed since he had seen his home. Returning to France for the summer would give him an opportunity to look for a steady job and introduce Kay to his family. At least two problems, however, stood in their way. Fearing that being pregnant would interfere with the trip, Kay underwent a series of operations with Dr. Mary Halion, a pioneer of women's rights, which resulted in a successful abortion. The other problem proved more difficult. The couple simply did not have enough money for passage to France. As summer approached they had all but abandoned their plans to go when, to their astonishment, Marjorie Loeb, Harold's shy, quiet, divorced wife, who lived in the magnificent house over the basement of the *Broom*, offered to loan them $250, a munificent sum they promised to repay as soon as Richard found a job and Kay sold her first book. It was a joyous and grateful couple who at the end of June stood on the deck of the French Line ship the *Suffren* watching the skyline of New York disappear.

Still weak from the abortion, Kay remained in their cabin for much of the voyage. It was a time to ruminate on the past and on what lay ahead in

France. Kay had her mother to thank for making her the "brave spirit" she believed she was. "I would have grown up a narrow-minded, smug, self-satisfied little Boyle with no visions or dreams," she wrote Katherine. "You gave me a thin, unadmirable body, but you also gave me a broad, rather admirable mind." There was no doubt which was more important to Kay. Since childhood Kay had felt her mother's influence as teacher and defender. Katherine had once read to Howard's friends selections from a diary Kay had kept while traveling with the family in Germany. Her daughter's writing, Katherine pointed out, was factual rather than allegorical, but just as original as Gertrude Stein's *Tender Buttons*. In the formation of literary tastes, Katherine had also been more influential than Howard, whose favorites included Sir Walter Scott and Robert Louis Stevenson. Katherine read Carl Sandburg, Jane Austen, George Moore, and George Bernard Shaw to her daughter. With Kay, Katherine always shared her modest but original views on art and music and her impassioned beliefs about what constituted a successful life. Long opposition to her husband's mercantile values had convinced Katherine that the principal function of money was to purchase freedom from those who rejected the belief that only that which the hand cannot touch is of value. It was a belief Katherine struggled all her life to keep and it was one her daughter would master.

Lola Ridge was as much of an inspiration for Kay as was Katherine. It was Lola, whose example prompted Kay's observation that "real rebels . . . build themselves tight little houses and sit within them all their years." By contrast, she and Lola were "swinging into the wide, hot rhythms of life," taking it exactly as it was, and "moving easily with its motions." However, for Richard, as Kay well knew, responding to the "hot rhythms of life" had far less appeal. It was enough for him to have a few months to hibernate, a time in which they could "really care about each other." As for Richard's family, she wondered if she could "embrace and love" these strangers. Would they understand that along with being a "brave spirit" she was also "an uncertain person who loved her mother more than life?"

On the morning the *Suffren* nudged into the port of Le Havre, Kay caught sight of her French in-laws. Papa Brault, erect, with short white hair, blue eyes, and tobacco-stained mustaches, was the epitome of the retired army colonel. Beside him stood Madame Brault, stoop-shouldered and dressed entirely in gray. Two of Richard's sisters, also wearing gray, completed the welcoming party: tall, elegant Charlotte, an "Ingresfleshed beauty," was married to an invalid; Marguerite, who talked and strode like a boy, persistently questioned the state of the weather during the crossing and this reminded Richard of the exaggerated importance the subject of weather had always had for his family. On the slow homeward journey, Kay discovered that the elder Braults considered another subject to be even more serious: clothing. A daughter-in-law who appeared in public without a hat, wearing a blue dress garnished with red roses, a crimson chiffon scarf, and huge white earrings, with her face smeared with rouge and lipstick, would have to be immediately remade. The transformation began at Rouen, where the travelers halted for the night. Madame Brault conveyed her objections to the colonel, who commanded Richard to inform his bride to remove the hoops from her ears, the crimson scarf from her neck, and the makeup from her face. That accomplished, Madame took charge and completed the metamorphosis by buying her new daughter-in-law a white straw hat. Such an item was de rigueur in Brittany and would lend respectability to the wearer and impress the Braults' censorious neighbors. Feeling as drab as the country house toward which she was being borne and as persecuted as the martyr of Rouen (in whose town of execution Kay had capitulated to conformity), Kay packed away the earrings and scarf. Only Charlotte questioned her mother's taste. Blue, she whispered to her American sister, is really your color.

The Braults' residence in rural Brittany came close to being an actual refutation of the metaphysical purpose of their trip. Kay and Richard had agreed to make the journey to France, among other things, a search for individual freedom, an investigation into the real meaning of democracy. Madame Brault's triumph in Rouen had struck a blow against individual freedom, however, and the family dwelling, "rigid," "straight-faced," enclosed by high walls, and where the occupants observed patterns as ritualized and restrictive as the Brault women's attire, seemed more a prison than a home. For weeks Kay stayed in her bedroom, complaining of fatigue, "nerves," and internal disturbances resulting from the difficult abortion in June. Ever solicitous, the Braults turned themselves into a deferential first-aid brigade. Papa even prepared her breakfast—an unprecedented courtesy—and regaled her with elaborate and incomprehensible stories. Each morning from the garden beneath her window, Madame Brault called, "Good morning, Kay"—the English greeting being, to Mama's mind, the equivalent of a tonic. Marguerite created a hat for her and talked animatedly about going to America. One day Richard's brother, Pierre, a doctor, examined her and prescribed more sleep, food, warm baths, and time away from the family; he predicted she would feel much better after she began having children. She did not tell him that she did not intend to have children for years.

Kay scarcely needed Pierre's advice. As "dear and devoted" as they were, the Braults made her impatient. Spoiling her with ministrations and constantly hovering, they denied her what she most wanted: privacy. Richard, too, was uneasy with them. Disputatious by temperament, he seized every opportunity to attack the institutions his parents supported —church, government, army. Each exchange deepened the hostility between them and made him more quarrelsome. For relief Richard and Kay escaped to nearby coastal towns. Long walks or an afternoon of fishing lifted their spirits. But nothing provided anything like the deliverance Kay experienced when Richard, on occasions, shooed everybody away, and she retreated, alone and unbothered, into what she later called a "delitescent life"—a separate secret existence that admitted of only Lola, her sister, her mother, the works of a few poets and novelists, and her own writing. She lived for such rare interludes.

"I am primed for good production," Kay boasted to Lola shortly after her arrival in France. She first wrote a ponderously titled poem, *The Book of Cincinnati*, a "specific and clear stroke of protest" that lambasted (with help from Sandburg and Masters) the decrepit and impotent Cincinnatians who had rejected Duane Swift, Lincoln Steffens, and the radical labor movement. About the same time she began a "pure and simple" autobiography in which Cincinnati, that "nest of reactionary stagnation," again provided the background. Called alternately *Source* and *Process*, it later became *The Imponderables* (an intriguing word she had found in a friend's letter) before it mysteriously vanished. For amusement, she tried translating Apollinaire's *Alcools*, not very satisfactorily, and from Glenway Wescott came a request to read the final proofs of Marianne Moore's poems for Monroe Wheeler's publication *Manikin*. To *Broom* (under its new management) and *Adelphi*, both of which she disapproved, she sent poems, rationalizing her action by contending that a "hungry stomach" as well as an empty intellectual life had to somehow be satisfied.

As the summer wore on, a decision on whether to return to America had to be made. Lola had offered to take up a collection for their return passage, but for Richard, who had not found a job, going back to New York offered few attractions; he was particularly reluctant to rejoin the Edison Company. Doing so, Kay wrote Lola, would be "hell" for him, although

Kay Boyle, c. 1928

for her, New York would be "vital and stimulating." But, since they had thrown in their "lot together in a spirit of understanding and love and wisdom," they would have to work out their immediate future "on the most colorful and happy lines" possible. For a while they decided to remain in France but not with the Braults. For Richard, homecoming had been an unhappy experience, and for Kay that "compact little existence" lacked "discrimination." She wrote: "The garden sadly needs weeding— but I would rather plant a new one."

The event that helped her cultivate her own garden was the discovery of a first novel by a twenty-year-old prodigy named Raymond Radiguet. *Le Diable au Corps* is the story of a love affair between the wife of a soldier at the front and an amorous schoolboy of sixteen. Radiguet, who died a few months after his novel appeared, had written it when he was approximately sixteen. The book, something of a moral tour de force, had become an unexpected success. Kay followed the boy's journey through sexual passion and pain as he struggled toward maturity, and this led her (she would later write) "out of the bleak silence" of the summer "into the clarity of speech again" and into "a reality . . . translucent and untroubled." But for all its welcome harbingers, the discovery of this book would forever be linked with the first faint tremors of a convulsion that would eventually destroy the union of purpose and "high will" that Richard and she had forged. In spite of the vows they had taken to uphold their marriage, she knew that it was vulnerable after all. Richard, suddenly and alarmingly, appeared as "a separate entity."

For a while, however, the tableau of France that Radiguet had so tantalizingly evoked filled her life. In September, like a vision materialized, the tableau was realized in the spectacles of Paris, where for a fortnight Kay and Richard exhausted themselves in the city so long denied them. A gift of 3,000 francs from Charlotte Brault made the visit possible. Whenever Richard left their hotel to call on prospective employers, Kay, costumed in a black silk dress, a broad-brimmed black hat, her crimson scarf, and white hoop earrings, explored the city on her own. She went everywhere. Once she lingered near the bookstore Shakespeare and Company. Would she dare, dressed as she was, appear before the proprietor, Sylvia Beach, who preferred sober attire? Overcome by timidity, she turned away. On another occasion, she called on Harold Loeb, this time depending on her sartorial splendor for the courage to tell him that *Broom*, under the new directors, had abdicated its responsibility to literature. The new editors had ignored all Lola's achievements, they had maneuvered writers into opposing camps, created cliques where none existed before, and had practically denied that the descendants of the *Seven Arts* (such writers as Sherwood Anderson, Waldo Frank, Conrad Aiken, Van Wyck Brooks, Louis Untermeyer, and Randolph Silliman Bourne) still lived. She reported to Lola how with "heat and bitterness" she had told Harold all this and how he had "apologized for almost everything in it [*Broom*] and had tried to excuse himself by claiming that he was practically out of the magazine and had allowed his name to appear only in order to draw a salary. It was an incredulous explanation, but typical: 'How Harold!'"

At a second meeting with Loeb, whom she had ended up liking without "having the slightest respect for him," Kay met Robert McAlmon. She had often heard his name in New York, mostly from William Carlos Williams, who had shown her a few of his letters, but it was Lola's "very graphic, detailed, and detestable description of the man" that she had retained. When she joined the two men at the Café de la Paix, McAlmon was in the midst of delivering a withering attack on the mystic Gurdjieff, who was seated nearby with two of his disciples, Jane Heap and Margaret Anderson. Regarding Kay indifferently, McAlmon seemed to fit Lola's description of a person so aloof as to be almost untouchable. Was this sour-visaged man with steel-blue eyes and a profile like John Barrymore's, she wondered, really castigating the mystic and his misguided followers? Or could his acrimony be traced to the ridiculous and spiteful rumor that he was James Joyce's mistress? When he suddenly demanded to know who and what she was, she could not reply. Silence, perhaps, was what he expected, for immediately he drew himself up and with an attitude of pride and high purpose he shouted: "God's got to be a good poet or a good composer before I'll genuflect." His words, totally unsanctimonious, flooded her with misgivings about her own dedication to literature.

Shaken, she returned to the hotel, quarreled with Richard, who was depressed after another day of unsuccessful job hunting and found her account of the turbulent encounter with McAlmon incomprehensible. Trying to make him understand seemed futile, and staying with him was impossible. Hours later, she wandered into the Bois de Boulogne, disheveled and still confused. At daybreak she resolved to find McAlmon and ask him for work that "would give a shape to [her] life," be "solid and symmetrical," and somehow serve the ends of art. But McAlmon had vanished. For the rest of the day, she languished in the Tuileries, reading a battered copy of *The Lake* by George Moore and discovering on the closing page a challenge as compelling as McAlmon's: "There is a lake in every man's life, and he must ungird his loins for the crossing."

At the hotel that night, an elated and relieved Richard greeted her. He had found a job in Le Havre. The occasion demanded a celebratory dinner, the best they could afford. Kay held back her news, aware that for a while it would be necessary to delay her departure across Moore's beckoning lake.

Before jet aircraft began routinely disgorging passengers at Orly and De-Gaulle, travelers just as routinely entered France through one of the major seaports, often Le Havre. After a week or so aboard a transatlantic liner, passengers welcomed the sights and sounds and smells of the active port, where a whole population seemed to be toiling to berth their vessels. Few tarried in Le Havre, an ugly, muscular, commercial city that seemed to pride itself on moving people away almost as rapidly as they arrived. Like most seaports, it contained two populations, a larger one—stable and efficient, composed of laborers, longshoremen, and merchants—and a smaller population made up of ex-sailors, prostitutes, derelicts, and other homeless transients.

Only the prospect that Richard's assignment with the local electric company might be short would make Le Havre tolerable. For 75 francs (out of his monthly salary of 350 francs) they rented two furnished rooms, clotted with the filth of the former occupants. The balance of Richard's paycheck was rationed at 10 francs a day. But after two months, more economizing was necessary, and they moved into a single room behind a café-restaurant, with a potbellied stove, water from a spigot in the alley, and a public toilet. There were some small compensations: a warm wall between their room and the kitchen and dinner at pensionnaires' rates at the restaurant. Also, the café they lived behind fronted the channel, and on the long seawall Kay could walk alone.

Housekeeping in France was a perpetual challenge. They had no telephone and no refrigerator. Drying laundry in the damp climate demanded infinite patience. For days it would hang indoors, sodden and leaking little puddles on the floor. Sewing, mending Richard's socks and shirts, and knitting became daily assignments as necessary as cooking. Kay fetched water, ground coffee, and bought fresh vegetables from the crowded markets and marvelous cuts of meat for low prices from a sympathetic butcher.

It was a surprise to discover that Le Havre, although dismal and perpetually wet, could at times be "oddly beautiful" and that its inhabitants could be absorbing. In the cavernous, "coldly-colored" Halles (markets), Kay observed the stout, bareheaded, heavily shawled women who sipped hot potage behind their stands; the quick-footed, rapacious housewives who contested the price of every purchase; and the caretaker, a man with Dostoevsky-like hands, who lived in a small room with a dozen amorous cats that were forever insinuating themselves about his arms and shoulders in appreciation of the food, the warmth, and sexual gratification (masturbation) he provided. She spied other types in cafés: a gawky little girl in a gray beaver hat who stared through immense gold-rimmed glasses; a man who wore a tight-fitting blue tam-o'-shanter and whose misshapen head—flat from the front and grotesquely bulged in the back—and missing front teeth gave him an aboriginal look.

Richard, despite the long hours he worked, remained a pillar of strength. For every inconvenience that depressed his wife, he assumed responsibility. Without him ("so utterly right, so understanding and complete"), she confided to Lola, she would certainly falter. Still, never before had she experienced such depths of loneliness. Following hours of writing, when she longed for a "companion-soul" to talk with or "to be dropped in on or interrupted," she had no one. And yet, she had to admit, being "so separate" nourished her, too: "I have come through a wide and deep period of being—I have lost a very peculiar sort of faith I had in circumstances, and I have shed a final skin. And since the final skin has dropped, I feel that I am at last able to write that an inner and unrarified strata, a pure inner strain, has come to the surface and can never again be submerged or corroded." Writing, much more than reading, took her entirely outside, or into, herself. Her letters abound with injunctions "to write like mad." She sent poems and stories to *Broom, Double Dealer,* and *Adelphi*. She dispatched copies of "Harbor Song," a poem about Le Havre, to Lola and Harriet Monroe at *Poetry* and to William Rose Benét at the *Saturday Review of Literature*. In midwinter she stopped working on the novel about Cincinatti and began another, which, at Glenway Wescott's suggestion, she called *Plagued by the Nightingale*, the title coming from a poem by Marianne Moore. The story was about the long and strenuous summer in Brittany and became her first published novel.

At Lola's urging Kay welcomed another into her inner world of permanent companions, Emanuel Carnevali, who after eight years in America (1914–22), had gone home to Italy. Carnevali's uncouth but highly poetic writing possessed all the sinew and verve of Sandburg's and Whitman's, poets he especially admired. McAlmon liked the Italian for his lack of cant; like McAlmon, Carnevali spoke what he believed. As associate editor of *Poetry,* Carnevali had rejected Lola's poems for the same reason he had dismissed Williams's, Kreymborg's, and Bodenheim's: all buried their true feelings under layers of verbiage. Now, in a remote village hospital in northern Italy, he was dying of a rare and incurable disease (encephalitis lethargica). Williams's prophecy that Carnevali was another firebrand foredoomed to expire quickly, an "obviously lost soul," seemed tragically accurate. For Kay, however, he was the epitome of courage. Without courage, how could he, as he daily watched his withering body succumb to uncontrollable shaking, continue to live as though he expected to rise from his sickbed and walk away? Joyously, he answered her letters, typing always on onionskin paper as weightless and fragile as his body. He gibed at America (where old hungers were perpetually exchanged for new ones), exalted Lola (a lioness "flinging herself madly against the walls of the ugly city"), and complained that too many poets composed a poetry of death. He sent poems and portions of an unfinished book. They exchanged self-portraits; his eyes, he said, had a Chinese slant, but otherwise he had the look of a poet. Kay complained that, besides the remnant of a broken nose, she was too thin and not pretty. Far from being a "lost soul," Carnevali was a true kindred soul, a poet, and a fellow victim of poverty.

To brighten a bleak Norman winter, Kay made plans for the following summer. She decided to spend it in America and to see publishers and discuss plans with Lola for a new radical magazine. She would apply for passage money to a foundation (the Garland Fund) that favored applicants with experience in the radical movement. Meanwhile, she looked foward to entertaining her first American guests, William Carlos Williams, who was coming with his wife to France on a "sabbatical leave." Although Williams had said that anything longer than a stopover in Le Havre would be impossible, she had proceeded with her "senseless plan" to entertain the couple just the same. She had even taken Carnevali's suggestion and painted a window on the wall of the one windowless room she and Richard lived in. On a cold, wet morning Kay met the Williamses at the dock. Gently but firmly, Williams repeated that they could not stay. McAlmon expected them in Paris. For an hour they stood talking alongside the boat train. From her disappointment Kay learned that "people of dignity are not to be dragged by the hair of their heads into the precincts of one's life, and that to attempt this is to violate their probity."

Gifts of books helped to turn the coldest months into an ardent "intellectual winter." From her mother came D.H. Lawrence's *Studies in Classic American Literature*. His "new and ruthless way of thought" invigorated her. From an aunt came Rebecca West's *The Judge*; Kay parsed West's

Emanuel Carnevali

Richard Brault

sentences and tracked down the meanings of her strange words. In Le Havre she found Norman Angell's *Political Conditions of Allied Success* —another of Katherine's favorites—and to clarify his difficult message, Kay transposed long passages into blank verse. She sent the "transformations" to Katherine, from whom two more books arrived. *Holiday* by Waldo Frank disappointed her. The other, however, was pure joy. Although Glenway Wescott had found Evelyn Scott's autobiography, *Escapade*, too cluttered, too rhythmless, and too unplanned and overwritten, none of his complaints dampened Kay's appreciation. Here was "hot intense real life. I can't leave her. I love her," she informed Katherine. "She has gone deeper than Lawrence, because she never had to learn what Lawrence is trying to forget." Here was the "utterness of reality and truth." What Kay had been trying to learn about "getting beyond words," Scott had admirably demonstrated: "Her words do not have to be exotic or strange, because the emotion behind them is more expressed than her expression. She does not have to leave out verbs or play with adjectives—she is real." Here was a person Kay vowed some day to meet.

As the winter wore on, Kay contrasted her isolated and impecunious existence with life her contemporaries had in clique-ridden centers like New York and Paris. "Weeded out" of such places and left to themselves, though, they would no doubt go "all to pieces." That fate, she could be certain, would never happen to her. As mean as her conditions were, she could take satisfaction in the growth and accumulation of her work. Breaking away from the Braults had been the first step. Living virtually alone for months had proven that she could both write and sustain herself. It had also developed a "tremendous obstinancy to believe in [her] own importance."

Would returning to New York, she wondered, be more than a summer interlude with Katherine and Lola? Afterward, she would return to France and to the same "voids," the same "needs." Nothing would have been solved. What had to be worked out was a tenable alliance between her "new faith" and its "material expression." She described how this might be effected in a letter to Lola. "I know there are people who believe . . . that civilization, the business of money-making, money-spending, money-saving, is done." But as certain as these people were that the "establishment of a new supremacy" was needed, they often remained hopelessly enchained by the old. She thought of Raymond Duncan, walking majestically around Paris wearing flowing robes that he had woven himself. He operated a theater "wholly free from false tradition," but he had weakened his own remarkable, even inspiring protest against the mercantile system by selling his "created garments at unspeakable prices." Perhaps Duncan illustrated the difficulty of freeing the mind and then finding that the body protested. "I want to get my body away, out of the accepted basis of life and into its own reality. Would a commune, she asked Lola, be possible? To it she would invite all those who believed in a "subexistence"—certainly Katherine, Lola, and perhaps Evelyn Scott—to live there, just as they pleased. "We could live in sandals and smocks and be free to escape each other when bitter moods were upon us." Just believing that it could be done, combined with a willingness "to give up everything for the very last thing we want," would be tantamount to linking an "assertion of the artist spirit, without pose or sentimentality, to the progressive spirit of civilization." "Get subsidized," she urged her friend, "and revolt with us."

Responsive though Lola may have been to Kay's idealistic "clarion call," she could not answer it with action. Insofar as Kay had addressed a challenge to herself, she was prepared to act. She would give up the American trip, stay in France, and "be free!"

In April Richard and Kay learned that reassignment to Paris or to anywhere else had been delayed. To temper their disppointment, they moved to Harfleur, a small, unpretentious nearby town where they had often gone on weekend rambles. Their new home, the third floor of a former Carthusian monastery, was the inherited property of Madame Henri, the mistress of a small, exquisitely furnished chateau just beyond Harfleur. Here Madame Henri served tea to her third-floor tenant and bit by bit divulged the details of her husband's infidelities and violent outbursts of temper as well as accounts of her own secret acts of cruelty against her *bonne*. Grateful to have someone to talk to at last, Madame Henri was as profligate with her produce as with her confidences, never failing to send her young listener away laden with fruit and vegetables.

Harfleur offered more than a meager livelihood. Gradually, Kay realized that within it lay an "entire spectrum" of French life that she never knew existed before, one that was far more compelling than that of the Braults of Brittany. Invigorated by the people around her and the events they recounted, Kay immersed herself in the life of the "unhappy town." For the second time, she decided to put aside a "work in progress" (*Plagued by the Nightingale*) to start a new book. Originally titled *March Minot* and later *Gentlemen, I Address You Privately*, the book would, despite the elements of intrigue and sexual deviation, resist her efforts to transmute the sad life of Harfleur into satisfactory fiction. She began the task with a burst of enthusiasm. For this, as well as for her other projects, came encouragement and support from Lola, and Kay responded with grateful thanks. "I feel that you whom I love stand alone in my life as the one person who has any depths of faith in me." Unlike Katherine, with whom a "too personal" relationship practically ruled out "any unprejudiced belief" in what she could accomplish, Lola possessed "a remote dispassionate knowledge" and could provide frank evaluations.

Regardless of Katherine's opinions of her work, however, her presence in Harfleur was indispensable. For months Kay had begged her mother to join her, insisting that life would be a mere marking of time until she did. In July, a month after Kay and Richard had moved to Harfleur, Katherine arrived, bearing a check for $100 from Lola, and as Kay anticipated, an insatiable curiosity about her daughter's surroundings and friends. Over the next year both Katherine's curiosity and Kay's need for companionship would be amply satisfied.

A few months before her mother arrived, Kay had completed the saga of her youth (*The Imponderables*). While she liked individual chapters, the book as a whole, she had to admit, failed to say what she wanted. The characters had not become the "symbols of conflicting forces" that she had tried to make them. She doubted whether she would even try to publish it. She had had similar misgivings about "Harbor Song," and yet she had never stopped circulating the poem. Eventually, Harriet Monroe agreed to publish it, if Kay would replace the word "buttocks" with a less offensive anatomical term; Kay suppressed her outrage and grudgingly substituted "thighs." From Evelyn Scott, to whom she had also sent the poem with the note that the poem was filled with "Scott material," came an encouraging answer. Mrs. Scott pronounced "Harbor Song" "most satisfactory." She especially appreciated the parts Miss Monroe had objected to; she also liked the poem's "harshness," that trait being "half the distinction of beauty."

Evelyn Scott and Lola Ridge had become close friends in New York before Kay's arrival in 1922. Each had made a deep impression on the other. Evelyn's critical writings, examples of which appeared in *Dial* in 1920, inspired Lola to call her friend "perhaps the most brilliant critic in America." Born in Tennessee in 1893, Evelyn had lived in many places—Brazil, New York, Bermuda—before settling in 1922 in the French village of Cassis, a town nearly as remote and sheltered as Le Havre. Her writings before *Escapade* included a play called *Love*, a popular mystery, *Blum Rum*, and a volume of poetry, *Precipitations*.

Meeting the woman who had found such striking qualities in her work was the climax of Kay's month-long summer tour with Katherine that ended in Paris, where Mrs. Scott and her husband were staying. Kay wrote of her first impressions of Evelyn to Lola: "I had not visualized her as *simple* and as *untouched* as you must surely have told me she is . . . She is wholly without defenses. Her capacity for suffering has never grown less, and that is the significance of youth. Her whole personality struck a note almost the very farthest removed from the one I had expected, and that freshness of her enthusiasm and the purity of her belief was good to find."

Certainly her new friend would give her an honest report of *The Imponderables*. Mrs. Scott's estimate was exalted, if at times confusing. *The Imponderables*, she began, was unquestionably "the best first novel in an immediate and personal sense" she had ever seen. The "portrait of the author" presented in the book reminded her of a "very lovely and effulgent young moon with a blot of rainy atmosphere obliterating its most cruel definitions." For the book's "purely lyric expression," however, she reserved her "supreme compliment." Only the author's "absolute will of being" could have produced it. Compared to Waldo Frank, William Carlos Williams, and E. E. Cummings, Kay was a better artist, because she alone had the "sense of the beautiful as a palpable subjective sensorial texture" and "a capacity to preserve the persistent oppositions as in a fugue of individuals . . . who . . . stem out of an identity in her [the author's] emotions [and] keep their own consistent melodies." If Kay Boyle succeeded in preserving her "sense of differences," she would surpass the best writers in America and England and "do something that contains their measure of beauty and the other measure in which their beauty . . . can never be a full expression. In other words . . . you are, or you ought to be, our coming novelist—our very best."

Concerning the practical matter of publication, Mrs. Scott was fortunately more lucid. Send the manuscript to Lola, she advised, with instructions to deliver it to Thomas Seltzer ("If anybody is capable of talking convincingly about an enthusiasm, Lola is"). Should Seltzer refuse it, she continued, instruct Lola to ask Waldo Frank to introduce it to Liveright. As directed, Kay sent the manuscript to Lola. It was enough, Kay wrote her, if she (and now Evelyn) got "something out of it." She would be satisfied if her effort served only to discover "our similarities." The mere thought of courting public prestige was acutely painful. Still, there was never "enough money," and whatever the book earned would be welcome. She added, however, that she did not see how "one can lose money on a book, even if one doesn't make any." If she "could write the kind of stuff that sells," she would "be more avid about it." As for Evelyn's glowing "letter of recommendation," she asked Lola to include it with the manuscript when showing it to any publishers.

Those who have survived a winter in Normandy often complain of too much rain and the dolorous effects of too many days spent inside damp houses. For the Braults, the winter of 1924–25 was calamitous. Battered by incessant bouts of the flu and attendant complications, first Kay and then Richard succumbed to "raging fevers and biliousness," which often led to "vile retchings and agony" that confined them to bed for long stretches. When the maladies subsided, each found ways to convalesce; Richard repainted furniture and grumbled about returning to work. Kay continued work on her novel about Harfleur and finished an impressionistic sketch for Ernest Walsh's new magazine *This Quarter*. It was the second of her pieces that Walsh would print. Carnevali, impressed by "Harbor Song," had sent the poem to Walsh, who, unaware that Miss Monroe had already taken it for *Poetry*, asked to print it in the first issue. Kay quickly stitched together the deleted parts of the original version, including the objectionable stanza, and added to them a few new passages. She sent the amalgam, entitled "Summer," to Walsh with the hope he would find it as good as the original. He did and paid her 120 francs.

At the first tentative hint of spring came news at least as welcome as the season. Richard would not only receive a "fine raise" but would also travel (first class) to his company's American headquarters for two months. The only "bitter part," Kay wrote Lola, was that his absence would be "quite hell" for her; for Richard, it would mean "independence and stimulation." They welcomed the additional income as a relief from "material stagnation." She would send with Richard a segment of *Nightingale*. Although she believed it was a better book than her first, she would await her friend's opinion.

In October, Kay's always precarious health deteriorated, weakened by repeated respiratory complications. A month later her condition worsened. Exactly what ailed her she did not know; just moving around was agonizing. As well as she could determine, the main problem was a "sore lung or something in [her] ribs." Doctors, she complained to Richard, only prescribed tonics guaranteed to make one live forever. Whenever possible she divided her time between *March Minot*, now off to a good start, and *Nightingale*, portions of which Evelyn complimented. In December she was again confined to bed; her weight was down and she was unable to throw off a persistent case of bronchitis. This time she sought medical attention. A local doctor diagnosed her sickness as tuberculosis; if she intended to remain in Harfleur, he warned, she would have to give up all her duties as well as writing and remain in bed. The Braults urged her to go to a warmer region; the Scotts invited her to join them in southern France. But the person who conducted her away from Normandy, away from Richard, away from a workaday existence that had sapped her energies was a man she had never seen.

It was the irrepressible editor of *This Quarter*, Ernest Walsh, who had learned of Kay's condition, and insisted that she join him in Grasse on the French Riviera and that she stop over in Paris to be examined by a lung specialist. He explained that the money (1,000 francs) he had sent for the trip was an advance payment for her novel *Nightingale*, which he would serialize in *This Quarter*, and assured her that his co-editor, Ethel Moorhead, also looked forward to her arrival. Kay's presence in Grasse, he thought, would liven up a place that tended sometimes to be "dull and lonely."

She was "tearfully grateful" to this good samaritan. Ernest Walsh must be "about the most human person" alive. Leaving Richard, she convinced herself, would be unthinkable were it not for her "absolute physical inability" to remain in Harfleur and recover her health. Nonetheless, it was in something close to an "orgy of self-pity" that she said good-bye to him and sped to Paris at the end of January. But as the distance from Richard lengthened and that from Ernest shortened, it was as though she knew "exactly what was going to take place."

The man so eagerly awaiting her arrival would be dead in eight months. Walsh was himself a victim of tuberculosis, due partly to a wartime accident that had left him totally disabled and dependent on a small monthly pension. He had drifted to France in 1922 after spending four years in military hospitals. Walsh, like Carnevali, as William Carlos Williams might have said, was another "firebrand foredoomed to expire quickly." The only surviving son of James Walsh, a tea and coffee merchant, and Sara Lampson, a zealous Roman Catholic, Walsh had spent a carefree childhood in Cuba, roaming the plantations his father managed, riding horses bareback, and cavorting with Portuguese tramps. But at fourteen his father's death and his mother's Catholic bigotry made staying at home intolerable, and he ran away. A few years later he contracted tuberculosis. After a two-year rest at Saranac Lake, he emerged cured. He took to the road again, holding odd jobs, studying at Columbia University, and once even walking from San Francisco to New York, a journey made pleasanter by his ability to persuade wary farmers along the route to exchange a night's lodging for an hour of his talk. A brief marriage ended in divorce. In 1918 he joined the infant U.S. Aviation Service, and on a training flight in Texas crashed and severely injured his lungs. In Paris in March 1922, he looked up Ezra Pound, to whom Harriet Monroe had given him a letter of introduction. Pound read his poetry, explained how one should write a poem, and sent him to Brancusi, with a note (in French) informing the sculptor that Walsh still seemed to be feeling the effects of the plane crash. Whatever his disabilities, Brancusi liked the young American, whose height and pallor accentuated his fragility and whose ivory brow, heavy dark hair, and chiseled features gave his head, always drooping slightly, a strong, bold prominence. From the sculptor's studio would come within a year the stone that marks Walsh's grave in the Monaco Cemetery. Twice in Paris, Walsh had fallen ill, and both times he was released from the American Hospital before he had recovered. After the second confinement, because his pension checks had not arrived, he ran out of money, and the hotel where he was staying, the Claridge, seized his luggage. It was at this uncomfortable moment that Ethel Moorhead entered his life.

Also a guest at the Claridge, Miss Moorhead had noticed the tall, good-looking, young man with the underfed look and the cheeks that reddened at night. Like him, she was also alone, having left all her suffragette friends behind in England and Scotland. Ernest read her his poems, and Ethel told him she would some day write about the suffragette movement. She read his poetry appreciatively; he studied her paintings appreciatively. When Ethel learned that the hotel had commandeered his belongings, she paid his overdue bill, and together they left Paris.

For a year Ethel and Ernest shuttled north to escape the heat and then south to escape the cold. They visited Germany, Italy, Sicily, Tunisia, Algeria, and France. Everywhere Walsh avoided sightseeing. It was a strain on his fragile condition. Mostly he did what he liked best—sitting in cafés, talking, drinking wine, and observing. Everywhere he depended on doctors to stop his hemorrhages. At Miss Moorhead's home in Edinburgh in the summer of 1923, he read his poems to Harriet Monroe. She accepted

Robert McAlmon, 1925

William Carlos Williams, mid-Twenties

several. On a drive with Miss Monroe to see the Trossacks, he caught cold and hemorrhaged badly. While recuperating, he fell in love with his nurse. Warned by a doctor that falling in love for one in his condition was a "bad thing," Ernest replied that she was "a damned pretty girl." Ethel packed up and moved away. When the affair ended, Ethel returned and they traveled together to the French Riviera. There he again became ill. After recovering, he went to California, where he once more fell in love, this time with a woman who might have loved him had his illness not frightened her. He rejoined Ethel in Switzerland. But when Ernest complained that the Alps and Lake Leman depressed him, they moved to Italy. At Bazzano they called on the ailing Carnevali, who would always remember the "generous, happy, strong man" who showered him with a "wagonload of cigarettes [and] eau de cologne."

After that the two traveled ceaselessly. In October they were in Paris. Among the Americans Walsh knew, there was Hemingway, who early in 1925 had presided over the closing of the *Transatlantic Review*, where he had been Ford Madox Ford's associate editor. Walsh and Hemingway talked of starting another magazine, but according to Ethel Moorhead, Hemingway made it clear that Walsh's contribution would be money, not poetry. To soften the rebuff, Ethel and Walsh decided to produce their own magazine and finance it from a legacy Ethel had recently received. But before they could begin, Walsh suffered several severe hemorrhages, and when he was strong enough to travel again, Ethel took him to Pau to rest and regain his strength. There they assembled their magazine. Dedicated to their mutual friend Ezra Pound, *This Quarter* appeared in the spring of 1925, and a second issue, printed in Italy, followed a year later. By this time, doctors in Milan had diagnosed Walsh's condition as "extremely grave." When a move to a more moderate climate became imperative, the couple chose Grasse. Ethel rented a villa, and Ernest went to bed for three months; his sole visitor, besides Ethel, was the doctor. Ethel read him Dickens. He composed "experimental" poetry, perfecting a language that closely resembled Middle English. In January, his rest cure complete, he awaited, with undisguised ardor, the arrival of his stricken friend from Normandy.

In Cannes, Ethel and Ernest met Kay's train. Walsh, Kay noticed, wore a soft light-colored overcoat draped over his shoulders. His skin was ivory, his eyes dark, his lashes long and black, his eyebrows joined above his nose. She spied a copy under his arm of Carnevali's *Hurried Man*, which McAlmon had just published. Ethel was dressed in an expensive plaid suit and wore her graying hair in a bob. Her voice reverberated with a Scottish clang, but her small brown eyes and tense mouth betrayed shyness or perhaps just uneasiness. She carried a pince-nez. She informed Kay that she was hard-of-hearing. Their villa was a stately, wisteria-clad abode perched on a steep hill at the edge of the perfumed town of Grasse overlooking the Mediterranean. At dinner the first night, Kay heard how Ernest and Ethel had met and where they had traveled and lived since. After the meal Ernest read poetry—McAlmon's, Carnevali's, and James Joyce's.

On warm days they toured the region. Ernest, like his neighbor Francis Picabia, loved driving, and he expertly guided Ethel's automobile along the twisting roads. Kay's health improved precipitately, her cough disappeared, and she gained weight. Her examination in Paris had come out well too. Except for deep scars, her lungs were sound. Rest, good food, cod liver oil, and sun would restore her health completely. To Katherine she reported that her "charming" hosts served her American delicacies like Shredded Wheat, Heinz baked beans, and Campbell's tomato soup— luxuries that made her feel suddenly "less expatriated and more American." Could she ever again be a "good French woman"? Thanks to them her life had once more become "very exciting" and "stimulating."

Certainly Ernest Walsh was endlessly fascinating. She had never met anyone who charged the atmosphere with so much animation and gaiety. He was a bottomless spring of inspiration. At once she had felt his "spirit"—intrepid, cavalier, gay; he was like Carnevali, another stricken soul exuding poetry and life-giving forces. In her novel *Year Before Last* (New York, Harrison Smith and Robert Hass, 1932), in which she depicted this period of her life, Kay portrayed herself as Hannah, a woman in love with Michael, a man clearly modeled on Ernest Walsh. Michael, Hannah muses, "had lived through thirty years of life and this seemed like an age of reason to her and she could find no words adequate to say. On one side of her heart, he stood with his gravity or merriment and his wild wondrous talk that led her into endless places, and above him the flare of his spirit such as she had never known before nor thought could be. And on the other side was her misgiving that her own spirit and strength could not match him. She was humble before him and speechless, because of the belief and purpose in him that was never turned away."

Before long it became apparent to Ethel that once again Ernest had fallen in love with another woman, this time with their guest, who had also fallen in love with him. Ethel refused to stay around and packed up her belongings and went off to Monte Carlo, leaving the lovers to fend for themselves until the lease ran out. What had happened to change the balance of their relationship so suddenly was something Kay tried to describe to Lola: "All would have been delightfully simple had I not realized that what had been missing from me since I began was some very exciting and necessary quality in life which Ernest Walsh had got. So it has just developed as [it] has. . . . I do not know how it will end, but that is the exciting part of everything. That is all I have to say . . . and that I am very much in love and writing poetry again."

Although several months passed before Richard became aware of his wife's feelings, he was much on her mind. She who had "preached fidelity and denounced betrayal," she wrote later, now "accepted faithlessness as if it were the one thing . . . [she] had been waiting for." What might happen to Richard—or even to Ethel—counted for less than did Walsh's "beauty and his courage." To pay homage to his example for the rest of her life was all she wanted. Already he had shown her that gaiety was one of the "postures of courage" and that the "loss of heart [was] an indulgent name for cowardice." Like him, she, too, would be courageous, at least courageous enough to go on believing that somehow she could preserve him from death; it was less an arrogant belief in her redemptive powers than a conviction that through love and care and belief in his survival, Ernest Walsh would live.

Although Ethel had taken with her all the contributions to *This Quarter*, new ones arrived almost daily. Opening and reading them never failed to inspire from Ernest a spate of poems celebrating the joys of receiving mail. Besides answering letters, returning rejected manuscripts, and taking dictation—all tasks she had done with Lola—Kay shopped, cooked, and washed. Few visitors disturbed their routine, but among those who did were Joan Boyle, now working for *Vogue* in Paris, and a fellow staffer named Pauline Pfeiffer, for whom Ernest Hemingway would soon leave his first wife, Hadley. Pauline explained to her hosts that the letters she received daily from Hemingway contained instructions about what Ernest wanted her to buy for Hadley's birthday. When Walsh read aloud to them an editorial in which he praised Robert McAlmon, Pauline denounced it, doubtlessly aware of Hemingway's growing antagonism toward the publisher of his first book. Ernest bristled and left the room. After the visitors had gone back to Paris, Walsh noticed that Hemingway no longer wrote to him.

One day after Kay and Ernest had spent a few days at Mougins with Francis Picabia collecting information and illustrations for a supplement on the artist for *This Quarter*, they returned to find the door of their villa literally plastered with unpaid bills. When their lease expired shortly afterward, they abandoned the villa for a small hotel on a hill above Mougins, one of several in the region that provided meager accommodations and many inconveniences. Here Ernest suffered another hemorrhage. To escape the summer heat as well as the rumors spreading through the village that Walsh might infect the whole town, they pushed north into the Alps-Maritimes, where suspicious, jittery hoteliers forced them to vacate one hostelry after another. Days later, exhausted and nearly penniless, they stopped in the village of Annot, "high and lovely enough to stand above and beyond the judgment and condemnation of man." As they sat sipping a drink on the terrace of a hotel, "silently reluctant" to go on, they watched as a faunlike man, young and stylishly clothed, approached their car; he paused, squinted at the heaps of manuscripts and copies of *This Quarter* on the rear seat, and then abruptly turned around and walked directly to their table. "I recognize you from your picture," he said, looking at Ernest. "My name is Archibald Craig."

Craig, whose real name was Cedric Harris, was a Scot who was exactly Kay's age. He had arrived in Paris in 1923, and after working for the *Times* and *Tribune*, he had decided to devote his life to poetry. He too had suffered from tuberculosis. Now he lived with his cousin, Gladys Palmer, the only daughter of A. A. Palmer (of Huntly and Palmer biscuit fame), at her lodgings nearby. If providence had brought Ernest and Kay to Annot, Craig hoped that something stronger could keep them there. His cousin, he confided, was also the Dayang Muda of Sarawak, a title she acquired through marriage to the brother of the Rajah of Sarawak. An inveterate entertainer, she regularly filled the local hotel on whose terrace they sat with her friends. If they agreed to remain in Annot, Craig assured them that the Dayang Muda would direct the proprietor to provide them with a remote room so that guests would not hear Ernest coughing. They agreed.

With serene and secure lodgings guaranteed, Walsh turned to the complicated problem of how to produce the third issue of *This Quarter* without having to print all the contributions and without depending on Ethel's cooperation. He could not invite her to Annot as long as Kay remained with him. Without her, however, *This Quarter* would never appear. This was Walsh's quandary: Kay, who (he believed) had relieved his despair and given him that necessary "concern with something else" and who would also now become the mother of his child, was in all respects his wife; Ethel, on the other hand, for whom he felt a deep compassion ("If you close your eyes . . . it might break your heart, the solitary kind of life she leads," Michael says of her in *Year Before Last*) and to whom he was indebted for underwriting a magazine primarily intended as an outlet for his poetry, could not be expunged from his life without almost certainly losing what meant much to him as a sustaining human relationship. With the arrival of each new contribution, Walsh's desperation increased: *This Quarter* would never appear again without Ethel's help, but to gain that he would have to give up Kay, and that he refused to do. Years later, in the McAlmon-Boyle book *Being Geniuses Together*, Kay reflected that it might have been "reasonable and logical" for Ethel and Ernest to have reunited at this time. And this might have happened if "logic and reason" had been part of their deliberations. Instead, Ernest clung to his dream that he could retain Kay, regain Ethel, and produce another issue of *This Quarter*.

Richard, too, clung to fond hopes. In the six months Kay had been away, it had become increasingly clear that she would not return to Harfleur. But in July when Richard took a job with the Michelin Company in Clermont-Ferrand, he went to Annot to ask her to rejoin him. With Walsh, who alone knew that Richard was Kay's husband, Richard got along well. When a heavy round of parties forced Ernest to take to his bed, Kay and Richard cared for him, Kay administering injections, sterilizing instruments, and packing ice on Ernest's chest, while Richard fetched fresh prescriptions and allayed the guests' suspicions with a story that the patient suffered from stomach trouble. When his condition worsened, Richard went to Monte Carlo to replenish the dwindling ampoule supply. He also delivered a letter to Ethel in which Kay had described the gravity of the latest crisis. Ethel returned with Richard and found Ernest improved. For several days she lingered, consoling Ernest and observing Kay suspiciously. Had Kay's letter been a ruse to bring her and Walsh back together? One time when Kay left the sick man's room and was detained, causing Ernest, who could not bear to have her out of his sight for long, to suffer a paroxysm of jealousy, Ethel, who all the while remained at Ernest's bedside, greeted Kay's return with a barrage of abuse. The following morning Ethel reclaimed her car and descended to Monte Carlo, convinced that Ernest would have made no such demonstration if she rather than Kay had left the room for twenty minutes. Richard left, too, his relationship with Kay as ragged and unresolved as Ethel's was with Ernest. Loath to grant Kay a divorce lest it upset his still unsuspecting family, he preferred to do nothing, hoping that in time she might return to him.

Ernest Walsh, 1925

His strength regained, Ernest resumed his efforts to bring Ethel and Kay together long enough to complete preparations for *This Quarter*. Despite what had happened, this plan did not seem completely improbable, for as Ernest's fictional counterpart (Michael) concludes, since he was all that Eve (Ethel's name in *Year Before Last*) had, she might reconsider her actions and accept Hannah (Kay). Hannah has meanwhile decided that love is somewhat less Whitmanesque than she once believed: "As narrow as a coffin and as sharp as a thorn," it "casts everyone else out." Although she can admire Eve's "bravery, her ferociousness," and even her unjustness, she cannot abide her cruelty. When Michael asks Hannah if she could live with Eve, she concludes that "in his love for them both, he was playing them one against the other," and that when he is well, "her own pride" must take her away.

When Walsh resumed work, however, Kay did not go away—at least not far away. At the end of August, when Ethel unexpectedly returned to Annot, Kay moved in with the Dayang Muda. Ethel had bad news for Walsh. She had decided to publish the magazine either alone or with Robert McAlmon. Either way, Walsh's name would not appear as editor. But when she requested the contributions he had received, he refused and demanded she relinquish those she had confiscated weeks before. She refused. They argued and Walsh flung a carafe of water at her. She departed.

The reconciliation Ernest so fervently desired finally happened, but not because Ethel recanted and retained him as editor or because she accepted Kay. Soon after Ethel's turbulent visit, Ernest began to hemorrhage, at one point at a rate fast enough to half fill a chamber pot in five minutes. Kay summoned Ethel who, after watching Kay pack ice on Ernest's chest and plunge injections into his arm, exclaimed, "You're a wonderful woman. I've always excused my inability by my love and thought others could do it because they didn't care about him." When the worst had passed, Ethel, grasping their hands firmly in hers, insisted they both join her in Monte Carlo. Ernest glowed with relief. A few days later, an oxygen tube in his mouth, he was placed in an ambulance (hired by Ethel) for the long descent from the mountains to her villa above the sea. For a week he continued to bleed, averaging two hemorrhages a day. Ethel fought with the specialists who daily attended the dying man and charged her bills of 1,200 francs. Determined to prove she too could care for Ernest, she became "fiercely injured" whenever he asked Kay to do some chores. She dropped things, knocked Ernest's bed whenever she came near it, and spilled water down his neck. When he chided her for being so clumsy, she stayed in a vile temper for days.

Ernest Walsh died on October 16, 1926. He was thirty-one. With him were Ethel and Kay. In his final moments of life, just before dawn, each woman told him what he most wanted to hear: *This Quarter* would go on. At dawn that same morning Ethel asked Kay what she would do. Return to her mother, to her sister Joan, to Lola, she replied. Ethel proposed something else. "I had only him, and now I have only you and the baby that's coming. We must try to work it out together. We owe that much to him and his child." The next day the two women followed Walsh's coffin to the Monaco Cemetery, which faced the sea and the royal palace. The occasion might have passed in quiet mourning had it not been for a telegram from Eugene Jolas announcing he was starting a magazine (*transition*) that would continue the work Walsh had left unfinished. Would Kay, he asked, send him poems and stories immediately? Again Ethel had been ignored. Why had Jolas wired the vexatious "usurper," she complained, when she had been Walsh's co-editor?

Although Kay decided to remain with Ethel, she had considered a few other alternatives, one of which she proposed to Katherine and Joan. Since her child would not be born until March 1927, why should she not return to the United States and live with them until the baby came? She hazarded that it might even be possible to convince the American consulate in Nice that she was Walsh's legal wife and thereby become eligible for free passage home as well as for his monthly pension. Katherine and Joan, however, had some misgivings. They described the horrors that might await her at Ellis Island (Kay had had to give up American citizenship when she married Richard), pregnant, penniless, and without a husband. Joan went farther, speculating that Kay might be accused of "moral turpitude" if she returned to America. Their reaction, sincere and motivated by genuine concern for her welfare, was nonetheless a shock. Their objections seemed more important than the fact that she wished "to come to them, not for support, but for the sort of love and understanding only they could give." It "has been one of the bitterest things to me," she confided to Lola.

For three months they stopped writing. Christmas passed without a greeting. And then in January, having heard (probably from Joan) that Katherine was ill, Kay wrote to her mother, explaining that a "new life" had emerged around her, one separate from Katherine; she was making a "new person" of herself so that she could accommodate herself to "this new living." She explained how much she had wanted to return to Katherine ("as someone to come back to") after Ernest's death, and how others—Lola, Evelyn, Richard, and Carnevali—had wanted her to; since then, they had comforted her by putting "their fear and their sorrow" with hers and discovering "something else with it." Now that it appeared her own family had abandoned her, she would try to create a new one; it would consist of Lola and her husband David, Evelyn, Carnevali, Archie Craig, the Dayang Muda, and Picabia. "My kid," she boasted, "will have his own family." Surprisingly, it would even include Ethel. "There's the blood and the tradition and the future of my kid."

One she had not included in her "new" family was Richard, who at the end of January, one year after Kay had left him, came to Monte Carlo with the news that he had been appointed manager of the Michelin branch in Stoke-on-Trent, England. He would leave for England in mid-February, and he hoped she would join him after the child arrived. With her he would share his salary but not his quarters, that is, if she preferred not to. His generosity overwhelmed her. By living separately, she knew she could write and "be merry." But it would be impossible to accept Richard's money. If he were rich she would take it, just as she would from anyone who would not miss it. Whether she could ever again live with him, even occupying "separate rooms," was a more difficult decision. If she did, it would only be because she had found a way to support herself and Michael Kent (one of several names she had considered for her child) and because Richard remained the "only possible person in the world" with whom she could live. She loved him and knew she could be "happy and contented with him," but she also knew she could never again become his wife. As she said to Evelyn, "When a thing is done it is done," and the bond that had once existed between them was irrecoverable.

In the final months of his life, Ernest Walsh had yearned to have two wishes granted: to live with a woman who loved him and to father a child. Kay provided both. In Annot, after her pregnancy was confirmed, Ernest's joy approached delirium. Kay, however, could not always be certain just what her feelings toward motherhood were, especially now that she would face it alone. At times she longed more for Ernest than for their child. "I want him reborn again because he was something to have gone on with and a child is sad because it is an ending of something beautiful even though it is the beginning of itself." Sometimes she felt an urge "to tear the lungs and the hearts out of . . . people for his poor body." What sustained and nearly destroyed her was a belief that Ernest's spirit lived. It lived so intensely and so painfully because they both had believed, out of an awareness of life's brevity, that only what people said and were to each other "now immediately" made them important. If she had not believed while they were together that "everything" they said or felt was important at that moment to each of them, Ernest would now be only a "dry regret." Similarly, if Carnevali had waited for the certain tests of friendship to be passed before giving Ernest "everything at once," he "would have been a much less happy man," and Kay and Carnevali would "not have each other." First impressions "are the only ones of any value," she wrote Katherine. "We had our eight months, and we did things for each other that no one else had ever done. I made him happy, and no one else ever did that for him. And I am going to have his child. . . . He did for me what no one can ever take away from me. It is there solid and sharp in me like love or pain, but it is something better than these." That Walsh had been the "greatest and most exciting person alive" she would never forget.

But for Kay to preserve and nourish the memory of Ernest Walsh while living with Ethel Moorhead demanded more and more stamina, patience, and tolerance. At the worst of times, she vowed to leave Monte Carlo as soon as the baby came. "I want to do what I can for *This Quarter*," she wrote Evelyn, "but if a process of living takes from me the only thing of any importance remaining, in my case what Michael [Walsh] was and in particular what he was to me, I don't see any way but escape." More than anything, Ethel's "English" superiority and righteousness piqued her. Her habit of staring at her while she bathed was particularly annoying. After inspecting her from top to bottom, Ethel would slowly shake her head and sigh: "I'll never understand it. You're really not that beautiful." Ernest's preference for the "usurper" remained an unfathomable mystery to Ethel.

Once admitted to the Clinique Ste. Marguerite, in Nice, Kay's views of Ethel softened somewhat. Ethel was "fundamentally one of the greatest women alive," she explained to Lola. "She alone has stood by me, and I am not ungrateful." It was just that she was no longer "nervously equipped to exist" with her. Being away from Ethel and alone in a clean, sun-filled room, surrounded by paintings—Picabia's and Ethel's—proved enormously restorative: "I think the world's good to me." Again she had a chance to write. Archie Craig came often and never left without reading aloud Carnevali's or Walsh's or Lola's poems. Picabia, whom she asked to be still another godfather (the others were Carnevali and the French doctor who last attended Walsh) also came and promised to bequeath to her baby the "historical cradle of all the baby Picabias." The baby's name, she told Picabia, would be Michael Francis.

Four hours after Sharon Walsh was born on March 11, 1927, Ethel cabled Katherine that Kay had delivered her daughter without a whiff of chloroform. Picabia delivered the family cradle and amused himself trying to clothe his sleeping goddaughter (he called her the "image of Stieglitz") in a blue lace coat and bonnet. Ethel came by daily, and Archie resumed his regular visits. Nothing in the nature of this "sensitive, grateful, and very real comrade" was stronger than his devotion to poetry. Kay agreed with him that a new outlet was needed for the "two hundred good poems" printed each year—and then forgotten—perhaps an anthology of the "best" American and English verse that would demonstrate that "the true, the adventurous, the romantic spirit of poetry" remained alive and possessed with a "new fire and vitality." It would be a formidable answer to the "girly-girly off-moments" of Harriet Monroe's "crew or the mouthings of Eliot." Together they would select poems from magazines like *transition* and *This Quarter* and perhaps as early as January 1928 would publish the first collection. Archie was confident that he could borrow money for a printing of a thousand copies, which if the price was fixed at $2, might earn enough to pay for a second anthology.

Two weeks after Sharon's birth, Kay returned to Monte Carlo. She had several reasons for changing her mind about going back to live with Ethel: first, *This Quarter* had to be proofread; and second, until Sharon was older, she would not travel far. Also, there was Ethel to consider. She had taken Walsh's passport to the Mairie in Nice and registered Sharon as his legitimate child. Perjuring herself before the authorities was her way of showing contempt for officialdom. She had done the same thing earlier by swearing before the American consul in Nice that Kay was Walsh's widow, even claiming that she had witnessed their marriage in Edinburgh and that Kay was therefore entitled to Walsh's pension. Such fearless defiance of authority was inspiring, even touching. Moreover, Ethel had been exceedingly attentive throughout Kay's confinement and had paid all the medical bills. "I don't know what would have become of me without Ethel," she confided to Katherine. To leave her now would not only be ungracious and ungrateful, but Ethel's life would be "almost empty of any human contact." Going back with her would of course not be easy. "My reason, my gratitude, my convictions are all with her," she wrote Evelyn, "but my sympathy is awkward and unreal with her." She was prepared to find Ethel unreasonably and maddeningly mistrustful, particularly in relation to *This Quarter*. To "be simple and honest to a fault" with her was all she could do.

Back in Monte Carlo there was hardly time to develop new "personal spites" with Ethel. Preparing *This Quarter* consumed every minute. In the midst of all the activity, Robert McAlmon appeared, unannounced, and for three days Ethel tried to turn him into a bullying inquisitor. Convinced that Kay had only the feeblest opinions on most subjects she dared him to ask her what she thought of Negroes, and when he refused and she asked the question, Kay admitted she did not know what she thought of them but that she liked them. Ethel squealed with delight, but McAlmon quietly noted that Kay's reply was one few Americans would say. Another time, Ethel advised McAlmon to leave Monte Carlo before Kay "ruined a third man's life." By contrast, a generous and considerate Ethel tried to convince McAlmon that Sharon was Richard's child, pointing out that Richard sent money for the baby.

This Quarter finally appeared in April. Ethel blamed the delay on Walsh's last illness and the failure of the American government to refund 16,500 francs due Ernest's estate. As a memorial to Walsh, it fulfilled all Ethel's goals. First came three drawings of Walsh—one by Picabia and the two Ethel made the day he died—followed by a selection of poems Walsh wrote while living with Kay in Annot. Plaintive, playful, joyful, contemplative, and trivial, they are the observations of a man who must have believed he was living the happiest days of his life. Kay, sometimes called "wife," appears as his constant companion. The settings exude domesticity: "The oven is getting warm. She sits in her apron with the big/ Orange blocks cleaning the birds and I smell the potatoes/On the stove boiling and I see how her face is pale from/My child in her belly." The observer-poet draws inspiration from his equally watchful subject: "She wants to know my thoughts. She peeps under my eyelids/And listens to my footfalls going from her. Even when she peels/Potatoes in the kitchen and I wait for dinner to be ready with my eyes closed/She listens. She watches me. She wants to know everything/Because she loves me and cannot be alone." At the end of a selection of Walsh's unfinished essays— violent literary dicta and equally violent comments on morals, manners, and fashions—Ethel placed a verse reverberating with Ernest's promise of vitality: "I promise you/Every thought of me shall be/Cognac to your blood/Every thought of me shall be fire to you/I who am dead shall warm you and urge you."

In her own tribute to Walsh, "A Word More," Ethel maintained that since Walsh had spoken for himself, she would write only of his force and gesture—both those of a big man—and of his fearless outspokenness and his belief in "other young great writers" to whom he acted like a flame. Kay's poems, "To America" and "For An American," reflect her—and her country's—loss; and three others—"Poems," "Carnival 1927," and "Comrade"—reveal her grief. Archie Craig and Emanuel Carnevali expressed their sorrow—Craig delicately, Carnevali robustly. Following the installment of *Plagued by the Nightingale* came Ethel's spirited "Editorial," which defended the goals she and Walsh had set for *This Quarter* and detailed an "unrecommended List" of her enemies, the foremost being the American consul in Nice. Kay, invited to add her own list, included both Ezra Pound and Harriet Monroe. The special supplement of Picabia's poetry and painting completed the issue.

The letter McAlmon wrote Kay the day after he left Monte Carlo had the force of a summons. After apologizing for butting into her life, he got to the point: the best thing she could do was leave a place where she did not belong. If she needed money, which he thought likely, she could have it whenever she wanted. Early in May, Kay reported to Evelyn that she and Ethel had had their "inevitable bust-up," and that "on the spur of a hot argument," she had decided to join Richard in England. McAlmon wired her $50. Her relations with Ethel, she told Evelyn, had deteriorated rapidly after the magazine had appeared. Staying on with her would be like remaining "married to someone who gives you everything—consciously gives—and will have nothing in return. Not love, not interest, or belief." For seven months Kay had tried to convince herself that "self-justification" was unimportant and that she herself was also difficult and objectionable. What she had discovered was that she wanted to be "neither right or wrong, but simply to be, and [that] contact with people equally indifferent" was all that mattered; that is, "equally indifferent to anything but sort of flat fundamental swinging sympathies that don't have to be explained." In spite of all the difficulties, however, leaving Ethel made her "sick at heart."

At the same railroad station where she and Ernest had met her the year before, Ethel turned to Kay and said: "Tell the baby's father that its resemblance to him is striking." Minutes later as the Paris-bound train gathered speed, Kay watched Ethel walking along the quay, "her mouth twisted like acid and tears running down her stricken face."

Marguerite, Richard's sister, met Kay in Paris and took her and Sharon to a hotel. That act of thoughtfulness (the Braults had sent her) only compounded the "evil and perfidy" of her decision to go back to Richard. In London Katherine and Joan received her. A "greater humility" she had never before felt. "I, who had always talked so madly, so foolishly, of the

Kay Boyle and Harry Crosby, 1929

things in which I believed and the things I was certain I would do, stood in failure and defeat before them." Joan's achievements increased her humiliation. It was Joan who had worked hard and won independence and who now took care of their mother. It was Joan who had assumed the responsibility that she had dreamed of accepting and might now never have. How strangely ironic was this return, this retrogression, for if this was what she had meant when she had once said to Richard in Harfleur that she wanted to go back to where she had been, she now realized the futility of trying to recover the past. To her mother and sister she could not admit that she had broken and betrayed all the vows she had made to others, as well as all the promises she had made to herself.

Stoke-on-Trent, one of the grimmest of the five Staffordshire pottery towns in Arnold Bennett's novels, was England at its worst—stolid, conventional, and dirty. It hardly seemed like a place likely to relieve one's gloom. But soon after her arrival, Kay met the wife of another Michelin engineer, Germaine Garrigou, a beautiful, sensuous, animated woman (a *jolie femme*) whose companionship provided unexpected and joyful diversions. Germaine swooned over Kay's account of her tragic love for Ernest Walsh. She studied the photograph of Walsh that Kay had kept hidden in the bottom of her trunk and solemnly agreed that Kay should never "embrace another" and should wear black forever. She helped Kay clean Ernest's clothes, which she had brought from Monte Carlo, and dispatch them to Carnevali. Germaine, like Kay, had stopped loving her husband and now wanted a life of her own apart from her spouse. Together the two women gloried in their private experiences. They traded favors. Germaine "adopted" Sharon while Kay typed the final copy of *Nightingale*. When Germaine's husband would appear unexpectedly while Germaine was entertaining her lover, Kay pretended the traveling salesman in question had come to see her. Because of Germaine and an Englishman or two, one of whom invited her to walk the Continent with him, Stoke became what Kay had least expected: a place alive with "people and conversation and energy."

But no one, not even the compassionate Germaine, could replace the "spirit" of Ernest Walsh, in whose company Kay still steadfastly lived. To his spirit she reported every change in Sharon, every detail of her growth, even though she could now no longer hear, but only remember, his laugh. It was a "particularly nauseous" madness, she confessed to Lola, "practical only because he still exists for me as a standard of achievement." At the same time she realized that "some sort of source becomes exhausted, some source of emotion, when it has been used so intensely and deeply in life with another person whose emotions responded so completely and so generously." Before time eroded his memory, she would somehow have to give Sharon an understanding of the man who was her father. But how? How could she show her that this "gayest, bravest, simplest, and most gallant of poets" was what she meant by "a rare companion"?

From the time she arrived in Stoke, Kay had heard nothing of Ethel Moorhead. Then from Archibald Craig, who had called on Ethel with McAlmon, came the news that Ethel had decided against printing additional installments of *Nightingale* in *This Quarter*. Craig also reported that Ethel had reported that their divergent views on motherhood were the reason that Kay departed from Monte Carlo, an explanation Kay dismissed as being far from the truth and almost certainly prompted by vengeance. Ethel took the "prize as the rottenest dealer going," she told Craig, and she reminded him that Ethel had turned down two of his poems because she had detected Kay's influence in them. Archie, unmoved by Kay's animosity, answered with soft words. Ethel was a "sweet, lovely, and great, great woman," with whom he had had a "good talk." McAlmon, too, was wonderful, "natural and simple."

McAlmon had become a figure of contention in another embroilment, this one between Kay and Evelyn Scott. Evelyn strongly objected to McAlmon's being a contributor to Kay and Archie's anthology. She had even hinted that if McAlmon remained a contributor, her friendship with Kay might suffer. For five months they had wrangled, and Kay defended her action by claiming that she had overcome any lingering prejudice toward McAlmon that was inspired by Lola. McAlmon had been included, she explained to Evelyn, because the editors had invited him. Also, she admitted that McAlmon had become attractive for a number of other reasons: "He makes no pretenses. He writes because he writes and admits no understanding of what self-respect demands of an artist." He had no "aesthetic pretenses." Nor did he resort to "subterfuge," apologies, or explanations to cover up his mistakes. He was direct and consistent.

The disagreement exposed some disturbing things about Evelyn Scott. For one, she was inclined to judge people summarily, without really knowing them or their work. Kay also suspected that those that Evelyn took into her confidence tended "by deception" to protect her from recognizing her "extravagances in her loyalties to others." Kay admitted being defensive of her own enthusiasms, including McAlmon. But inducing her friend to accept McAlmon had never been her intention. It was enough to know that with Evelyn, she was always able to speak the truth and that their relationship rested on a "sacred belief in each other." It also rested on her lasting respect for Evelyn's *Escapade*, a "direct and simple" book that accomplished what no woman had ever before done. Eventually, however, Kay would conclude that the reality of her friendship with Evelyn really resided in their letters, which each had always addressed a facet of themselves.

McAlmon made a few testy observations on the debate. Miss Scott's "emotional prejudice" had obviously extended beyond him to ideas. Her mind, a "collegiate one," dwelt on abstractions and ideas rather than actualities, as *Escapade*, in his opinion, had proven. Most disturbing was her brand of idealism that included a "friendship-breaking clause." What else could be said about someone who intended to force a person to terminate one friendship in order to retain another?

After her appearance in the maiden issue of *transition*, Kay had kept Jolas supplied with poems and short stories. In May he printed a poem, "Complaint"; in June, a story, "Portrait"; in August, another poem, "And Winter"; and in September and December, two more stories, "Polar Bear and Others" and "Bitte Nehmen Sie Die Blumen." Although grateful for his support, she nonetheless took a dim view of the *transition* critics ("feeble and bloodless") and found the editors' hero worship of James Joyce and particularly Gertrude Stein appalling. Certainly not everything Miss Stein wrote was worth printing. A few other *transition* contributors also annoyed her, notably Hart Crane and Laura Riding.

Although censorious of the work of others, Kay rejoiced when admirers recognized strengths in her own writing. Archibald MacLeish considered her poems addressed to Walsh to be her best. So did Evelyn Scott. Lola found the segment of *Nightingale* in *This Quarter* "full of a running sap" and filled with language that was "luminous with a light that shines within." But it was Bill Williams's appreciation of *Nightingale* that surpassed all praise. "Your story," he wrote her, "is superbly written. I read last night until I was weary-eyed. I regretted to have to quit. Then I went to bed disgusted with my own novel that I am finishing. I wanted to tear it up. My sentences seem boorish, infantile, beside your beautifully informed inventions. What eyes you have! I am blind by comparison. . . . You have a quality that I must call feminine. The most feminine I have ever seen and fully equal to the best male stuff. No man could write like you. This is what I have always looked for from a woman. I am happy now, permanently happy to know you can do this good work. The poetry too, your poetry, is burning with intense feeling. It makes everything easier for me. Except, as I said, I dread to look again at my novel. . . . You have done well." He concluded with a rousing hope: "Here's to the next ten years! May we all somehow see each other and burn each other up—somehow."

In Stoke, Richard remained a model of tactfulness and consideration. He had agreed that they should live apart and meet only for meals and parties and for occasional excursions into the countryside, and like his industrious and independent wife, he had gradually built up a circle of friends and appeared to be happy. But, for Kay, to continue to be supported by Richard was a humiliation that would have to end.

During the winter, Archie Craig had proposed a plan that would make a return to Europe possible. If Kay agreed to join him and the Dayang Muda in Paris, they could resume work on their poetry anthology (now entitled *Living Poetry*); also, since Craig had persuaded his cousin to begin her memoirs, he and Kay could assume much, if not all, of that writing project. For her part Kay would receive a salary and room and board. The position had some strong attractions. Besides living with the princess (which thus solved the housing problem), being paid for her work, whatever it might turn out to be, would enable her to support Sharon and herself while maintaining some degree of independence.

In April 1928, Kay and Richard separated for the second and last time. Again they assured each other that they would be apart only a little while. But each must have known, as Kay wrote later, that what they "had been to each other once had come finally to an end."

The move from a French compound in England to an English compound in France brought Kay more than security and partial independence. It plunged her into a world of opulence. She lived in comfort in luxurious accommodations in the same apartment with the princess. In the mornings, a maid drew her bath and served her an English breakfast in bed. From her wardrobe of discarded "creations" by Molyneux, Lanvin, and Poiret, the princess chose dresses for her new companion. Most of the Dayang Muda's wealth came from the family biscuit business, but while still young she had married a man named Brooks whose brother was the white Rajah of the kingdom of Sarawak in northern Borneo. Through marriage she had acquired her title as well as a large share of the royal fortune. Being married to Brooks had also inspired in her an alarming profligacy that expressed itself in what her husband and in-laws considered wild and wasteful expenditures, which included thousand-acre farms in Ireland and ships that never sailed. Gradually the family had cut off her funds; then Brooks had sued for divorce and taken custody of their six children, having convinced a court that the princess was morally unfit to raise them. Shaken by these acts of outlawry that had left her alone, the princess coveted two things: revenge on her ex-husband and publicity. The surest way to accomplish both, Archie had convinced her, was to write and publish her memoirs.

The problem, however, was that the princess, for all the splendor of her background and associations with minor royalty, had only the haziest recollections of her past and almost no conception of her own identity. It was infuriating to extract from this passive and often inarticulate woman, "with a face at once wise, sad, petulant, surprised, and infantile," only a few flimsy scraps of information. She had obviously suffered from being controlled first by a dominating mother and then by conspiratorial in-laws. Her whole life seemed composed of disconnected faces and facts without meaning. For the ghostwriters, the situation demanded drastic action—nothing less than inventing a life for someone whose existence already seemed closer to invention than actuality. Kay and Archie drew up a vague outline of the princess's history, and their plan to provide her with a life she had never lived produced spectacular results. Whole scenes emerged from their imagination, replete with celebrated persons like Oscar Wilde. The princess waited eagerly for each new installment and invariably approved everything the makers of her past did. By June a goodly portion of the memoirs was finished, and a young Canadian writer and friend of McAlmon's named John Glassco was hired to help with the final typing. Glassco would often read the day's work to the princess, whose appreciation, he noticed, heightened whenever he read passages depicting her former husband as "a fool, a snob, a coward, a lout, a tightwad, and a nitwit." Obviously, Kay and Archie had served the punitive princess admirably by making everybody in the book, except the princess, look ridiculous.

Between turns at the memoirs, Archie and Kay worked on their anthology, making additional selections and arranging those they had already accepted. Archie remained as close and confidential a companion as he had been the year before in the south of France. On long strolls in the Bois de Boulogne with Kay and Sharon, he and Kay talked of Ernest Walsh and Carnevali. As part of his effort to ingratiate himself among the most celebrated artists and writers in Paris and to entice as many of them as possi-

Eugene Jolas, Paris, 1931

Kay Boyle, 1930s

ble to the princess's apartment, Archie attended all the important parties he could wrangle an invitation to and often took Kay along with him. Soon after she arrived in Paris, they went to the Jolases (Kay made the arrangements) for a gathering of the *transition* contributors. There she met the Joyces, the Gilberts, the Colums, Archibald MacLeish, Elliot Paul, and Robert Sage and watched, amused, as Gertrude Stein and Alice B. Toklas walked in, silently, imperiously, and directly in front of Joyce, and established themselves in a distant part of the room. In their wake followed Archie and a bevy of young admirers who clustered at Gertrude's feet. The scene dramatized one of the deep and lasting divisions in literary Paris, a division that would eventually require the Jolases to make a choice between the two commanding figures—Stein and Joyce.

The redoubtable Miss Stein never made a deep impression on Kay Boyle, and James Joyce would remain an imposing and distant person. She saw little of them, and she neither sought nor wanted a friendship with Miss Stein. The influential figures in her life for the next several months were two publishers: Eugene Jolas and Robert McAlmon. Of both men and of their pivotal position in her development at this time, she wrote in *Being Geniuses Together*: "It seemed to me that summer, just as it seems to me now, that had my tastes been formed by academic standards, or had I felt compelled to give allegiance to any group or state of mind, rather than allegiance to individual women and men—or to give consideration to the requirements of American publishers and editors—I could not have loved both McAlmon and Jolas so deeply and wholly without question as I did. I was grateful then, and I am still grateful now, that I lacked the intellectual effrontery and subsequent embitterment that might have diminished my acknowledgment of all these two men stood for and all that they had done."

Although she gave her allegiance to two men, rather than to two groups, Kay knew that there were strong literary and personal differences between Jolas and McAlmon. The ideas Jolas espoused as the "revolution of the word," McAlmon dismissed as mumbo jumbo. Complicating this admixture of warring beliefs and attitudes further was her own feeling about both men. Even before coming to Paris, she realized that she had been in love with McAlmon, and the time would come when they would agree to marry; but for a simple altercation, they might have. With Eugene Jolas things were and would remain different. In Paris it would be Jolas who would make all the advances and who, she had little reason to doubt, had fallen in love with her.

Born of immigrant parents in New Jersey, raised in Lorraine, self-educated and trained on the job as a reporter in America and Paris, Eugene Jolas had finally found a backer (his wife, Maria, a Kentuckian with an extraordinary voice and a considerable fortune) for *transition*, six issues of which had appeared at the time of the celebratory party Kay attended with Archie. Jolas, in his early thirties, was as compact of build as Walsh was frail, with broad shoulders and the "head of a Roman senator." His eager, impassioned talk, so simple and even tentative in contrast to his prolix and convoluted articles, testified to his deep devotion to literature. Jolas's idiosyncratic views on the importance of dreams, myths, hypnosis, automatic writing, and the borderland experiences of half-sleep, however, were sometimes confusing if not incomprehensible; at best, Kay admitted, they helped her define the nature of her own "undefined revolt." With him she entered for the first time into a linguistic, cultural, and metaphysical realm that, although puzzling, infused her life if not her writing with provocative new ideas. His counsel and stimulating thoughts and ideas notwithstanding, she continued to write in a realistic manner, perfecting her own style with sure and careful attention to the power of ordinary words. She remained essentially a romantic among revolutionaries, a conventional writer who contributed to an unconventional magazine of the arts; her writing was closer to McAlmon's in spirit and style. Recently, however, she observed that Jolas's emphasis on the importance of the "word" did make her discontented with "nine-tenths of American writing."

Knowing Jolas was to be included in the search for the "few great simple truths" that every artist seeks to discover through his work. With him—for a while they met daily for drinks and lunch or dinner, and after the Jolases had moved to Colombey, they dined whenever he came to Paris—she met those who were making *transition* a citadel of the avant-garde—Philippe Soupault, Tristan Tzara, Louis Aragon, André Derain, Robert Desnos, Moïse Kisling, Alexandre Noll, and on one of their rare visits to Paris, Laura Riding and Robert Graves. With Jolas she went to the fete at the Champs de Mars, to a Russian fortuneteller, whom Aragon saw regularly, and to the Bal Negre, where in the early hours one morning Jolas introduced her to Harry and Caresse Crosby. Jolas's personality was as many-faceted as the cultures that had formed it. His response to women was "Latin in its eloquence." His curiosity about men's minds, the stimulus he derived from their talk, the sense of camaraderie they provided, was German. His humor seemed at times "disturbingly American," but his passion for justice transcended nationality. Basically, this genial, gregarious, and loquacious man seemed almost provincially French.

A month passed before Kay met McAlmon at Lipp's, one of the calling places on his nocturnal rambles in search of interesting company. Since 1921, when he arrived in Paris already married to the English writer Bryher, whose parents had bestowed on their new son-in-law a bounty generous enough for McAlmon to form his own publishing company (Contact Editions), he had been an ubiquitous figure in Montparnasse. But the city to which he had come to write roughhewn prose accounts of his western upbringing and his experiences in Europe had never nourished him as it had others. Paris, of course, was never a talisman that miraculously bestowed talent upon the talentless, but McAlmon had talent. His friend Hemingway, whose first book McAlmon printed, and others, like Harold Loeb and Glenway Wescott, placed their novels with New York publishers, but McAlmon, like Gertrude Stein, had either to go on printing his own books or suffer the alternative of neglect and certain obscurity. Moreover, by the close of the decade, the ambience that had once made Paris a stimulating place was fading.

Dispirited and bitter, he often retreated to the countryside, seeking quiet, privacy, and rest, and when his energies were restored, he would come back to the place of his aspirations and his defeat.

From Lipp's that night, McAlmon conducted Kay to Le Grand Ecart, a Montmartre cabaret, where at times he found "some lively people." On the way he ridiculed *transition*. Why, he demanded to know, did Kay stick with Jolas? How could she abide his monotonous and obfuscating jargon? To go on paying obeisance to something called the "revaluation of the spirit in its intercontinental relations" was to remain insulated from reality. McAlmon's snarl depressed her, and she was glad to leave him at the bar and dance with the son-in-law of the patron of the Boeuf-sur-le-Toit, who scarcely differed from the other parsimonious and overfed bourgeois on the dance floor. From Le Grand Ecart, they shuttled to Bricktop's, a fashionable hangout for international celebrities. Kay marveled at Bricktop, the carrot-topped proprietress, her great white teeth flashing in smiles, who directed the swirling activity around her with the insouciance of a warmhearted and confident policeman. Bricktop, reared in tough American bars and clubs, had mastered the art of quelling fights, and regular customers knew they could depend on her if they got into trouble. Once she had bailed McAlmon and Jimmy (the Barman) Charters out of jail. From Bricktop's they recrossed the Seine to the Left Bank and joined McAlmon's friends Kiki (the model) and Hilaire Hiler at the Coupole. The long night ended hours later across the street at the Sélect in the company of Harold Stearns, whom McAlmon dismissed as another "modern myth" like Jolas, Hiler, and Kiki—all wasted survivors of a gayer, wilder, more adventurous time. Kay, alas, had come to Montparnasse too late. Those remaining spoke stale lines, the scenery needed changing, and, worst of all, the drinks had lost their transforming potency. Countless nights of perambulations through Montparnasse cafés, and other cafés beyond, in search of that elusive person who might briefly arouse his curiosity and brighten an otherwise sodden evening—a Nancy Cunard or Mina Loy or Djuna Barnes—had ended as this night had—in exhaustion, dejection, and a futile hope that one more drink might relieve the hours of unbroken boredom. But now even alcohol failed. In her story "I Can't Get Drunk," Kay depicts McAlmon (Denka) as a "dromo-maniac" who ceaselessly quests but never finds anything new, who ceaselessly drinks but remains agonizingly sober. Condemned to sobriety, he listens with bitterness to friends' tales of times when alcohol transformed their meetings into romantic interludes. McAlmon, restless, impetuous, hard to pin down, resisted committing himself to anyone at any time; yet, as Kay knew, he unfailingly came to the aid of those who needed help. His nighttime forays (with or without a companion) to find the one who might put things to rights again betrayed his terrible insecurity.

Archie Craig's manipulations to satisfy his cousin's lust for publicity reached a climax when he inveigled Miss Stein and Miss Toklas to come to tea in the rue David. According to Kay, the only reason they came was out of a snobbish interest in finding out just who this wealthy woman was that Archie so often talked about. Kay, still living at the Dayang Muda's, was also invited, despite the fact that after the single visit she had made (with Archie) to Miss Stein's, an embarrassed Craig had informed her she would not be welcome again in the rue Fleurus salon. Both Miss Stein and Miss Toklas had found his companion as incurably middle class as Hemingway.

Bringing together the three publicity-conscious moguls nearly ended in disaster. What Archie hoped would be a convivial confab that would magnify everybody's glory began ominously with the participants anxiously eyeing each other; the aphonic princess was even more silent than usual. After a flurry of polite pleasantries, only the animated conversation of Archie and Miss Toklas prevented the tea party from expiring in silence. To their immense relief, the painful situation suddenly ended with the unexpected appearance of Raymond Duncan. Raymond, ordinarily the only guest at the Dayang Muda's teas, was as surprised to see Gertrude as she was to see him. In fact, she could hardly contain her delight to find, standing before her and still speaking with a flat American twang, another scion of Allegheny, the small town in western Pennsylvania where both Gertrude and Raymond had begun life in the middle seventies and from which they had made early departures to pursue the joys and rewards of eccentricity. Raymond's sartorial transformation was a masterpiece that released gales of laughter from Gertrude. Swaddled in a flowing tunic, his long gray hair wound in a crown around his small "eaglelike head," his stockingless feet bound in plain thonged sandals, and his lean muscular body belying his half century of years, Raymond looked as imposing as a retired Roman emperor. Both expounded on the heights to which fame had brought them and their common origin, which now seemed so laughably incongruous. "Raymond," Gertrude exclaimed, "I knew you when you worried about the crease in your trousers!"

While Miss Stein saw in Raymond Duncan a saving diversion, Kay had begun to regard him as the magnetic leader of a commune where she and Sharon might go to live. At the Dayang Muda's, Duncan had often described the colony he had established in the Paris suburb of Neuilly. There, he told Kay, adults and children worked at common tasks and provided for themselves. The children formed a group of their own, eating, playing, and working together under the direction of an experienced member of the colony, usually Ayah, Duncan's companion since the death of his wife in Greece many years before. The adults made belts and sandals and other articles, he told Kay, all of which were sold at the two shops the colony maintained in Paris, one in the fashionable rue du Faubourg St. Honoré, the other in the Boulevard St. Germain on the Left Bank. In July, when the princess announced she would leave Paris for the summer and Archie entered a sanatorium for treatment of a serious recurrence of pulmonary trouble, Kay and Sharon moved into Duncan's colony.

To celebrate their induction, Raymond organized a party. He urged Kay to invite all her friends but to inform them that, in accordance with commune regulations, no alcohol would be served. Besides McAlmon, the celebrants included Eugene Jolas, Robert Sage, Hilaire Hiler, Bill Bird, Man Ray, and a young writer from Texas already familiar to Kay, named Ed Lanham, who would marry Joan Boyle the next year. Faced with the unprecedented challenge of attending a dry party, McAlmon arrived carrying a covert supply of his favorite brandy with which he spiked the punch. Everyone else he had managed to forewarn did likewise. Duncan, smiling and satisfied, noted that nonalcoholic parties could be festive too. But Kay suspected that he knew exactly what was happening and had decided to pretend ignorance.

The initiatory party for Kay and her friends turned out to be a farewell party as well, for soon many would leave Paris, and some, like the Jolases, would be away for the summer. Then in mid-July, Duncan's companion, Ayah, a shrewd, suspicious woman who ruled the colony with Napoleonic zeal, announced that she and Raymond would take all the children, including Sharon, south to Nice for a long vacation. Kay, she made clear, would remain behind to look after the two shops. For eight hours each day, in one shop or the other, Kay sat surrounded by heaps of tunics, shawls, and sandals. Occasionally, a curious passerby would enter to inspect the unusual things. Most of the time she wrote, seated on one of Raymond's uncomfortable Grecian benches, hiding her writing beneath the heavy cushions whenever visitors approached. Among the visitors were James Joyce, who inquired about the fabrication of the rugs and tunics; his daughter, Lucia, who wanted to enroll in Elizabeth Duncan's dance school near Salzburg; George Davis, later editor of *Mademoiselle*, who read chapters from his novel and shared with her a few dry figs and goat cheese; Harold Stearns, who ate nothing, but discussed plans for a biography of Rabelais; and Harry Crosby, pallid and gaunt, who always arrived bearing poems that he would read animatedly and leave behind for her criticism.

When Richard unexpectedly walked into the shop one day, explaining that he had come to Paris on business, Kay took him to the Coupole, where they found the café regulars—Flossie Martin, Kiki, Hiler, Kisling, John Glassco, and Graeme Taylor—in various states of drunkenness. Serving as self-appointed host was McAlmon. Whether provoked because Kay had come with Richard or more likely because of some deep dislike for her literary sensibilities, McAlmon that night committed an act of cruelty she never forgot. From the bar she watched him walk to the end of the counter and tear from the wall behind it the announcement of *Living Poetry*, hers and Archie's oft-delayed poetry anthology. Then, looking straight at her, he slowly tore it to pieces. "That's what I think of your crazy, senseless undertakings!" he shouted. "That's what I think of your taste in poetry!" It was too much to bear. As he started back to the bar, she hurled a stein of beer at him, which missed its target, clipped the counter, and splashed the contents into Glassco's face, thereby provoking uproarious laughter. Hastily, she retreated to the Boulevard Montparnasse with Richard, leaving behind a weeping Glassco and McAlmon grimly laughing.

The stormy night at the Coupole was the prelude to a season of shattering events that would twist Kay's "summer in Paris" into a nightmare. As

Paris filled up with tourists and her friends drifted away, a sense of desertion overwhelmed her. Besides withdrawing physically, her friends had taken their "complete, articulate lives" away with them. The Duncans' departure with Sharon left Kay bereft. Alone and afraid, she stopped writing to those like Carnevali who had always sustained her and whom she might have called on now. What was about to take over her life, she later wrote, was the "fatuous ego." Consumed by self-pity and desperately lonely, she slipped into a routine of promiscuity—reeling and stumbling from bar to bar, sleeping indiscriminately with random lovers. For the first time she regarded her "fallen sisters" compassionately, for like them love had no place in her behavior. It was ironic that Papa and Mama Hiler, who had often seen Kay and their son, Hilaire, together, chose this time to inquire whether they intended to marry. Such a "fine and respectable thing" it would be, intoned the old man, unaware that marriage was the last thing on her mind.

Kay's self-indulgence went on for weeks. When she could no longer bear the company of the man she was with, she would leave his room and rush back to the shop and sleep on the floor. Behind the self-indulgence that was close to being self-flagellation was a cold, ineradicable puritan conscience, "its little gray bonnet tied under its chin," which made every act of abandon a "sin" for which she would be accountable. Promiscuity, it seemed, demanded as much inner resolve as redemption might require. Pregnancy—a predictable result of this Celine-like spiral—was something she contemplated but never dared accept. When it happened, she summoned up the "cold calculation of an executioner." The child, she determined, would never be born. "All I knew was that it could not, must not be born, and I denied it its life." To the question, whose face would the child have? she replied: mine. To her aid came the Crosbys. Caresse found an abortionist, and Harry paid the huge fee.

As agonizing as the physical pain was the mental distress the abortion occasioned. How could she, who had had the care and cultivation of a "privileged upbringing," have allowed this to happen? The accusatory question elicited only an awful, earthshaking answer: "I was faced with the knowledge that if I, with the love of a gently bred family to shape me, had become what I was, then the whole moral fabric of our society was in jeopardy." While still contemplating the meaning of this stunning conclusion, her body suddenly and totally collapsed. What accounted for so rapid a decline remained unknown for several days. Unconscious, her mother at her side (Katherine was again living in Paris), she was trans-

Kay Boyle, 1946

ported from the colony to the American Hospital nearby. For over a week she hovered between life and death. When the illness was finally diagnosed as meningitis, a spinal tap brought her back to consciousness and saved her life.

For six weeks Kay convalesced. Joan came back from London, and seeing Kay made Joan resolve to be a better sister. Katherine's daily visits, however, inspired self-reform in her stricken daughter. "I would wait for Mother to come through the door . . . and I knew I was not going to be a failure any longer. I was going to live humbly and soberly."

Among the "missing" friends who returned to Paris in September was Eugene Jolas. On one of many visits to the hospital, he accepted a short story she had written about the events of the summer. The story, "Vacation Time," told how the narrator descended deeper and deeper into a morass of regret, guilt, and self-pity. "I was going like a crazy woman from one place to another thinking that tonight I must get into something deeper, the eyes full, the mouth full, to be sunk in it, to wallow like a sow." She wanders into a café and pours out her complaints to a lethargic listener, insisting that old errors and losses cannot obviate her belief in the future. But memories of a dead friend in Monte Carlo [Walsh] overwhelm her. Why, she wonders, had she not "spat [her] way to heaven with him"? No less torturous is the impossibility of drawing strength from her mother's example: "Oh wonder-wonder mother-love why didn't I have a bit of you instead of this fierce agony which betrays me this decision of the soul which is decided for happiness and which results in complaint?" On leaving the café, she thinks of drowning herself in the Seine, but when a stubborn taxi driver agrees to take her home but not to the "dark Swanee Seine," she ends up back in her room, alone, beating her fists against a mirror and "soothing the sad old face that was crying in it." From this impasse, sickness mercifully rescues her.

By October Kay had returned to Duncan's colony, and although still weak—she relied on two canes for support—Raymond reassigned her to the shop in the rue St. Honoré. His reaction to her illness was unexpected. "Mother sickness," he charged, was her real trouble, an observation he left undefined and undocumented except for saying that whenever the family appeared on the scene there was bound to be trouble. What was clearer was that he had withdrawn his confidence in Kay, and that she had harbored similar feelings of mistrust of him for some time. Among several unsettling discoveries she had made was that the Duncan-embossed tunics, sandals, and other things supposedly crafted in the colony were either machine-made or had been brought from Greece years before. Ayah had also upset her. Besides eyeing her suspiciously as a possible rival for Raymond's attention and affection, she had often barred her from seeing Sharon except at times she designated. Furthermore, when she did go to the children's quarters, Kay found Sharon as well as the quarters filthy.

In *My Next Bride* (New York, Harcourt, Brace & Co., 1934), the novel in which Kay described her life in Paris, Duncan appears as an engaging mishmash of wisdom, quackery, intelligence, and just plain nonsense. As producer and director of his own one-man show, he adroitly weaves together the conflicting roles and responsibilities of artist, charlatan, idealist, and slick advertiser. All he purportedly creates makes money, and when his career as a shrewd businessman threatens to make a mockery of his long unrealized aspirations—aspirations that had attracted Victoria John (Kay) to him—she resigns from the colony. The event that actually precipitated her departure occurred shortly after she returned to the commune.

Into Duncan's shop one day came two wealthy ladies from Kentucky who were prepared to spend the colossal sum of $25,000 for an assortment of his crafts, all of which would be installed in a museum in their home state. When Kay allowed the two angels to leave the shop without handing over the entire amount and then reported to Duncan what had happened, he remained in a state of anguish until the next day, when he met the ladies and divested them of the rest of their fortune. With the money in his possession, Duncan revealed his true colors. There would be no reward for his enterprising clerk (Duncan was well aware of Kay's desperate need of money), there would be no money for a printing press and hence no books of poetry (she had gone to the colony expecting to work in his "printing affair"), there would be no money for kilns or looms like those used years before in Greece, and no money for decent accommodations and proper clothing for the children, who slept on sheep hides on the floor and, being inadequately clothed, had to remain indoors during the winter. Not only would he keep all the money, but he would spend it exactly as he wanted. How he decided to use a goodly part of it became shockingly clear one day when he rolled into the commune grounds behind the wheel of an enormous Chrysler, which he had got at a discount because he agreed to have a banner attached to its side reading: "Raymond Duncan Drives a Chrysler."

Whatever trace of respect Kay might have retained for Duncan vanished with this betrayal of his ideals. Like Victoria, her fictional counterpart in

Bride, Kay perceived at last what he was: an old man clinging to his youth
(the time of his real influence, his genuine revolution) and, despite himself, succumbing to the lures of profit, all the while surrounded by sycophants who saw through him and by a grasping woman who ceaselessly
badgered him. What Victoria had hoped to find in communal life never
materialized. "I am ready to take each act of my life as a stone in my hands,
never to be denied," she vowed when she joined the colony. "My words will
be like stones to myself, as hard and irrevocable. Now I have ten francs a
day in my pocket and people to go back to at night. I can look at the days
ahead or behind me and think of what they will make in the end." All her
determination and organization vanished, however, in the long summer
orgy of sex and sickness, a lapse which Sorrel (Duncan) ridicules. There
is even the suggestion in *Bride* that Sorrel, after delivering an oration of
appreciation to the departing Kentuckians, tries belatedly to extend his
gratitude to Victoria by attempting to seduce her.*

Resigning from the colony proved to be more difficult than joining it.
Once Kay had announced she intended to leave, Ayah refused to release
Sharon. The child, she claimed, had been given to the colony, and the
colony had assumed responsibility for her upkeep and training and now
she belonged to them. In Ayah's opinion, Kay had really bequeathed her
daughter to the Duncans. In *Bride*, Sorrel speaks reverently of the "children in my house"; the children "do not belong to this or that woman.
They are not property. They belong to life, and that's the secret of their joy.
I have no children of my own, but I say these are my children because I
have opened my house and my heart to them. I have no heritage to give
them. . . . But I believe they will have something better than most men
receive from the fathers of their blood. . . . We have given them a relation
to life, not a relation to the standards made by man."

The claim Duncan made on Sharon, sanctioned by the precepts he had
himself drawn up and enforced, would be impossible to circumvent by
argument. Getting herself and Sharon quickly and safely out of the colony would require stealthy planning and a foolproof method of escape. If
she fumbled, if the Duncans suspected her intentions and thwarted her,
or if she left the colony and was later apprehended, it would be difficult to
prove that Sharon, who had been illegally registered in Nice, was her

*Although Kay Boyle believes that Raymond Duncan was much too cautious to try out-
right seduction, she remembers that Duncan expressed his gratitude by murmuring in her
ear that she was "the honey which drew men and women to the beehive" of his shop. At that
point he held her close and whispered that he would like to be privileged to taste that honey.

daughter; the result could very well be the loss of her child to the colony forever.

The plan she devised at first involved only the Dayang Muda. Whenever Kay was alone at the colony, the princess came to help her load boxes crammed with books, papers, and clothing into a chauffeur-driven Daimler that Harry Crosby had made available. The next step was crucial: where would she go once she had made her escape? Not back to Richard and certainly not to the princess, for Duncan would surely come looking for her there.

The matter was still unsettled when just before Christmas Kay met McAlmon at the Coupole. With him was a couple she had never seen before. The man, tall and slender, wore bright clothing and had an aristocratic face and streaky golden hair. The woman, short and attractive, had hair of the same color. Both possessed beaklike Roman noses. The woman was Clotilde Vail, the man with her was her brother Laurence. He rose, removed a bouquet of mistletoe Kay was carrying, held it over her head, and with exaggerated courtliness, bestowed kisses on her nose, eyelids, and mouth. Clotilde nervously pulled Kay down beside her. "I'll sit between you and my brother," she said, "so he won't eat the mistletoe." The attention Laurence had paid Kay, while perhaps no more than he would show any young woman, would shortly be regarded as an augury of considerable consequence.

After the Vails had gone, Kay told McAlmon what she and the princess had accomplished and asked if he knew where she and her daughter could hide after their escape. McAlmon suggested that the Crosbys' mill, Le Moulin, located a few miles from Paris, was a safe hideaway. With the Dayang Muda, Kay worked out the final details. They agreed that on the last day of the year, the princess would give a party for all the colony children and that Kay, after chaperoning them in taxis from Neuilly, would direct the children inside her apartment; once they had disappeared, she would drive off with Sharon. The scheme worked flawlessly. From the Dayang Muda's they went straight to McAlmon's hotel, and from there he escorted the runaways to Crosby's mill, where a party celebrating the new year had begun.

By the end of this year, which Harry Crosby was that night excitedly anticipating, he would be dead—a suicide. With him was one of many mistresses he had retained in both Paris and America. Crosby's frequent visits with Kay at the Duncan shop did no more to arouse his wife's suspicions than dozens of other meetings he had routinely arranged with various women. For that reason Caresse no doubt assumed that her husband and Kay were having an affair. They were not, and Kay made this point the single, overriding purpose of *My Next Bride*. Dedicated to Caresse, the novel attempted to clarify an admittedly murky situation and to prove that, despite all the time they had spent together, she and Crosby had never become lovers. That they had not was probably due mainly to Kay's resoluteness, for if the portrait of Crosby (Antony) in the novel bears a resemblance to the original, Crosby doubtlessly foresaw a time when their relationship would cease to be platonic. Antony demands to know how many lovers she has had, a question that Victoria (Kay's alter ego) prefers to leave unanswered, except to say that she is a puritan, lives alone, and is insignificant. Such revelations, however, only encourage Antony to press his demands: "I ask everything. I ask that people give up their brides." His vision of mass betrayal portends moral chaos: "The whole universe on a honeymoon of horror, wedded to their daggers, stabbing their way from one betrayal to the next. Even your own family and friends are eager to do it to you." One day while Antony and Victoria are drinking together, he confesses he loves but fears her. She replies that she has never been in love and does not know what it is, but Antony insists that their love will be "history . . . like nothing else has ever been." They join a houseboat party in progress (probably on the barge of Vert Galant, owned by Crosby's close friends Frans and Mai de Geetere), and in the midst of the bedlam and ubiquitous bedding down, Antony announces that his next bride will be Victoria. More confusion follows his declaration, and Victoria totally blacks out as Antony delivers her, drunk, to her quarters. Later, she wakens to find herself covered with mud, her blue cape (a badge of her degradation) dirty; she is also disconcertingly uncomfortable in the wrong places. She is certain, however, that her "assignation in the filth" was no different from what befalls any girl. Antony, she is sure, is innocent. When pregnancy brings her to a state of near collapse and she is befriended by Fontana (Caresse Crosby), who insists she give birth to the baby if it is Antony's, Victoria reiterates that it is not. "It was never anything like that between us," she tells Fontana. "He has you all the time, he always has you; I had no one. I used to think it was good to have no one, but when Antony talked about you, I wanted someone. It happened the first time on the boat. . . . I don't know who it was exactly. And after that it happened very often. . . . It was never Antony." The escapades, she assures Fontana, were like a madness, "to find someone you don't hate as much as you hated the one before."

Kay Boyle, 1943

Crosby's practice of compelling Kay to listen to his poems and then provide comments, immediately or later in writing, tested her gallantry as well as her critical probity. Generally, she combined encouragement and tepid disapproval. "The poems you left I liked. They all seemed to me so far better than any in any book of poetry I've seen lately that I should think you could do something definite with them." Poems having only comparative value did not interest her. She suggested that he had a more arresting subject at hand. "In all your things there is a center and a warm glow that I like. But if you wrote out what is there churning about inside of you, there'd be something else again." She passed on the advice that Bill Williams had once given her, that clarity was the important thing. That comment had strengthened her belief in long poems, where a poet can say what he wants to say, and also in Harry's poetry—"solid and good to the core of it." It was during their many meetings in the fall of 1928 that Crosby, probably encouraged by Jolas, asked Kay to select some of her short stories to be published at his Black Sun Press early the next year.

Although Laurence Vail's affection that night in the Coupole may have seemed no more important than that which he bestowed on any number of others, he and Kay began to meet often after she left the colony. By the spring of 1929, they were together constantly and had decided to move to Ste. Aulde, a small town two hours' drive from Paris. That year Laurence would turn thirty-eight and Kay twenty-seven. A third-generation Paris-American, an artist and writer, and a dadaist in perpetual revolt against all forms of conventionality, Vail had earned his title of "king of Bohemia" the hard way. In his unpublished autobiography, he remarks that a family friend predicted at the time of his birth that his life would be influenced by liquids. Looking back over several decades filled with considerable ocean traveling, light washing (laundry), and heavy drinking, he could only marvel at the accuracy of the prediction. His drinking was something few had failed to notice, either at his big parties, which he enjoyed giving, or in the cafés of the Quarter. Inebriety often provoked him to violence or outlandish misconduct, which Kay attributed partly to the breakup of his marriage to Peggy Guggenheim after seven stormy years. By caring for him "in every way," Kay naively but understandably believed she could alter his behavior. As for herself, joining Vail would mean that she would never again be alone. With him she looked forward to pursuing common interests—writing, translating, painting, mountain climbing, and raising children. It was soon after the new year began that she discovered they would have their first child, an addition that would increase their family to four, since Laurence's marriage to Peggy Guggenheim had produced two children, Sindbad and Pegeen, both of whom would spend considerable time with their father and Kay over the next dozen years.

In her lively autobiography, Peggy Guggenheim admits that she gained more from her marriage to Vail than motherhood. It was Laurence who introduced her to Bohemia, to the artists and writers as well as to those who did nothing at all—Vail seemed to know everybody—and with that introduction, she gradually shed the conventions of her bourgeois upbringing. They married in 1922, the same year Kay and Richard had married, but they had hardly the same equanimity. Vail had no sooner proposed to her than he regretted it. After much hesitation and evasion, he reproposed, and still uncertain, skulked into marriage. The man who so warily consented to be her husband entranced Miss Guggenheim: "He appeared to me like someone out of another world," she wrote. "He was the first man I knew who never wore a hat. . . . I was shocked by his freedom, but fascinated at the same time. He had lived all his life in France and he had a French accent and rolled his r's. He was like a wild creature. He never seemed to care what people thought. I felt when I walked down the street with him that he might suddenly fly away—he had so little connection with ordinary behavior." Seven years later Vail did fly away, at least from Peggy, and for reasons not the least important of which were Vail's discovery of his wife's affair with John Holmes and their basic disagreement over where to live. Years before, Vail's artist-father had turned his son into a "mountain fanatic." I would "give up anything for a climb," wrote Vail—even writing, painting, maybe pipe tobacco, and children. Peggy felt differently. She had never liked the country and she had an ineradicable distaste for the mountains. Living anywhere but in Paris was like being buried alive. Unfortunately, the excitement of Paris that stimulated her usually overstimulated and exhausted Vail. Like McAlmon, he would regularly retreat to the country for rest and restoration. Vail's preference for the country fortunately made no difference to Kay. She liked living there, Vail remembered; she "didn't care what sort of country so long as she had time to pound out her romantic novels on the typewriter."

Shortly before Kay and Laurence left for Ste. Aulde in February 1929 they went to a party at the Crosbys' mill in Ermonville, one of the hundreds the Crosbys hosted. There Kay again saw Hart Crane (she had met him earlier with the Vails), who having arrived in Paris the month before, was finding the city, with assistance from Crosby and Jolas, an "incredibly free and animated" place. Crosby, as enraptured with Crane as Crane was with him, heard the poet read selections from his still-unfinished opus, *The Bridge*, and begged Crane to allow him to print it at his Black Sun Press. Crane agreed and at the time of the party was about to move into the mill, at Harry's invitation, to finish his work. Although Crane had attracted a number of influential defenders, such as Allen Tate and Yvor Winters, he had not impressed Kay. In her review of his poetry collection, *White Buildings*, which Jolas had reluctantly printed in *transition*, Kay complained that Crane appeared to be finished with "life, civilization, emotions, and human ambition." Further, only a vast emptiness existed behind his plethora of words. She castigated him on the missing element in his work: "Words are shallow troughs for the deep water of the mind, and it is only the fierce, the living, the simple, the clear, the angry mind which can overflow the troughs and go out over the mud, and over the grass, bearing the light of the sun on it like an angry shield." *White Buildings* failed because it was false, dull, humorless, and full of empty words "hiding a human fear." Crane, she concluded, was as "phlegmatic as a Rotarian, as entertaining as the American Legion."

Kay's "explosive boil" (Crane's quip) irritated him, and at the Crosbys' party, he took his revenge. Seizing a copy of *American Caravan* containing a story by Kay, he tore it up and threw it into the fireplace, apparently forgetting that the book also contained one of his poems. Paradoxically, that temperamental outburst brought a noticeable improvement in their relations. Soon afterward, Crane wrote to a friend that it pleased him that Kay Boyle had decided she liked him. In the summer, Kay and Laurence again ran into him in Paris. He had just come back from a working trip in the south of France that had failed to bring *The Bridge* to completion. They were delighted when he agreed to come to Ste. Aulde, where, it was understood, he could stay as long as he liked. But when he failed to appear at the agreed-on time, they learned from Maria Jolas that, after a nasty altercation with Madame Sélect (the café proprietress was not known for her tolerance of Americans) and a swinging battle with the police, Crane, battered into insensibility, had been dragged off to jail, where he remained despite all efforts to secure his release. Kay and Laurence marshaled everyone they could find to protest Crane's confinement. Crosby coordinated the rescue efforts, and a week later a bearded and bruised prisoner was permitted to pay a fine of eight hundred francs (supplied by Bill Widney) and depart.

That spring Crosby's Black Sun Press published Kay's first book, seven stories entitled simply *Short Stories*. All but one had appeared in periodicals, four in *transition*. A few days before publication, Harry sent her one of fifteen copies printed on Japan paper and containing a dedication that read: "To the greatest in America, Kay Boyle." "I'm so proud of my book," she replied, "and had you been here the moment it arrived, you would have known."

Two stories, "Summer" and "Portrait," draw on the period when Kay lived with Ernest Walsh and Ethel Moorhead. Her ambivalent relationship with Ethel is finely delineated, as is the effort each woman made to accommodate herself to Walsh. In "Summer" (the summer of 1926), an aging woman, hard-of-hearing and tired, lies in bed while a girl reads to her. After she falls asleep, the girl muses on the potentialities of language: "She wanted to believe in a language that burned black the tongue of the one who spoke and scarred the one who listened. She would demand nothing of it, but to serve it, and be humble before it." From the next room the "hard quick beating" cough of the man they both love wakens the sleeping woman, who wonders if she will be able to sleep again. The girl writhes in silent agony, unable to go to him and help him expel the demon that is suffocating his life. The next morning the man and a woman companion, with whom it was his practice to spend long periods in the countryside, appear on a terrace. The man, seeing the woman and the girl seated nearby, asks if he may remove an unoccupied chair at their table for his companion, but the woman instructs the girl to tell him that the chair has already been claimed.

In "Portrait," a woman, alone, recreates the emotions and events of a played-out drama involving herself, another woman, and a dead man whom each had loved. The narrator's remorse has overcome her impatience with the other woman (Tara), whose incessant questions and preoccupation with death suddenly seem acceptable human concerns.

A third story, "Bitte Nehmen Sie Die Blumen," describes a tug-of-war between the French and English residents in a town that resembles Stoke. The narrator accompanies her husband (Peleser), who will pull for the French side, to the tournament. Opposing him is a member of the English team towards whom she has felt a powerful attraction, despite fears that she has lost the capacity to love. During the contest she admires the Englishman's "clean unsubtle beauty"; she remembers seeing him in the refectory reading the *Times* and sitting in a park drinking tea, his gloves and cane on a chair. "For a turn of his body" she would leave Peleser and make "a new life with this man," simply because he is "beautiful" and because his small ambitions are more important than hers. The French lose, and the Englishman helps the fallen Peleser to his feet. Later, the wife and the Englishman meet in the boardinghouse where they reside. She accuses him of flaunting his English superiority under the guise of being a gentleman. At dinner that evening she sits across the table from him; she feels again his intense anguishing attraction and realizes he has been "silenced by the sad proud humility of his heart." He offers her the menu, across which he has written: "Aber Gott Bitte, Nehmen Sie die Blumen."

"Vacation Time" recaptures the excoriating summer in Paris. "Spring Morning," an exercise in poetic prose, harkens back to happier times with Ernest Walsh. The two other stories tell of families in disintegration. "Uncle Anne," a romantic nomad, a "lost man," who is viewed through the eyes of an adoring niece (Eve), has come home to rediscover his roots and his country. For Eve's parents, however, he becomes a man unfit to remain in their company when they discover he has impregnated a servant girl. "Theme" translates a lonely woman's love for her son into the daytime fantasies that sustain her until he returns at night.

Crosby's high estimate of his friend's writing prompted more than his adulatory dedication. In his *Diary* he wrote: "Again I say that Kay Boyle is the greatest woman writer since Jane Austen." Agreeing with Crosby, Jolas attributed the "savage beauty" of her narratives to her "organic impulses." In prose that was "hard, yet flexible enough to present the 'limitstates' of her consciousness," she had captured a "universe of anguish, confusion, and a desperate search for liberation." *Short Stories*, concluded Jolas, marked "a turning point in the evolution of American literature." McAlmon, not surprisingly, dissented. The stories, he argued, were not as good as some others she had done, but he acknowledged that they had helped her "get recognition from more commercial publishers." With one firm, newly founded by Jonathan Cape and Harrison Smith, she would soon arrange to publish a second collection of stories as well as her first novel and a translation.

In her letter thanking Crosby for the inscribed copy of *Short Stories*, Kay agreed to undertake a translation he had suggested, a portion of *Babylone* by René Crevel. It would supplement her income and provide at least a diversion while living at Ste. Aulde, which, although hardly an ideal living place—the climate was uninspiring, the walks too flat, the house too small—was nonetheless convenient to Paris, a necessity as long as Kay continued working as secretary for Bettina Bedwell, the fashion editor for the *Paris Tribune*. Moreover, Laurence's complicated divorce proceedings also made proximity to the city necessary.

As her pregnancy advanced, Kay traveled less often, and in the fall she and Vail moved to a Paris hotel. In November her translation of *Babylone* appeared in *transition*, and in the same issue, Jolas printed Kay's poem "Dedicated to Guy Urquhart." A few months before, McAlmon had used this name (his mother's family name) for two of his poems, which Kay had then submitted to Jolas in the hope of challenging his low opinion of McAlmon's writing with disguised examples of his work. To her delight, Jolas published one of the poems. But when she revealed that the author was McAlmon, Jolas fumed and warned that he would tolerate no more subterfuge. In June Jolas printed her story "On the Run," another episode about the summer of 1926, which recounted her exhausting and aimless perambulations with Walsh in the mountains behind Nice, as well as her review of *John Brown's Body* by Stephen Vincent Benét ("a dull book"). The centerpiece of the issue, however, was the "Revolution of the Word Proclamation" in which Jolas listed the twelve principles that he and fifteen signatories believed would cleanse contemporary writing of such offenses as the "banal word, monotonous syntax, static psychology [and] descriptive naturalism." Not surprisingly, the statements themselves, despite supporting citations from Blake and Rimbaud, possessed a few of the very faults they scorned and were almost impenetrably ambiguous. What, for example, was one to make of: "The revolution in the English language is an accomplished fact," or "Time is a tyranny to be abolished"? Although the final statement—"The plain reader be damned"—sounded the familiar challenge of almost all manifestos, those among the signers who accepted it could hardly have numbered more than Jolas himself, the self-appointed Joycean stylist Abraham Lincoln Gillespie, and perhaps Vail. Certainly other signers, like Stuart Gilbert, Whit Burnett, Elliot Paul, and Robert Sage, although doubtlessly in sympathy with Jolas' complaints as well as his means of expanding the creator's ken, were not about to disabuse the "plain reader." Nor was Kay Boyle. Except for some free-flowing sentences that lacked standard punctuation and a few paragraphs of easy-to-follow stream-of-consciousness writing, her work was hardly beyond the comprehension of the plain reader. Nor was it intended to be. Jolas's theories generated considerable interest, if only mild respect, and they became guiding principles for only a few whose work appeared in his magazine. The contributors to *transition*, certainly Kay Boyle, Gertrude Stein, and Hart Crane, for example, and later Samuel Beckett and Dylan Thomas, worked out their own creative methods and developed their own styles.

December was a month of life and death. In New York Harry Crosby finally kept his oft-postponed rendezvous with death. Caresse asked her friend Archibald MacLeish to identify Crosby's body, his arms around a second victim, the wife of a Harvard graduate student, in the Hotel des Artistes. The same month, in Paris, Kay gave birth to a girl whom Laurence—delighted to have another daughter to replace Pegeen, who resided mostly with Peggy Guggenheim—named Apple-Joan. (Had it been a boy, Laurence announced later, he would have been called Apple-Jack.)

By mid-December Caresse Crosby, bearing Harry's ashes, had returned to France. Eugene Jolas collected tributes for his friend and printed them in the June 1930 issue of *transition*. Kay's "Homage to Harry Crosby," composed soon after his death, is understandably laudatory. Crosby was a man "who took his time and his contemporaries to heart. With all the nobility of his belief in them, and all the courage of his determination to make his life a testament of stern and uncompromising beauty, he wrote his poems . . . and his diary in words that never faltered in their pursuit of his own amenable soul." Among his achievements she cited his *Diary* ("one of the few important diaries ever printed"); in it were "some of the finest and most moving descriptions of foreign places, of weather, of times of day; the speech of [one] so absorbed in the display of life that he had no time nor inclination for pessimism or for slander; some of the most delightful love poems of our time; and a lively sense of humor." Drawing from an introduction intended for an edition of the *Diary*, she provided a more complex view of her friend. Crosby was "in no sense a modern." He had "no place, no interest, no taste for experiment in modern life." His gaze was inward, fixed on himself, until the very end. In his complicated sun-worshipping system he had found his refuge and a shield that protected him from "his Boston environment, his position in the bank, his education, and above all, against people, against all kinds of people. His soul rejected them, they dismayed and bewildered him; he wanted himself. . . . People were the enemy." His true intimates consisted of a "collection of old keys, illuminated manuscripts, stained glass windows, the *dame à la licorne*, old bookbindings, the sixteenth-century bed."

*Kay Boyle and children (left to right: Ian, Kathe, Clover, Apple, Faith),
Central Park, New York, 1946*

*Kay Boyle and daughters (Faith, Clover, Kathe, Apple),
Central Park, N.Y., 1946*

When Caresse Crosby went on alone with the Black Sun Press, she asked Kay to translate the complete novel of Crevel's *Babylone*, this one to be a Black Sun book. Not satisfied with the portion of Crevel's work that had appeared in *transition*, and certain that on her next try she could do better, she agreed and offered to send Caresse a sample translation at once. "I want to make it the most wonderful book in the world." She finished by early summer, and still as fascinated as ever by Crevel's "emotional imagination," she sent it to Paris, noting that the book lacked only one thing, a "sort of foreword." It would not be a "dry thing, not documentary," rather "a sort of literary note," very similar to one she was writing for another translation, Joseph Delteil's *Don Juan*, which she had undertaken for Jonathan Cape and Harrison Smith.

With Caresse's approval she wrote "An Open Letter to René Crevel." She began by mentioning the feeling of inadequacy that many a translator has doubtlessly felt at the end of an assignment. She apologized for making an assault on Crevel's mysterious language—she an intruder from a country where a spirit like Crevel's would most certainly have "perished in the walled garden of Mr. Dickinson." Her greatest problem was rendering the elusive quality of Crevel's prose in a language as relentless as English. Only a few who wrote in English had accomplished a similar beauty— Poe, who found it in blood and in the flesh of corpses; Carnevali, who spoke of it in poverty and anger; and Joyce, who created a new language in order to speak "out his heart." Crevel's book belonged to France.

With the Crevel book finished, Kay turned to the much longer translation of Delteil's *Don Juan*, which after the "wonderful discipline" of Crevel was "comparatively simple." By the end of the year, she had finished and sent it to her new American publishers, Cape and Smith, who paid her 8,000 francs (the translation came to 206 pages) and published it in April 1931, with Kay's foreword.

After passing the summer in Ste. Aulde, Laurence and Kay moved south to Villefranche, near Nice, where after a short stay in the villa of Mary Reynolds and Marcel Duchamp on the Route Nationale, they took a house high above the town on the Moyenne Corniche, with a terrace that afforded a view of the harbor. Laurence hired a cook and an Italian girl to look after the children, and Sindbad and Sharon started school. Nearby lived Alfred Kreymborg and his wife; Frank Scully, editor of *Variety*; in the writers and artists village of Cagnes-sur-Mer were Bob and Rose Brown—energetic, lusty, productive Americans—whom they would see often. Brown, after several colorful careers—playing the New York Stock

Market; publishing magazines in South America; and writing (by his own count) one thousand stories, a best seller, a collection of detective stories, and a large quantity of just about every form of hack literature ever conceived—had ceased being a "writing machine" and had invented a contraption he claimed would make the book obsolete. A forerunner of the microfilm reader, Brown's reading machine used a "tough tissue roll," no larger than a typewriter ribbon, on which was printed the complete contents of a book and which could be unrolled beneath a magnifying glass at any speed. According to Brown, this device would make reading as fast as hearing. (The eye, he claimed, was faster than the ear.) It would also save fortunes normally spent on the manufacture and storage of books. To demonstrate his reading machine, he invited friends to contribute specimen "readies"—short passages of "telegraphic" prose (articles, pronouns, connectives, and adjectives were expendable)—that could be run rapidly through the machine and still give the viewer some idea of what he had seen. Brown supplied Kay with a sample readie and asked her to try her hand at one or two of her own.

From Cape and Smith, in November 1930, came Kay's first trade book, a collection of thirteen short stories called *Wedding Day and Other Stories* (New York, Cape and Smith, 1930), all but two of which, one being the title story, had already appeared either in *Short Stories, transition, American Caravan,* or *Hound and Horn.* "Wedding Day" describes the final agonizing hours preceding Clotilde Vail's marriage in April 1930, when she and Laurence wander for the last time through the city (Paris) where they had grown up and where they had forged an alliance never before seriously threatened. Their respectable, upper-crust parents, by making them feel they were in the way, contributed to the powerful bond that for years had held brother and sister together. Such "intransigeant loyalty," their "strength and comfort," had been, Peggy Guggenheim complained, a "thorn in the side" of her marriage to Laurence. In the Bois de Boulogne, with their "yellow heads" and proud arched noses erect, they look like people chosen to begin a new race. "It isn't too late," the brother whispers to his pensive sister. Again at home they find their "fine arrogant old" mother (Mrs. Vail, a New Englander, maintained a household noted for its puritanical exactitude) as inflexible as they had left her a few hours earlier, when in an outburst of "black arrogance" she had thrice denied her daughter a gift of the family heirloom copper saucepans. As much in protest against his mother's hardheartedness as against the now inevitable separation from his beloved sister, the son angrily kicks a silver platter (a receptacle for calling cards) and sends it spinning down the hallway. Behind it the mother follows in silent pursuit. For brother and sister, the marriage ceremony unfolds like a mime; neither is aware of anything except the now broken bond. Around them flutter the wedding guests, polite people their mother summoned from the American colony, all totally unaware of the wrenching experience that is taking place. Their mother, seemingly as imperceptive as her guests, dances by in the arms of a general, noting with satisfaction and triumph that the wedding has turned out to be a "real success."

In 1931, five months after the appearance of *Wedding Day*, Cape and Smith published Kay's first novel, *Plagued by the Nightingale* (New York, Cape & Smith, 1931), heavily revised since its inception in 1924. Kay had done most of the rewriting the previous year, and since it was the same year she and Richard were divorced, toiling on the story about her sojourn with the Braults must have often been trying. She grafted one major invention to the original version: an unrealistic love story of a young doctor's attempt to spirit Miss Boyle's alter ego, Bridget, away from her melancholy husband (Nicholas) and his family. Although it had probably helped to sell the book, she remained convinced that it had been a better novel before she dragged in the "love interest." *Nightingale* also introduced a soon-to-be-familiar character in Kay's fiction: an American woman of indeterminate age—innocent, idealistic, impulsive, and vulnerable—who is a victim, "a depressingly glorified figure." Bridget's only refuge from her morbid, disputatious, and even suicidal husband and his rigid, conservative bourgeois family (with the exception of the sister, Charlotte, who is generous and sensitive) is the delitescent life of her own making into which she admits a few figures from her past. Yet Bridget resists the temptation to become an aesthetic recluse. When her stubborn old father-in-law offers the couple 50,000 francs if they produce a child during the first year of their marriage, a proposition that plunges her husband into another cycle of frustration and rebellion, she calmly suggests that they have a child and use the money to escape the suffocating family. But Nicholas, who suffers from an undefined family malady (a rare and fatal bone disease), refuses to be responsible for transmitting the disease to his children. Her contention that his reasoning is only another "pretence of his own bitter wit" makes him more irritable, and he retaliates by accusing her of being responsible for their return to France where he has been so unhappy. Nicholas bungles an attempt at suicide, Charlotte dies, and when Luc (Bridget's suitor) offers her the chance to escape, she declines, although she agrees with him that she must somehow extricate herself from the family; however, she refuses to leave without Nicholas, whose need to escape she recognizes as greater than hers.

The reviewer Charles Hanson (*New York American*) proclaimed the novel to be as powerful as Edith Wharton's *Ethan Frome*, Greek in its development, with dialogue that sounded like a magnificent translation from the French. Without making comparisons to other literature, Katherine Anne Porter (*New Republic*) marveled at the author's precision ("nothing is misplaced or exaggerated") and at the masterful use of "symbol and allegory" to illuminate the book's great theme: "the losing battle of youth and strength against the resistless army of age and death." A *Nation* critic, while admiring the "Turgenev-like peace" that permeated the novel, objected to the second half, where the author's treatment of death and disaster lacked verisimilitude. *Nightingale* would remain for Kay a story of colliding cultures, divisions separating generations, marriage imperiled by contradictory priorities, revolutionary beliefs strained by economic necessity, and the surprising configurations that love often assumes.

The New York literary agent Virginia Rice, whom Kay had retained in 1930 and with whose services she had up to this time been entirely satisfied, failed to maintain her record of successful placements in May 1931, when she was unable to sell three of the author's short stories. Although Miss Rice's performance for the first part of the year was impressive—six stories published in *Harper's, Story, Scribner's*, and the *New Yorker*, four of which would eventually appear in E. J. O'Brien's anthology *The Best Short Stories of 1931* and *1932*—Kay was ruffled by her suggestion that stories about the English would sell much better than some of the others Kay had sent. The trouble with Virginia Rice and with publishers generally, Kay told Bob Brown, was that "nobody wants me to be a great woman. . . . As long as I write nice girlish novels and short stories about the English, everything will be alright [sic]. But just let me take a drop too much and lose my temper, and I'll be right back where I was to begin with." Her annoyance notwithstanding, she reported to Brown a month later that in two days she had written two new stories, both "pretty English," and hopefully "English enough to sell." Virginia Rice also reported that Harrison Smith looked forward to publishing everything she wrote, but that he was particular about what she wrote. He took a dim view, for example, of an "aviation book" she had proposed but was more enthusiastic about her new novel, *Year Before Last*, on which she had worked steadily through the spring. Her difficulty in writing about Ernest Walsh, his death, and the troubles with Ethel Moorhead—the subjects of the new book—was compounded by working around Laurence, who knew what she was writing and who occasionally went over parts of the book with her. Unlike her other unfinished novel, *Gentlemen, I Address You Privately*, which she admitted to Brown suffered from prolonged tinkering and over-writing, *Year* would give him a "kick in the *caleçons*." However, she had some misgivings about the first version. In February she had been pleased with the narrative form, but now it seemed long-winded. As for Brown's suggestion that she try to be more inventive, she had to admit that she had lost all her inventiveness. In August, with the novel still in rough form, she hesitated to show it to Brown, who always expected such "great things from her." Still, she was sure it would be a better book than *Nightingale*.

In the throes of writing about her relations with Walsh, she learned from McAlmon that he had extracted from Ethel Moorhead a batch of Walsh's poems; he had sent these to the American editor Bessie Breuer, informing her that he would consider publishing them himself if she declined. McAlmon was also the author of a book Kay had begun discussing with Caresse Crosby. For the leadoff volume in her new Crosby Continental Editions, Caresse had selected Hemingway's *Torrents of Spring*, a choice Kay believed could hardly have been worse. An empty and lifeless thing, Hemingway's satire of Sherwood Anderson had led to her first disillusionment with Hemingway as a writer. McAlmon, she told Caresse, was a far better writer than Hemingway, more honest, a true man of the American West, and one worthy of a place in the series. Although Caresse admitted being ignorant of what Hemingway had written about in his book, she saw no way to drop or switch the piece. She agreed, however, to include a collection of McAlmon's stories in the series, with the provision that Kay would be responsible for gathering them. She agreed at once, aware that sorting out the "best" would be difficult, for if McAlmon were allowed to help, he would "leave out all the sentimental, childish ones," which she considered his finest. She did ask McAlmon for his choices, but assured Caresse that if someone besides McAlmon picked the stories, the book would probably sell.

Caresse, she hoped, would also be interested in the aviation poem, which she would begin when she learned whether she had won a Guggenheim Fellowship. She had already assembled some six hundred pages of notes, mostly biographical citations on Count von Zeppelin. She would rummage in reference books for other necessary facts or rely on Laurence, who had the idea for the poem. For the "wind," she told Ca-

Kay Boyle, 1946

resse, she was counting on Harry Crosby's "spirit." For additional information, she would depend on Alan Ross McDougal (Dougie), who had recently visited them in Nice. There was no telling how well the three would work together or how compatible the two parts (a life of von Zeppelin and a history of aviation) of the poem would be, but the project could easily take two years. When Virginia Rice had first presented the idea to Cape and Smith, the publisher conceded that the book might be a bestseller. Nonetheless, they did not offer an advance and later in the year seemed opposed to the project, feeling that during the time Kay would be writing the book she might lose her reading public. However, in late May the Guggenheim Foundation rejected Kay's project, and her plan to write the poem and split the proceeds with Dougie and Laurence collapsed.

Fortunately, at this time Caresse asked Kay if she would undertake a translation of Raymond Radiguet's *Le Diable au Corps*, the novel of adolescent love that Kay had read so ardently nearly ten years before. Even if this project had not brought in money—now necessary to augment a dwindling income, Kay would have said yes with gratitude. It was an opportunity too good to miss: "I shall die if you don't let me do this one! It is one of the greatest simplest books—the most beautiful in that generation of Frenchmen. I have done battle for it—read it a dozen times. Please, take anything from me, but let me translate that!" Caresse also had an assignment for Vail. Would he attempt a translation of Colette? Laurence, although willing, suggested that Charles-Louis Philippe's *Bubu de Montparnasse* would be a better project for him and asked Caresse to reconsider her selection. Caresse's terms were below their expectations: 2,000 francs down and a royalty arrangement that would guarantee them up to 10,000 francs if the books sold well. When T. S. Eliot assured Caresse that both *Le Diable* and *Bubu* were "better worth translating" than any two French novels he knew, she asked the Vails to start at once.

For all her admiration of Radiguet, Kay found translating the novel "fatiguing, driven work," and she confided to Bob Brown that she continued only because she loved the book and Caresse; never again could she afford to do something like it. Twice in October she had retired to bed in tears after pushing herself all day and half the night. As other commitments piled up, she restricted herself to translating at night. Finally, with the end in sight, she fretted over the title, an extremely difficult one to translate. *Devil in the Flesh* seemed less and less satisfactory; it was neither "exact" nor "significant." While the French title *Le Diable au Corps* was "a familiar, almost childish expression," *Devil in the Flesh* certainly was not. Only "devil" had a satisfying sound. Other possibilities like *The Thorn in the Side* and *Limb of Satan* probably came closer to the meaning of the original, but the last sounded "a little literary." In November she finished, many months ahead of Laurence, who had stopped translating *Bubu* until Caresse cleared up some censorship problems that threatened to block publication.

In June, in Paris, Donald Friede, an editor with Horace Liveright, offered Kay a three-year contract. And in July an invitation came to join Harper's in London. She decided to use the second offer as a lever to force Smith (of Cape and Smith) to pay her a $1,000 advance for *Year*. If he refused she would give Harper's both *Year* and *Gentlemen* and ask for $100 a month so that she could begin a third novel or continue the aviation poem. In October she heard directly from Harrison Smith that *Gentlemen* had been a disappointment. Since a weak book could only harm her reputation, he suggested she let it "hang over" for a while. Although in agreement, she let him know that after making a few changes, she expected to see it published without delay. Before anything could be done, however, Jonathan Cape, Smith's English partner, visited the Vails and informed Kay that after reading the copy of *Gentlemen* that she had entrusted to Dougie, he wanted very much to publish it. He also revealed that on his forthcoming visit to New York he intended to fire Smith. Although the "foxy, obscene, dishonest" Cape seemed to be working for her best interests, he made her uneasy, and this feeling was strengthened when Virginia Rice wrote that in New York, Cape had succeeded in upsetting everybody, and that she, for one, intended to do everything possible to keep "that horrid man" from getting her client's books, although she agreed to consider any offers he submitted. Miss Rice kept her word. In December she sent Kay an advance of $1,000, along with a proviso from Smith stating that if *Year* failed to earn back the advance within one year, the deficit would be subtracted from future royalties. Furious over what she regarded a practice both unnecessary and unfair, Kay returned the check, demanding that henceforth no strings be attached to advances. Nearly convinced that her angry letter would produce a break with the agent—and half hoping it would—she was surprised when the matter was dropped. Eventually, however, Miss Rice wrote that Smith, after being dismissed, had hastily formed his own company and had agreed to publish both *Year* and *Gentlemen*, without any strings attached.

The highs and lows of Kay's writing life appeared and reappeared as rapidly as the blustery mistrals that sweep along the Riviera and that raise and lower temperatures by ten degrees in as many minutes. She described her alternating moods to Bob Brown. In April, following the publication of *Nightingale* and the Delteil translation and while working well on *Year*, she wrote: "Today I feel like a great writer. It's a wonderful feeling. Only it lasts such a short time." But in just two days in July she wrote two short stories, and the same month, with the creative urge still on her, she exulted: "I feel like a million dollars. I could write ten novels with one hand and five epic poems with the other." A follow-up note reaffirmed her ambition "to be a prolific writer and [to] write tomes and tomes." Productivity, however, had drawbacks. "I think . . . I write my short stories too quickly, in the stress of wanting to make a little money, and that is a lamentable idea." The flaws in those works that Virginia Rice returned were obvious and were the result of pushing too hard. It was a silly way to work. "Writing goes in streaks," she had discovered, but when one depended on it to make money, one could not wait for the creative streaks.

Aside from occasional trips to Paris, Laurence and Kay celebrated their triumphs and relieved their frustrations in Nice or in nearby villages, with the exception of Cagnes-sur-Mer, a "horrible, ominous, destructive" place they had found confusing and overrun with artistic frauds. They preferred having cocktails with their neighbor Frank Scully, joining the Browns and Mary Reynolds and Marcel Duchamp, visiting with Emma Goldman and Alexander Berkman or having dinner in Nice and an evening in the cafés with the ubiquitous Dougie, occasions when Kay and Brown would exchange stories or sections of novels. In May she showed him *Year*, and about the same time he gave her large segments of two new books, *What Happened to Mary?* and *You Gotta Live*, which Kay meticulously criticized. She and Laurence contributed to Brown's *Readies* anthology, which along with a volume of verse (*Demonics*) and a wry sermonette on pornography (*Gems*), Brown published himself under the Roving Eye imprint. An imaginative and indefatigable worker, Brown was a shrewd and demanding critic. His company was always stimulating and relaxing and his friendship genuine and comforting. Unquestionably, he was one of the few at Cagnes she could admire and trust. Emma Goldman, the outspoken anarchist deported from the United States as a dangerous radical, occasionally joined the Vails for dinner. Although Kay described her as "a grand girl," a combination of "Stein, Carnevali, and her own sweet self all rolled into one," it was her companion, Alexander Berkman (Sasha), whom she liked better, partly because, unlike Emma, who had accepted support from Peggy Guggenheim, he had not compromised his beliefs for money.

By the end of 1931, Virginia Rice had sold six stories, three of them ("One of Ours," "First Lover," "Christmas Eve") decidedly English. In "One of Ours," which T. S. Eliot, then editor of *Criterion*, had rejected as being "too indelicate" for English readers, Kay trivialized, in the character of a formidable matron, England's reputed concern for the welfare of those it ruled. At an exhibition honoring the Empire's colonies, she approvingly acknowledges that each country is indeed "one of ours." Suddenly, however, she comes face to face with an enormous black Nigerian, who throws open his arms and appears to be about to rape her. Paralyzed, she watches uncomprehendingly as an obliging waiter pushes the weeping man away, saying that a doll-baby the woman holds in her hand had inspired his actions. "It all depends on whether you have a child of your own or not," he explains. "The poor chappie's like this the minute he sees a doll-baby." "First Lover," published in *Harper's* in June, the first of thirty-two stories reprinted in the O. Henry Memorial Award Prize Stories, describes the electrifying effect a young Englishman has on three vacationing German girls, the eldest of whom, with encouragement from her sisters, appropriates the young man and nearly swoons when he casually remarks on the coincidence of meeting the girl's father in the garden and recognizing him as his former teacher. "Rest Cure," published in the maiden issue of *Story* (April-May), recounts the final hours of an exiled English writer with a strong resemblance to D. H. Lawrence. No matter how hard he tries to expunge the black memory of his father, a miner, the dying man cannot free himself from his father's hold, a situation powerfully represented by a lobster into whose eyes the invalid stares while praying, "Father . . . father, help me . . . I don't want to die."

Additional incentive to complete *Year* came during a visit to England in January 1932, where on the advice of Virginia Rice and the help of Curtis Brown, Kay placed the novel with Faber. Back in France and working eight hours a day straight through February, she reported to Brown in March that she had finished it. "It's a glorious feeling, isn't it?" And to Caresse Crosby, towards whom she had felt so close throughout the writing, as though they had "gone through some terrible thing sometime together, somewhere," she wrote: "I want you to like it—for you, for me. In it I've said every Goddamned thing that I have never been able to say to anyone." What literary value there might be in "stripping oneself naked," however, she would leave to Caresse to decide.

Kay's qualms about the book made no impression on Caresse. She was overwhelmed. Hanna (Kay Boyle) and Martin (Ernest Walsh), she rhapsodized, were "real and thrilling and heart-breaking." As a necessary addition to the Crosby Continental Editions series, she would put it into production at once, and in September—a little too soon in Kay's opinion—it was published, eight months before the Faber edition.

Perhaps April was not the best month for Kay and Laurence to marry, but Kay had finished *Year*, and except for a few stories still in the planning stage, she had not yet begun a major new project. Although it seemed that nobody cared whether or not they married (except Laurence's mother, who received the news joyously), doing so would at least have the practical advantage of making the move to Austria the following year less complicated. Kay rejected Maria Jolas's suggestion that they marry privately and scheduled the event for April 2 in the Mairie, in Nice, and invited all their friends. Only four failed to come—Abraham Lincoln Gillespie, Caresse, Dougie, and Emma Goldman, who sent a message that read: "May love last in spite of legal bonds and sanction." Present for the simple secular ceremony were the Browns, Bettina Bedwell and her husband Abe Rattner, Emily Coleman, Peggy Guggenheim and her companion John Holmes, Hilaire Hiler, Peter Neagoe, Clotilde Vail, and Mrs. Frank Harris.

Even modest weddings cost money, and before many days had passed after the marriage, Kay resumed her full writing schedule, stepping up first her production of stories (the money-makers); working long and late, she finished four by the end of April. The expectation of receiving some payments for stories by summer may have affected her decision to decline a new project Caresse proposed. Still convinced that André Breton's *Nadja* would be a valuable addition to the Crosby Continental Editions series, she asked Kay to translate it, and offered her 2,000 francs. This time Kay had to tell Caresse that the payment was too low. Furthermore, since Caresse had been unable to place Laurence's translation of *Bubu de Montparnasse* in America, it was doubtful whether an equally obscure novel, and one far more stylistically complicated, would fare any better. Also, translating *Nadja*, a demanding work, would take at least a month, and 2,000 francs simply would not cover living expenses for that period. It was worrisome to live "too much from hand to mouth, with absolutely nothing set aside" and never be able to "let down" for more than a few days.

Rewriting *Year* had been a costly expenditure of time, and now, in order "to make life possible," she would have to write stories all summer. Unfortunately, neither *Wedding Day* nor *Nightingale* had brought in any money. How *Year* would do she did not know, but she hoped for "great things" so that she could write more of what she wanted. Turning Caresse down was an economic necessity. "I wish [she wrote her] I could offer you translation and everything for nothing at all to help put your grand thing over, but this year it's impossible. If things sell well, I want to help all I can later on and not ask you a penny in advance."

The same month, after consulting Brown, Kay switched agents, dropping Virginia Rice, whom she now called "grasping and lecturing" and "more like a woman than any woman has a right to be" for "a nice hard-boiled baby" named Ann Watkins, an agent, she had been assured, who earned "diamonds from literature." Although Miss Rice had improved her record of story sales—in the first four months of the year she had placed "The Man Who Died Young" (*Yale Review*), "I Can't Get Drunk" (*Contempo*), and a much-altered version of "Black Boy" (the *New Yorker*)—she had displeased Kay by not submitting her stories to the best magazines and by neglecting to follow up on serial rights. Kay aired her complaints in a long introductory letter to Ann Watkins, noting that since her second novel (*Year*) was about to appear, she expected her new agent to sell her work quickly and for higher prices.

In June her novel *Year*, a ten-page poem, "A Statement" (For El Greco and William Carlos Williams), and two stories, "The Man Who Died Young" and "To the Pure," were published, making this her biggest single month of publication. She had dedicated *Year Before Last* to Carnevali, with whom she had always linked Ernest Walsh. The novel a reviewer called "a chronicle of the shuttling of one doomed male life and two female shadows" drew generally favorable comments from American and English critics (the English edition appeared the same month), but the local critic, Waverley Root, of the *Paris Tribune*, paid it perhaps the highest tribute. Calling her writing "as tense and vivid" as that of any of the moderns (the "words glow and bite and eat their way into the soul"), Root proclaimed *Year* as "near perfect" as any novel he had reviewed since Faulkner's *Sanctuary*. "Let's pray for a million," Kay wrote Brown.

Laurence, whose novel *Murder! Murder!* had come out in England at the beginning of the year, was nearly as optimistic about profits his book might earn. A surrealist experiment, *Murder! Murder!* had sold out by March. In July, with neither a second printing nor an American publisher in sight, Kay reviewed it along with Brown's *Readies* anthology in *Contempo*, calling both books exceptional and the only worthy ones out of a large crop of recent mediocre offerings. But in spite of Kay's praise as well as a complimentary notice Peter Neagoe printed in *New Review*, neither a second English edition nor an American publisher materialized. Laurence had obviously expected better things from his work.

Along with several new stories, Kay sent Ann Watkins a generous portion of the aviation poem (now called *Epic Poem on Aviation*) and most of her third novel, *Gentlemen, I Address You Privately*, on which she had begun to work again. Miss Watkins's report was mostly encouraging. She liked *Gentlemen* and the stories, but said little about the aviation epic. What would certainly sell, she advised, was another collection of short stories, which should appear before the new novel.

In August the Vails (including Sindbad and Pegeen) traveled to Italy and Austria, where they climbed glaciers and saw "wonderous things." In Salzburg they attended the Mozart Festival with the Jolases and then accompanied them to Feldkirch. The rest and change had been good for everybody. In November Kay was sailing along on *Gentlemen*, which she described to Ann as a "new and infinitely better book." In the same month, Caresse issued McAlmon's collection of nine stories, *Indefinite Huntress and Other Stories* (Kay's title), the contents arranged according to Kay's suggested order. When Waverley Root complained that McAlmon had tried for effects comparable to Hemingway's by stripping his sentences of both "unessentials" and "feeling," Kay rushed to her friend's defense. If a debt was owed to anyone, she argued, Hemingway owed one to McAlmon, the "sound and almost heedless builder of a certain strong wind in American letters." The "gentleman who came in afterward and laid down the linoleum because it was so decorative and so easy to keep clean" was Hemingway. In fact, she concluded, as many as a half dozen writers owed McAlmon a "debt of influence."

First Lover and Other Stories (New York, Harrison Smith & Robert Haas, 1933), the collection Ann Watkins had suggested, appeared in March 1933. Of the fourteen stories, four had never been published. In her dedication to Eugene Jolas, Kay quoted one of his favorite dictums: "Follow the voice that booms in the deepest dream, deeper go, always deeper." The stories form two groups: those precious and attenuated, such as the title story and "To the Pure." In the latter an English contessa, residing in Italy, receives a young man who tells her that her former paramour has asked him to call on her to determine whether she is still beauti-

Laurence Vail

ful. A surprising turn develops when she realizes the young man is her erstwhile lover's lover. "Black Boy," a story both agents had had difficulty placing, belongs to the second group, those with a strong social realism. Set in Atlantic City, where Kay lived for several years as a child, it describes the bond of friendship and trust that links a young girl and a black boy who pushes tourists up and down the boardwalk in rolling chairs. The boy speaks to her of the things he would like to do but knows he cannot. One day when riding on the beach, the girl falls from a horse. The boy nurses her to consciousness and carries her to her home. There the girl's suspicious and prejudiced grandfather (patterned on Puss) takes the girl and strikes the boy "square across the mouth."

Although by 1933 Kay and Carnevali had been corresponding for ten years, they had never met. From time to time he had sent her parts of an autobiography (*The First God*), and in the spring she volunteered to transcribe and give the various sections to Caresse Crosby, who had agreed to show the manuscript to publishing friends in New York. In two months Kay finished forty-one pages that, with an introduction by Dorothy Dudley Harvey, who had paid Carnevali's passage back to Italy, she then turned over to Caresse. Working on the autobiography came at a time when the Vails had decided to move to Austria. There were several reasons to leave France: Austria would be much cheaper, the climate would be better, and for Laurence, there would be magnificent mountains. In July on their way to Vienna, they stopped off in Bazzano to visit Carnevali.

Like Ernest Walsh, Carnevali was inspiring. It was painful to see the physical toll of years of suffering, but it was awesome to see how suffering had strengthened his spirit. With him Kay felt a kinship she had never before experienced. Here was the man who had loved Ernest Walsh and had received his love in return. "Being with him is not as easy to explain as love," she wrote Caresse. "It is a necessity." Sensing that being in the same room with this man, even remaining with him, meant more to Kay than she would admit, Laurence said: "You do not need to tell me. I know if it were not for the children what you would do."

Temporarily settled in Vienna in two hotel rooms, Kay wrote to Caresse in America that she had authorized Ann Watkins to tell any publisher willing to publish Emanuel Carnevali and Ernest Walsh that he could also have her new novel, *My Next Bride*. "I believe in those two names, and I know how much they would distinguish any publisher's list, and they are, in the final analysis, the two things I care most about putting over." Then, in quick succession came messages from Caresse and Dick Simon, her friend at Simon and Schuster, saying that Carnevali's autobiography had been rejected; within hours still another cable arrived from Ann Watkins with the welcome news that Harcourt Brace had offered a $500 advance for Carnevali's book, immediate publication of Walsh's poems, and a $1,500 advance on *Bride* as well as $2,000 on her next book. Ecstatic, Kay accepted at once. At this point Simon changed his mind and agreed to publish Carnevali after all. A victory for Caresse became an embarrassment for Kay, who had prevailed on her friend to show Simon the manuscript. It was impossible to undo what had been settled, and Kay could only try to patch things up with Caresse. She and Laurence had reached "rock bottom" before Harcourt came to their rescue. She had even had to borrow $500 from Ann to help them get through October and November. "I am absolutely heartbroken that there should be these difficulties between you and me about it [Carnevali's book]." And as for *Bride*, she went on, it would be dedicated to her, and was "in every way" her book. She had even wanted Caresse to publish it at the Black Sun. She had acted in the belief that Simon's refusal was final and absolute.

In November the novel Kay had begun in Harfleur in 1924 was published. *Gentlemen, I Address You Privately* (New York, Harrison Smith and Robert Haas, 1933) (the title comes from a poem by Ernest Walsh), despite numerous rewritings and revisions, remained what it had been at the beginning: the story of vagabonds moving uneasily among vagabonds. An expelled Anglican brother (Munday), a renegade seaman (Ayton), and a trio of homeless lesbians mingle with rapacious French peasants (including several who resemble Kay's Harfleur neighbors) and local officials. The practices of the latter remain unaltered by the presence of the former. About the French, Kay had made a discovery: all, or nearly all, possessed a trait she called "ponderability"—an inexplicable reverence for and a subservience to the substantial as opposed to the visionary and mystical. It was almost as though the differences that had separated her father and mother were embodied in the people of an entire country. Although the most fully developed figures in the book are French, the main characters, Munday and Ayton, bear the thematic burden. The harder Munday fights to resist Ayton's homosexual attentions—at one point Ayton says, "I want to be by you always, I want to live my life with you"—the more he is drawn to him, and finally he yields. Ayton, modeled after a Canadian seaman Kay knew in Le Havre, an attractive, innocent, "utterly common" man, with "no soft feelings, no falsities, no fear," and who just missed "being great," infects others besides Munday with his exuberance and zest for life.

"Strong and willful and gleeful," he was what "everyone wanted a man to be." Few could ignore his impassioned call to life: "If a man moves east like the stars and the tides do . . . there's no harm in anything at all." At the end of the novel, Ayton, moving ahead of the police, not only deserts the squatter's wife, whom he has impregnated but also steals Munday's possessions, including a piano, to finance his escape to Italy.

Showing the ravages of too much revision, *Gentlemen* suffers from disjointedness, incompleteness, and, inevitably, confusion. H. S. Canby (*Saturday Review*) pinpointed the problem in the author's fascination with the "shapeless confusion of emotion," and Louis Kronenberger (*New York Times*) blamed her "lack of coordination. Ornament is substituted for architecture . . . [and] each separate burrowing is more an end in itself than part of something larger and continuous." M. C. Dawson (*Books*) came closer to the difficulty the author herself had. "As Kay Boyle 1929," he wrote, "it is all you could ask . . . [but] as Kay Boyle 1933 it is less than the best; the material . . . seems rather willfully pushed into the waiting form." Counterbalancing the strong passages late in the book were the earlier portions that conveyed "a sense of backward looking." Kay herself admitted feeling very much detached from her novel, with the exception of certain descriptions, and "then not much."

After three "frightful" months in Vienna, the Vails retreated to the Austrian Tyrol, to Kitzbühel, a "deep, snowy place" overrun with English but which, Kay felt sure, would improve with the departure of the English and the arrival of spring and which would by summer be lovely. For Laurence its only defect was the absence of a glacier, but it did have long ski runs and walking trails. In Vienna they had witnessed depressing signs of the conflict soon to engulf the country. The Austrians were as miserable as they looked. Barefooted and grim-faced, they walked the snowy streets and stood, men, women, and children, begging at every corner. Impoverishment made the people increasingly responsive to Hitler's promises of economic recovery and full employment. Kay would soon depict the agonizing descent of this nation into Nazi control in *Death of a Man* (New York, Harcourt, Brace & Co., 1936) and the "White Horses of Vienna." "I've never known or seen such cold, such grimness, such misery," she wrote Evelyn Scott. "We lived in a couple of back rooms with the three children (who were in school until six every evening) in such darkness . . . I suddenly gave up . . . and couldn't move or think or work or want. I don't know what happened." Resettling in Kitzbühel "was like being born again." For the children there was a "country girl" who made life easier for Kay while she recuperated from some "uneasiness of [her] inner workings," not, she thought, due to pregnancy ("I am to have an addition to the family in the summer") but which nonetheless kept her confined to bed for long periods.

Almost as annoying as being physically indisposed was a joint project she had agreed to do with her friend and former employer Bettina Bedwell, the *Paris Tribune* fashion editor. In some ways, however, the project promised more than had ever come from the last collaborative effort, the Dayang Muda's memoirs, which after being published, had never earned a penny. She hoped no such fate would befall the new work, a mystery thriller called *Yellow Dusk* (London, Hurst & Blackett, Ltd., 1937) (Bettina's title). A "pot-boiler" pure and simple, it *had* to make money. With Ann Watkins's support and assurances (it will be a bestseller, she said), they went to work first exchanging chapters by mail, and then, after receiving some rather severe criticism from Ann, collaborating in person for a few weeks in Kitzbühel. But the forced, intense labor she was required to expend on something she regretted taking on often brought her "to the point of tears and rage." "I want to write my own pretty things," she complained to Evelyn, "and now have involved myself in this like an idiot." She had nonetheless managed to get a strong start on *Bride*, which she hoped would be "less Irish" than the others and closer to the part of herself that she had come to like best.

Kitzbühel was far more conducive to work than Vienna, although having magnificent "window views" of snow-covered trees and mountains instead of backyards was distracting. The only way to get anything done was to shut the window blinds and concentrate. Struggling with Bettina's book while lusting to get on with *Bride* and some stories took a toll. "I am in a state of nerves and ready to kill anyone on sight," she wrote Ann, but early in January her humor improved, and she reported that they had finished five chapters. Why anyone would buy the book, though, she had no idea. But perhaps that was reason enough. When she objected that the plot had become too involved, Bettina, a reader of detective stories and "other very worked-out books," overruled her. Still if Ann insisted on cuts or any simplifying of the plot, they would follow her advice. Finally, in February, they finished, and Bettina left for Paris to have copies typed for Ann.

One other extraliterary responsibility had also begun to absorb her time. Harcourt had decided to proceed with publication of Walsh's poems but not with Carnevali's autobiography, and Kay, partly because Ethel

Moorhead had been named executrix of Walsh's will and partly because Kay wanted Ethel "to have one thing" of Ernest's in which she, as far as Ethel knew, was not involved, had entrusted everything to Ann with instructions never to mention her name to Ethel. Since the publication of *Year*, Kay had learned that Ethel had become wilder and wilder and had several times threatened "to shoot" Kay if she ever found her. Only absolute secrecy would safeguard publication of Walsh's poetry. But Ann quickly discovered that "hard-boiled methods" hardly impressed Ethel. She not only objected to the publisher's conditions but demanded to see the manuscript "for revision" as well. Suspicious, she believed that since turning it over to McAlmon, it had probably been "tampered with." She was right. Kay had in fact retyped the poems and had added those which had appeared in the memorial issue of *This Quarter*. She had also asked Archibald MacLeish to write a foreword after Ford Madox Ford (Harcourt's choice) had refused. Now with the book in galleys, Ethel insisted on seeing the original manuscript as well as MacLeish's foreword. Although Kay had read what MacLeish had written and had asked him to remove the reference to Walsh's "being loved by a beautiful and gifted woman," he had not done so. Not only did the remark seem tactless and ridiculous, but she was also sure that if Ethel read it, she would do all in her power to stop publication, perhaps forever. She was right. Ethel tore the foreword to shreds and halted publication. A few months later, however, she changed her mind and agreed to allow the book to proceed, but only on condition that her introduction be substituted for MacLeish's and that she retain control of the book until it appeared.

With *Yellow Dusk* and Walsh's volume both behind her, Kay could again concentrate on *Bride*. But despite the problems Ethel had created, she reiterated that Harcourt would not receive *Bride* until she had guarantees that Walsh's book would come out. Work on the novel progressed so well in February that she promised Ann typed copy soon and inquired about serial possibilities. Regrettably, however, she had to report that Carnevali had fallen behind and would not finish his autobiography by November.

In April, after several tries, she received a Guggenheim Fellowship. It could not have come at a better time, but before receiving the stipend (1,800) she would have to produce a physician's certificate stating she was fit to start work at once. Since she expected her child in June, she feared that news of her advanced pregnancy, were it to circulate in New York, might jeopardize the award. "I don't see any reasons to advertise the fact that I will have to lay off for a fortnight . . . when the moment arrives," she wrote Ann. After all, "being pregnant makes little difference to me in the work line." Producing a certificate and accepting the money, despite the necessity of having "to be laid up awhile," hardly constituted a breach of faith, and, furthermore, the "peace and quiet" she expected to enjoy in the Innsbruck hospital would be all she would probably have for many years. Having babies was "a nice kind of relaxation" after months of non-stop writing and typing. Besides, time away from the children would provide the leisure she needed to think about her poems.

The peace and quiet Kay looked forward to in Innsbruck vanished in an explosion that might have seriously injured her and Laurence. Staying in an old-fashioned hotel next to the offices of an anti-Nazi newspaper, the Vails were nearly blown up when a group of Nazis planted a time-bomb on the roof of the adjacent building. Minutes before it detonated, a watchman at the newspaper office found the bomb and threw it into the hotel beergarden, where it exploded, destroying trees, chairs, and tables, and the glass-enclosed balcony off Kay's and Laurence's room. "I wouldn't have missed it for anything," Kay wrote Ann. "We are now . . . surrounded by Heimwehr troops all night who do sentinel duty up and down the roofs and gardens." It was all "very warlike." Bearing a baby after so much excitement was almost an anticlimax. On July 7 Kay gave birth to another girl whom the parents named Kathe, after the owner of the Kitzbühel Hotel who took such loving care of them all. As soon as the Guggenheim money had safely arrived, Kay broke the news to Ann.

A mammoth writing project that Laurence had conceived and begun as soon as they had arrived in the Tyrol and which had come to occupy all his time and much of Kay's was almost totally destroyed in the explosion. Kay outlined the project to Ann: there would be three books: the first, entitled *1934*, would be "a symposium of events [in 'concise rewrite form'] which have interested the world, or have not, during 1934." The second, *Crime 1934*, would concentrate on "outstanding murders" and lesser crimes. The third, *Short Stories 1934*, would be a collection of stories by people involved in the project. Each of the three volumes would be 365 pages long, one for each day of the year. Laurence had taken parts of volume one to Innsbruck, and everything had been blown to shreds in the explosion. As he and Kay sifted through the debris in search of salvageable remnants, the police extricated what they believed was evidence related to the placing and timing of the bomb—badly mangled magazine and newspaper clippings with Laurence's arrows and dates clearly readable. But for ineffective detective work, or the condition of the manuscript, Laurence might have been implicated in a bombing that had imperiled his life and destroyed his work.

Laurence continued work on this project and it completely absorbed him. His concentration and patience were remarkable. Daily he pored over French, German, Italian, and English newspapers, cutting out articles and stories that would make suitable entries and stacking up the mutilated remains around his room. Friends everywhere—Joan, Katherine, Hiler, Brown—supplied fresh newspapers and some short stories as well. Seeing Laurence involved in work he enjoyed and considered valuable was a relief to Kay after his many rebuffs from publishers. Both were counting on the series to earn some money too, but just keeping Laurence's spirits up meant more. "It's awful for him to have not a single word of encouragement or a penny coming in," Kay confided to Joan. "I'd give five years of my life (which sounds darn little) to see Laurence working with the assurance that what he wrote was going to see the light of day. I'm quite certain that his industry would put to shame half the businessmen in the world today—and it's doubly brave because he never gets anything for it except a kick in the seat of the pants."

Convinced that only a contract for the "1934" books would give her husband "a new lease on life," Kay urged Ann to act quickly. And to assist with the immense labor of compiling, sorting, and editing, they invited an English journalist, Nina Condron, to join them. Nina had often visited them in France, and it was a comfort to have her in Kitzbühel, for as much as she wanted Laurence's project to succeed, Kay regretted losing the time that it took from her own writing. By working night and day, she had managed to push *Bride* almost to completion, but her production of stories had dropped off badly. When Ann asked her to accept an advance on another novel, she replied that she did not want to be under any obligation for at least six months. Taking on more work would only put her in "too much of a state."

My Next Bride, Kay's fourth novel, the last one which drew on her experiences of the twenties, records the misadventures of Victoria John, a girl from the Middle West, from the time she joins Sorrel's colony outside Paris to the moment she places her future, and perhaps her life, in the hands of a wealthy American woman her own age. In three parts, it presents portraits of the three people who profoundly affected Victoria's (Kay's) life during the year she lived in Paris: Sorrel (Raymond Duncan), Antony (Harry Crosby), and Fontana (Caresse Crosby). Antony, the inverse of Sorrel, the bogus simple-lifer, is an honest hedonist; by pander-

Kay Boyle, Rutgers University, 1978

ing to his passions, he destroys his genuine but slender literary talent and exacerbates his fatal agony—a displacement of time, place, and position. Offering comfort and love and practical help after events that have left Victoria part of the wreckage strewn in Antony's wake, is Fontana, Antony's wife. Despite her belief that Antony and Victoria are romantically entangled—a fact resoundingly refuted in the novel—and the shock of Antony's sudden suicide (Crosby died in December 1929), Fontana proffers the revivifying aid and concern that restores her friend's mental and physical balance. The uneasy relationship between Victoria and Fontana was one of the points Kay stressed in a synopsis of the novel she sent Ann Watkins. "It is particularly a history of women, and of that nameless and nonsexual thing that can bind women to each other closer than can any relationship with men." Dedicated to Caresse Crosby, it was, as Kay said it would be, a work "in every way" written for her.

Part Three, the Fontana section, begins with a verse from Carnevali: "Bathe me in the vision of my youth, communicate me forever. Do not let me go back with the rest to fornicate and forget." *My Next Bride* is a memorable account of youth. It is also a farewell to youth, an exorcism, and an apologia. Kay would seldom return to the fecund period that had provided material for four novels and dozens of short stories and poems. In *Nightingale* she had drawn on the experiences of her twenty-first year; in *Gentlemen*, on her twenty-second and twenty-third years; in *Year*, her twenty-fourth year; and in *Bride*, her twenty-fifth and twenty-sixth years. These books are the finely distilled products of a long gestation. They demonstrate the unity between her life and her art. The wish she once expressed to Richard had come true: she had gone back to where she had been, over and over.

She had examined, organized, and transcended the experiences of the years from 1923 to 1929. Against them she had tested her reactions and discovered their significance. In all Kay Boyle's fiction, there is a need to catharize the tangle of emotions of innocence, responsibility, loyalty, perfidy, and guilt. *Bride* defines and defends her relationship with Harry Crosby. *Nightingale* explores the crumbling bonds that theoretically more than actually kept Kay and Richard Brault tenuously joined. *Year* describes the compelling, desperate, tragically brief, yet lasting, union that linked Kay and Ernest Walsh.

To those on whom she had depended, whose loyalty sustained her, and whose help had often meant survival, she returned loyalty, affection, and love. For Walsh's poetry, Carnevali's autobiography, and McAlmon's stories, she found publishers. Soon she would assist in the publication of Vail's *365 Days* (the three-volume project was scaled down to a single book). She dedicated her books to Carnevali, Eugene Jolas, Vail, and Caresse Crosby. All had at one time or another been members of her "created family," along with Lola Ridge, Evelyn Scott, Francis Picabia, Alan Ross MacDougall, the Dayang Muda, Archie Craig, Germaine Garrigou, and the Browns. Each of them had helped her find the freedom and independence she and Richard had sought abroad. She had freed herself from the insularity of the Braults, fled in disgust from the cozenage of Duncan's colony, revolted from the labyrinthine enfoldings of concupiscence, and rejected the ruthless machinations of wealth. From her bourgeois background, she had also found release. And by the midthirties, she had gradually retreated from her "created family," too; Sharon and the children of her marriage to Vail took their places.

France, (Brittany, Normandy, Paris, the Riviera), which had given her a vision and provided mentors in the form of places, language, color, and people, had become the land of her fiction and one of the sources of her life. Steadily she had absorbed the life of her adopted country. "Yes, she was more completely abroad than the rest of us," Glenway Wescott said of her. Unlike other expatriates, she did not segregate herself from the French or live surrounded and nourished and sometimes supported by her countrymen in an American community. Instead Kay chose to remain a part of non-American life abroad. She almost never did what most Americans did in France, partly because she had not gone there on Harold Stearns's advice to get out of America's sterile and intolerant environment quickly or risk almost certain artistic emasculation. She went instead because she was married to a French engineer who wanted to introduce his bride to his family and to his native Brittany. Besides the obligatory visit to her new in-laws, however, the trip became a working vacation. She wrote a novel and launched a literary career.

Gertrude Stein is sometimes remembered for her pithy statements, one of which was on the advantage of living in France. "It was not so much what France gave you," she said, "it was what she did not take away." Although Kay Boyle never made such a statement, one can deduce from her life an equally easily phrased, quotable, and accurate an aphorism as Miss Stein's. It might go like this: it was not so much that you went to France, it was what you did once you were there. Kay Boyle worked. (Gertrude Stein did, too.)

By the midthirties, with Austria rapidly succumbing to Hitler and with the struggle between opposing ideologies already raging in Spain, Kay had served her apprenticeship, both in observation and craft. Ready for a new stage of her career, she might have thought of George Moore's beckoning challenge: "There is a lake in every man's life, and he must ungird his loins for the crossing." If so, she had prepared herself to accept it.

In the fifty years since the midthirties, Kay Boyle has continued an active literary career. Besides several novels, numerous short stories (which earned her two O'Henry Memorial Prizes), and many essays, articles, and reviews, she has edited books by two close friends she made in the 1920s. One was Emanuel Carnevali, whose autobiographical writings she compiled for publication by the Horizon Press. The other was Robert McAlmon, whose neglected book of memoirs *Being Geniuses Together* (1938, 1984) she revised and supplemented with interchapters in which she described her childhood in America and her early adult life in France. Both projects revived interest in her friends' work.

Annoyed by the tendency to distort and romanticize the 1920s, particularly what happened in Paris, Kay Boyle has recently offered some correctives.* To those who believe that Paris was a Camelot where artists and writers discussed their work in sidewalk cafés, she points out that writers (more often than artists) lived outside the city, frequently alone, and seldom talked about themselves or their work. Nor was life in Paris always as glorious as it has been depicted. Starvation, suicides, "all kinds of agonies" were commonplace. Perhaps the most serious distortion she cites involves those expatriates (a word Kay Boyle dislikes almost as much as exiles) who survived the period but whose lives time and memory have turned into the "fragile substance of myth." To rectify this final injustice, she remains firmly committed.

*Leo Litwak, "Kay Boyle—Paris Wasn't Like That," *New York Times Book Review*, July 15, 1984, pp. 1, 32–33.

MARGARET ANDERSON

My greatest enemy is reality.
(from *My Thirty Years' War*)

Margaret Anderson was a born dilettante. There was nothing else she wanted to be. She lived to talk, occasionally to listen, and always to eavesdrop. On every topic she took sides. Either she approved or she disapproved. She was never wrong; that is, if she was, she never admitted it. Her faith in herself resisted all challenges and all attacks, withstood all rebuffs, contravened all contradictory evidence. When friends told her that she was a writer, she denied it, partly out of stubborn resistance to the opinions of others, especially when they concerned her, and partly because she believed that she lacked the talent to write. That she had written scores of editorials for the *Little Review*, the magazine she founded in 1914, as well as three volumes of autobiography, a book on the mystic Gurdjieff, and several unpublished works, including a novella on lesbian love, did not count. She still refused to believe she was a writer, a writer, that is, in the same class with her favorites Henry James, Oscar Wilde, Charlotte Brontë, and the great French stylists Baudelaire, Flaubert, Stendhal, and Proust. On finding in Harold Nicolson's *Diaries and Letters* a sentence she considered the epitome of thought compressed into the tightest form, she exclaimed: "How I should love to write like this!* But I never shall. In fact

I have never thought of myself as a writer at all. I am not a creator; I'm an appreciator, a discusser, a moralizer, a propagandist, an illiterate, and a dilettante. Not a writer, just a person who loves to think about ideas." No more candid self-description ever came from Margaret Anderson.

Despite what she said, Margaret was a writer, albeit a minor one; she was also a creator with few creations, a person who toiled incessantly to make her life a work of art. In an attempt to explain what Henry James meant by the artist's mind, she identified the indispensable thing that dominated her life from the time she left her conventional middle-western family in 1914 until her death nearly six decades later. The experienced mind, James wrote, is one "whose operations are independent of experience." By "operations," in Margaret's view, James meant the experiences one creates or, more fancifully, the "fairy tales that one commands to come true." According to this interpretation, Margaret's life is an artistic triumph. Resisting reality was a duty she never forsook. One proof of her talent to make real what was considered impossible was the *Little Review.* On the opening page of the first volume of her memoirs, *My Thirty Years' War* (New York, Covici, Friede Publishers, 1930), where Margaret recounted the life of the magazine, she proclaimed her victory: "My greatest enemy is reality. I have fought it successfully for thirty years."

What vitalized Margaret Anderson's life more than writing, editing (of which she did little and that none too well), playing the piano, or listening to good music, was talking and listening to great talk (the two were virtually inseparable), the foremost ingredient of which was substance, content of high quality. Again, in Henry James, she found an example of what she meant. As the author lay close to death, he said: "Ah, here it is at last—the distinguished thing." "No one," Margaret maintained, would "ever talk like that again." But among her friends several tried, and a few gained her admiration and lively appreciation. Without them, her effort to make fairy tales come true might have been harder.

The first of these talkers, and, many would say, the best, was Jane Heap. In Berenice Abbott's well-known photograph of her, Jane is wearing a shirt and bow-tie. Her hair is as short as a man's; her eyes, dark brown and slightly protruding, are trained on something off camera. Her nose is prominent and firm, and her full lips are heavily coated with lipstick. Her head has the classical features of a Greek god—broad forehead, high cheekbones, full cheeks and chin. If Jane's appearance drew attention, her

*The sentence that inspired her admiration and envy was: "You have used every snub which ingenuity can devise and ill manners can perpetrate."

clothing attracted even more. Of the masculine attire she favored, the most conspicuous article was often a Russian fur hat. There were times when Margaret, not known to permit custom to dictate what she wore or with whom she was seen, would object to Jane's extreme mode of dress and refuse to accompany her into the street until she changed into something less conspicuous. Jane, she chided, was just trying to call attention to herself. There were also occasions when Jane might have retaliated; for example, when Margaret would appear in public wearing one glove—on her right hand. That was the hand, she informed the curious, she hated. The left, which she loved, always remained uncovered.

What drew Margaret to Jane was not her idiosyncratic appearance. It was her brilliant and stimulating talk. Jane was simply the "world's best talker." It was harder to identify what made her the best talker than it was to report it. "You're the best talker I've ever listened to," one impressed listener told Jane, "but I don't understand a word you say." Whenever Margaret tried to explain what was so spellbinding about Jane's talk, she would state that her genius lay not in her words, or facility, style, truth, or erudition; it was the way she expressed ideas, effortlessly and creatively, as she went along. Whatever Jane said could always be discussed. Her ideas provoked challenge and provided opportunities for argument, agreement, or resistance—ideal conditions for one of Margaret's mind and temperament.

Repeating what Jane said was useless. The only way to know Jane Heap the Talker was to listen to her talk, and that Margaret did. Years later, however, Margaret recorded some of Jane's best talk. "I don't keep a record of the frailties of my contemporaries," Jane once said. "I have no time . . . and much less interest. I know enough about everyone; news is never of interest to me." Another time she said, "A great many unpleasant things may truthfully be said of me. I do not belong to any 'school of light.' Whatever people say is justified up to their understanding." Jane's pithy epithets always brought from Margaret floods of superlatives. Brahms, Jane called "a lesbian." Scriabin was a man with "a sick spine"; and Robert McAlmon, the writer and publisher she would come to know well in Paris, was "an epileptic without gumption enough to have fits."

Jane Heap came into Margaret's life unexpectedly one day in the studio in the Fine Arts Building, in Chicago, where for two years Margaret had struggled to publish the *Little Review*. That day Margaret was discussing the grand passion between Eleonora Duse and Gabriele D'Annunzio with a wealthy backer of the magazine whom she had jocularly nicknamed

"Nineteen Millions." When this temperamental woman expressed displeasure with D'Annunzio's treatment of Duse, Jane, silent until then, uttered "a loud and tender laugh" and said that for her Duse had always been the source of a "large pain." Offended, "Nineteen Millions" stomped out of the room, mumbling that she disapproved of frivolity. Margaret's reaction was different. Frivolity of the sort she had just heard was something she never wanted to be without.

For four years Margaret and Jane would be companions and lovers. Together they put out the *Little Review*. When Margaret lost interest in the magazine and went to France with her new friend Georgette Leblanc, Jane continued to publish it, both abroad and in New York, at irregular intervals until 1929. In Jane Heap, Margaret found "the special human being" with the "special point of view." Jane became her prolocuter, producing the pungent phrase when needed, articulating what Margaret could not describe, or, whenever Margaret ran out of words, obeying her command to "say it" with a thrilling clarity and certainty that demolished the opposition. Where Margaret just blurted out what she thought, Jane expressed things tactfully. So enjoyable was this verbal combat that Margaret would invent quarrels in order to show off Jane's powers. "I am the buzz," she would say, "and you, Jane, are the sting."

Being on exhibition was not a role Jane always enjoyed, however. Margaret, on the other hand, enjoyed nothing more than vanquishing some intellectual whose arguments had piqued her, and for that Jane was indispensable. Margaret was always stimulated more by criticism than compliments; but to her great annoyance, Jane would sometimes refuse to play the part of demolisher. It seemed that even the most patent ineptitudes amused her. Rather than castigating the speaker, Jane would laugh. People liked her natural affection, verve, and elation. Her tone was human and full of good fellowship, like an evangelists's or a politican's. From such disappointing encounters, Margaret would emerge bewildered and furious. Why, she demanded to know, had Jane refused to expose the falsities they had just heard? "Because I was having such a good time," Jane would answer. The explanation only increased Margaret's fury.

Jane's stimulating talk inspired Margaret's other role for Jane. Her ideas had to be preserved. The logical place was the *Little Review*. Grudgingly, Jane agreed, but every month she repeated how hard it was to write anything, how much easier the work would be with a dictaphone, and then went ahead only when Margaret agreed to take her words down in long hand. Next to Ezra Pound's contributions, Jane was the reason the *Little*

Review survived. Not only did her words enrich it; her editorial decisions were also responsible for its becoming a major outlet for modern writing, as important as Harriet Monroe's *Poetry.* What Margaret had done, or had failed to do, up to the time Jane came along is a story of false starts and misdirections.

"Hysteric" is the way Gertrude Stein described Margaret Anderson after they met in Paris. "Wild" is how friends in Indianapolis, where Margaret was born in 1886, remembered her and her sisters, Lois and Jean. In perpetual rebellion, Margaret and her sisters spent their childhood plotting escape from their staid bourgeois parents, a mother, who was not as bad as Margaret later made her out to be, and a gentle, tolerant, and intelligent father whom she adored and pitied.

As a girl Margaret took up the piano. She played it precociously, memorizing only passages she liked. When she agreed to attend college, she made arrangements to study piano rather than Greek. Western College for Women, a backwater institution in rural Ohio, contained Margaret for three years. What held her that long was not her piano studies (she did little), but the pleasure of listening to the performances of advanced students, one of whom allowed her to sit on her balcony while she played Chopin and Bach. At the start of her senior year, Margaret advised her father that spending another year in Oxford, Ohio, before returning home to the "higher joys of country clubs and bridge" was not what she wanted. "What do you want?" he asked. "I want to go to Chicago," she replied.

Neither parent favored the idea. She was too young, too impetuous, too extravagant, too impressionable. Margaret, however, would not be denied. She wrote to a Chicago journalist named Clara Laughlin, who conducted a column ("So You're Going to Paris") in *Good Housekeeping* and edited a religious magazine called *Interior.* How, Margaret asked, could "a perfectly nice but revolting girl" leave home? Miss Laughlin suggested that she first read Edmund Gosse's *Father and Son* and then come to Chicago for a talk. Meeting Clara Laughlin convinced Margaret she could never again live at home, especially with a mother who had become "nervous," a word that meant she had discovered the pleasures of making everything disagreeable.

Persuading her parents to let her go to Chicago was made easier when her sister, Lois, agreed to accompany her. Clara Laughlin gave her a job interviewing stage celebrities. She also wrote book reviews for the *Chicago Evening Post,* where Francis Hackett, the literary editor, advised her

Margaret Anderson   Jane Heap

Ezra Pound, 1926

to stop using "big words" and to strive for simplicity, a recommendation she later blamed for the permanent loss of her vocabulary. After a few blissful months in the city, the sisters had a visit from their disturbed parents. What had brought the senior Andersons to Chicago was a report from Miss Laughlin that their daughters were "going to the dogs." Both had begun smoking and run up large debts at local department stores. In heavy silence, the family returned to Indianapolis. Margaret and Lois isolated themselves in the homestead they now called "The Great Divide," after William Vaughn Moody's popular play. When Lois suddenly fell in love with a young man who recited so much Swinburne to her that she forgot how attractive Chicago had been, she decided to remain where she was. Within two months, however, Margaret returned to "her city," with her father's approval.

Her first job was clerking in Browne's bookshop, located in the Fine Arts Building on Michigan Boulevard, which also housed the offices of *The Dial* magazine, then under the direction of Francis F. Browne, whose two sons operated the bookstore. Browne, attracted to Margaret, gave her a position with the magazine, which might have led to a career as the editor's assistant. But in the summer of 1913, Clara Laughlin unexpectedly resigned as editor of *Interior* and recommended Margaret as her successor. She accepted for two reasons: staying with *The Dial* would be difficult since Browne had allowed his amorous feelings for her to be expressed in an aborted kiss, for which he movingly apologized; and joining *Interior* (now renamed *Continent*) would allow her to travel.

By this time Margaret was calling Chicago her "chosen city." No other city provided music better than the Chicago Symphony—she seldom missed a performance—or more stimulating exposure to art than the classes of the Art Institute. She had begun circulating among such "literary radicals" as Ben Hecht and Maxwell Bodenheim. She had also fallen in love with a woman for the first time. It was "a great love," she remembered, "great in everything including disappointment." What produced the disappointment was "animal jealousy," brought on when her "first love" left to visit her husband. Consumed with jealousy, Margaret opened one of the man's letters to the woman and read things not intended for her to see.

For all that Chicago offered a young woman in her twenties, however, it was not enough for Margaret. She felt restless. The trouble, she decided, was that her life lacked form and completeness. What was missing was inspiration. "Organized inspiration," observed her lifelong friend Janet

Flanner, would be the "dominant force in her career." Years later, with a startling precision, Margaret described what happened next:

I had been curiously depressed all day. In the night I wakened. First precise thought: I know why I'm depressed—nothing inspired is going on. Second: I demand that life be inspired every moment. Third: the only way to guarantee this is to have inspired conversation every moment. Fourth: most people never get so far as conversation; they haven't the stamina, and there is no time. Fifth: if I had a magazine I could spend my time filling it up with the best conversation the world has to offer. Sixth: marvelous idea—salvation. Seventh: decision to do it. Deep sleep.

The following day Margaret made more decisions: the *Little Review* would be "the best magazine in the world," it would be devoted to the "seven arts," and it would carry the slogan "A Magazine of the Arts, Making No Compromise with the Public Taste." How she would raise money, solicit manuscripts, pay the printer, collect advertisements, and distribute it were all matters that would conveniently resolve themselves.

She was delighted to discover that raising money was a lot easier than she had thought it would be. At one of the novelist Floyd Dell's soirées, she met a young man named Dewitt Wing. Wing, as lively and energetic a talker as Sherwood Anderson, John Cowper Powys, and others at the gathering, listened to her plans and reached the same conclusion she had: the *Little Review* must become a reality. To make sure that it did, he agreed to pay for office rent and printing from his meager salary. Other expenses could be met by advertisements, and he advised Margaret to canvass New York publishers. She took his advice and in a few days of hard campaigning collected $450.

Finding material for the first issue required slightly more effort. Contributors understood they would be unpaid. George Soule agreed to write about the "cubist literature" of Gertrude Stein, Arthur Davison Ficke submitted five poems on Japanese prints, Vachel Lindsay offered an early verse ("How a Little Girl Danced"), Llewellyn Jones sent an article on Henri Bergson, and Eunice Tietjens contributed a poem. But the mainstay of the first issue was the editor's exalted opinions on Galsworthy's latest novel, on Paderewski's artistry, on William Vaughn Moody's letters, and on the visiting English poet Rupert Brooke, who, some noted, looked as svelte and beautiful as Margaret herself. What would enliven her new and independent magazine, she promised, was creative criticism, or as she liked to call it, "appreciation." "In a world whose high splendor" is man's "chief preoccupation, the quality of our appreciation is the important thing." Only criticism that was fresh, constructive, "intelligent from the artist's point of view," a blend of philosophy and poetry, and "really interpretative" would be acceptable.

It was not the editor's critical demands that irritated Floyd Dell. It was her unabashed praise of art and its rewards. Dell ended an editorial in the *Chicago Evening Post,* which resulted in booming sales of the magazine, by complaining that Margaret had betrayed her own aspirations by praising everything in sight and forsaking the art of criticism. But in Margaret's opinion, all that she had betrayed was her adolescence. Eunice Tietjens, one of many mesmerized by Margaret's vitality and persuasiveness, agreed. The *Little Review* was "the perfect flower of adolescence, the triumph of wide-eyed and high-hearted ineptitude." Whatever the verdict, it was off to a rambunctious beginning, and Margaret, delighted with the notices her magazine had received, hastily planned the next issue.

Containing almost as many errors as the first (Margaret did not proofread galleys before she made up the magazine), the issue featured Sherwood Anderson's comments on the failure of writers to search in themselves for their material and William Butler Yeats's recommendation to read Vachel Lindsay's poem "General Booth Enters Into Heaven" for its "earnest simplicity" and "strange beauty." Margaret toned down her "desperate ardor for art," but not by much.

Just before the third issue went to press, Margaret met the anarchist Emma Goldman. She had never met anyone so knowledgeable, so well educated, and so dynamic. She was enthralled. Her adulation progressed into love for this roly-poly authoritarian woman. Why, Margaret argued, in an article dashed off at the last minute, could people not learn to live as brothers and give up private property and understand the "anarchist religion"? But in conservative Chicago, Emma Goldman was anathema. Margaret's fervid praise of a woman who favored free love and the prudent use of bombs created a scandal that eventually cost her the support of her one steady backer, Dewitt Wing. If it were discovered, Wing explained, that he was connected with the "notorious" *Little Review,* he would almost certainly lose his position, and doing so would mean the end of his support. Always equal to any emergency created by opposition, Margaret assured the distressed Wing she would go on with the magazine without him.

The *Little Review* did continue, but Margaret was forced to return to part-time book reviewing, which she preferred to accepting an offer that might have solved her financial problems. To her studio one morning came Harriet Monroe, who had for two years edited *Poetry* and published Ford Madox Ford, Sandburg, Frost, and Yeats. With her was the American poet from Brookline, Massachusetts, Amy Lowell. It was soon clear why Miss Lowell had come. Having offered Ezra Pound her services as an "Imagist poet" and been rejected, she was seeking another outlet for her work as part of a campaign to promote Imagism as her contribution to modern literature. The *Little Review* was just the vehicle she needed, and if Margaret would allow her to direct the poetry department of the magazine, she was ready to contribute $150 a month for an indefinite time. Certain that Amy Lowell would control anything she became involved in, Margaret refused: "I can't function," she explained, "in association."

Contributions from others who offered to help were accepted, however. Frank Lloyd Wright gave $100. Eunice Tietjens brought in a diamond ring. "Sell it," she told Margaret, "and bring out another issue." People she had never met asked her to lunch, listened to her talk about art and beauty, her ideals, and—perhaps feeling as Eunice Tietjens did that this person, so "unbelievably beautiful, so vital, and so absurd" was herself the adventure—gave her money. Only those impervious to her feminine qualities, which she learned to use to the fullest, could resist her, and doing so was like resisting a piece of candy.

Despite the generosity of many, Margaret eventually ran out of money, and when her sister, Lois, and her two sons moved in with her, she had to move and do so quickly. In pursuit of "something modest in the country," she came on a cottage in the village of Lake Bluff, thirty miles north of Chicago. There was barely enough space to hold Margaret, Lois and her sons, a *Little Review* staffer named Harriet Dean, and a black woman, Clara Crane, and her son. Clara shopped and cooked when there was money, and when there was not, Margaret opened charge accounts. Nearby lived the family of Morrill (Bill) Cody, who would become a familiar figure in Paris in the twenties. Mrs. Cody, drawn to the Anderson ménage, visited their cottage almost daily and suggested that Margaret might occasionally charge supplies to her husband. She did so immediately, ordering enough to keep the group going for at least a week. But Mr. Cody, although a writer himself, had no sympathy with "flighty young women magazine editors," and the account was closed.

Miraculously, they survived the winter, but by spring their money was almost gone, and Margaret went exploring again. This time she found a spacious, unpopulated beach near Ravinia, on the shores of Lake Michigan. The only thing missing from what was obviously the site of a summer residence was a residence. Margaret solved that problem by erecting tents, joined by a floor that served as a dining "room." With her band of tenacious followers, she settled down to enjoy "a North Shore gypsy life" and the publicity she hoped it would create.

From Ravinia, Margaret commuted to the *Little Review* studio in Chicago, often leaving after a plunge in the cold lake and a run on the beach and returning in time to watch the sunset. "So this is nature!" she exclaimed as day receded into night. Occasional intruders, like the policeman sent to dislodge them, Margaret overpowered by persuasion or guile. Reporters from the *Chicago Tribune* were welcome, however. The more publicity she could get for the *Little Review* the better, but when the reporters identified the beachcombers as Nietzschean revolutionaries (Margaret was writing articles on Nietzsche), the owners of an empty house in Highland Park, who had agreed to let Margaret and her following have it free for the winter, changed their minds. Lending their house to someone who appeared so charming but was really so depraved was out of the question. Margaret weighed the consequences of saying she was not the degenerate person they believed she was and concluded that as important as the house was, it was not worth betraying an ideal. She nonetheless had to admit that renouncing a fortune or a diamond mine would have been easier than losing a house.

From the prospect of spending a cold winter on the beach, Margaret and Harriet Dean were rescued by a socialist friend of Emma Goldman's, who put at their disposal a vacant house he owned in Chicago. As the shock of losing the first house slowly wore off, they set about decorating this one as though they expected to remain a lifetime. The following spring, Margaret began looking for something novel to do during the summer. What came to mind was Mill Valley, California, where her friend "Nineteen Millions" lived and where Margaret had often been invited. She reminded "Nineteen Millions" of her invitations and informed her that she intended to move the *Little Review* to Mill Valley in the summer and that she would bring her new friend and helpmate Jane Heap, apparently forgetting the altercation that had separated the two women and had sent her wealthy friend scurrying from the room in a rage. From California came word that Margaret would be most welcome but Jane would not. Certain that "Nineteen Millions" would change her mind as soon as she met Jane again and that she would be so delighted to have the magazine in California that she

Margaret Anderson and Jane Heap

Margaret Anderson, Gardine, 1926

would invite them to stay, Margaret began raising subscriptions for the trip. Friends donated clothes, food, and money, but when Jane and Margaret boarded a Canadian Pacific train for their journey west, they had only five dollars and a few baskets of food between them.

"Nineteen Millions" found Jane as "odious" as she had been before. Nothing could force her to change her mind. After half an hour of hard but quiet argument, Margaret capitulated and left. She and Jane would have to live somewhere else and in less splendor. What they found was a dilapidated ranch house near Muir Woods, across the bay from San Francisco. Being old, simple, deserted, isolated, sympathetic, painted an ugly brown, with a roofless porch and a glass-enclosed room in the rear, it was the perfect place. For sixty dollars it was theirs. From a small inheritance check Margaret received as her share of her grandmother's will, she paid the rent and moved in.

That summer she devoted to Jane and to decorating. It was also filled with horseback riding and music. Margaret wrote to the president of the Mason and Hamlin piano company, confiding that his piano was, in her estimation, the "world's most beautiful piano" and that she, who intended to be one of the "world's most beautiful pianists," could not bear to be anywhere without an instrument. Mr. Mason's reply was startling. Thanking her for her loyalty, he invited her to choose a Mason and Hamlin BB (a concert grand, the largest made) from the company's store in San Francisco. Margaret turned the living room into her studio and practiced every morning. Jane used the glass-enclosed room for painting.

It was in California that Margaret and Jane produced one of the most celebrated and notorious issues of the *Little Review*. Dismayed by the mediocre manuscripts she had received and entranced by the talk she and Jane engaged in daily for many hours, Margaret decided to print the magazine with thirteen of its twenty-eight pages blank. Two pages in the center contained a few cartoons by Jane (now officially the associate editor) that depicted their pastimes. The device was effective protest and propaganda. Margaret's point was made: Why labor to perpetuate the dull? When Margaret found time for the *Little Review*, she preferred to plan future issues, all of which always included articles she intended to extract from Jane. Jane answered the mail and designed new typographies. But what made the summer in Muir Woods memorable was talking to Jane.

The verbal combat began at noon. It reached a climax at tea. By dinner their words had staggered them. By five the next morning they were "unconscious" but still talking. What they talked about was Art. Who made it and why. The "strange necessity" the artist felt was what intrigued them. Jane's "uncanny knowledge of the human composition, her unfailing clair-voyance about human motivation" enthralled Margaret. Jane's exposition was what she had been waiting for, searching for. But welcome as Jane's knowledge was, Margaret did not imbibe it easily. Although Margaret's dilettante mind was crammed with borrowed information, the flotsam of many poets and philosophers, Jane's was original. She almost never quoted anybody, and what she said she expressed in a personal way. She said nothing she had not thought herself. The result was usually argument, which was good for both. Margaret thrived on controversy—she never found enough people willing to argue for their beliefs—and Jane consid-ered talk worthwhile only when she had resistance. Each tested the other's weapons and explored the nature of verbal combat. Jane taught Margaret how to defend herself by improving her powers of speech, how to size up an audience and give only what was desired or merited.

Jane once demonstrated her verbal powers in the presence of Emma Goldman. Following a ferocious argument, she accused the great anar-chist of lacking a sense of geography as well as logic, whereupon Emma complained that Jane was too aggressive. At a second anarchist gather-ing, Margaret, feeling pressed to the wall, recklessly contended that "Sa-lome" was "better art" than "The Ballad of Reading Gaol," and then cited the example of the black swan in a poem by Amy Lowell as a way of "pointing emotion." Laboring men cared nothing about a black swan, Emma remonstrated, and, besides, the poem had nothing to do with rev-olution. Margaret complained that Emma was talking about economics while she was discussing art. She answered Emma by suggesting that if the anarchists realized their goal, the leisure that workingmen might en-joy would only give them more time to be insensible. Emma dismissed Margaret's esoteric art as incomprehensible and of no value. "Not so," Margaret replied. "Even an oppressed workingman understands the eter-nal human emotions." "Eternal poppycock!" Emma shot back. The ex-change brought Emma to nervous prostration (it was the first time Mar-garet had ever seen her in that condition), caused Margaret to be fully disappointed in the anarchist, and formed the basis of a series of letter-lectures to the anarchist which in summary form appeared in the *Little Review.*

Margaret's passion for living in nature, in discomfort if need be, waned as the annual autumn rains began drenching Muir Woods. It was time to go back to Chicago. At the first stop, Los Angeles, they collected enough subscription money to take them to Denver. There they addressed a large audience on the failures of the anarchist mind. Margaret was no longer charmed by anarchism. In fact, her attachment to it had always been sentimental, and her interest had been in anarchists like Alexander Berkman and Emma Goldman and not in their creed. Art, she had come to understand, was far more than revolt, and although the notion came to her later, it was also far more than workmanship or "some Flaubertian perfection of technique." What Margaret meant by art at this time was superior ideas, usually expressed in conversation. The artist was an exceptional person with something exceptional to say. Jane, according to this definition, was an exceptional artist. She expressed exceptional matter in an exceptional way and the result was style. Margaret believed that style was the man. She also believed there was nothing wrong with the phrase "art for art's sake." Cannot art exist for itself? "Should it be art for money's sake?"

When Margaret and Jane resettled in Chicago in the fall of 1916, they received a letter from the person who would transform the *Little Review* from an eccentric toy into a leading magazine of the arts. Margaret had had the good sense to send Ezra Pound a copy of the *Little Review* (the January-February 1916 issue) and to ask for his opinion. Pound provided polite encouragement and recommended that the editors first hire an efficient proofreader who could be depended on to rid the magazine of typographical "horrors." Then during the summer, he had urged both women to read James Joyce's *Potaayman* (they did) and to consider publishing two poems by Jean de Bosschere, the most modern writer in Paris, according to Pound, not excepting Apollinaire. Pound helped with subscriptions, too, and offered to spread the word about the *Little Review* if the editors supplied him with twenty copies of each issue. Then in November, learning that Margaret would soon move the magazine to New York, he took a deeper interest in its publication: What was the circulation? The financial condition? Would they consider paying contributors? Was a "foreign correspondent" (Pound was already European editor for *Poetry*) someone Margaret might want? Working for love only was not a tempting prospect—he had done too much of that already—but arranging for the magazine, with contributions by those he recommended, to go to the "right" people, especially in France, was worth doing. As for propaganda (philosophy), he saw no disagreement between them. Besides assuming that the editors also favored a deeper understanding of French life and art as a means to bring about improved conditions in America, he advanced the equally acceptable notion that their common effort should aim at enriching the individual and assisting him to escape from the "enslaving system" created by American universities. Pound's offer demanded acceptance.

As soon as he learned that the editors were amenable to his plans, he made demands. He wanted "an official organ . . . a place where I and T. S. Eliot can appear once a month (or once an 'issue') and where James Joyce can appear when he likes, and where Wyndham Lewis can appear if he comes back from the war." The vital matters were how much space Margaret would agree to allot him and the others, and how many issues she could put out each year. Pound suggested sixteen pages and eight issues. In exchange, he could offer no money, but he would pay contributors out of a guarantee ($600 to $750 a year) provided by an anonymous patron (the lawyer John Quinn), and Margaret could keep all the subscription money the new contributions would generate. For forthcoming issues, there would be "a lot of Fenollosa stuff, Chinese and Japanese," some criticism from T. S. Eliot, poetry by John Rodker and Iris Barry. Still uncertain were contributions from Joyce and Lewis.

Regardless of the line-up, however, Pound was convinced that the "new order of things" ought to open with a bang—sixteen pages of "new blood" —signalled by the simultaneous arrival of a new battery of writers. Their identity was clear by April 1917, when Pound announced that for the June issue he would supply work by Yeats, Eliot, Lewis, and himself; for the May issue, he was sending Eliot's "Eeldrop and Applelex" as well as Lewis's *Imaginary Letters* and his own *Jodindranath Mawhwor's Occupation* and an "Editorial" announcing his acceptance of the post of foreign editor.

So the *Little Review* was remade, transformed into Ezra Pound's mouthpiece and into a journal of the new literature. Transformed, too, was the editor. When a reader complained that the magazine had descended below its "earlier standard—almost below zero," and that he had lost patience with the foreign editor and "his contemptuous invective against the 'vulgus,'" Margaret answered with the ardor of fresh conversion: "A contempt for the 'vulgus' is the inevitable reaction of any man or woman who observes the antics of the 'flies in the marketplace.'" The June issue was as impressive as Pound had predicted. The next month came Eliot's French poems, a third installment of Lewis's *Imaginary Letters,* Pound's "Aux Etuves de Wiesbaden," and three vignettes by Pound's protégé John Rodker. August brought more poems by Yeats, a half dozen others by Iris Barry, another of the foreign editor's protégés, Pound's *Stark Realism,* and a review of Joyce's *Portrait of the Artist as a Young Man.*

The move from Chicago to New York was Margaret's idea, and it took her a little while to discover why it was a good one. Chicago, she had come to believe, had taken all it wanted from them, and they had received all it could give. The time had come "to touch the greatest city of America," where their position as editors of the *Little Review* would be more commanding. However, for Jane, who loved Chicago, the move to New York was inconvenient, and only the Christmas party she organized on the day of their departure buoyed her spirits during the journey. By the time they arrived in New York, she was unhappy. Margaret was too. New York was a "hideous reality." While Jane remained in the hotel, sullen and strangely uncommunicative, Margaret struggled with the new reality. Their situation seemed hopeless, and at times Margaret wondered if they should perhaps live apart. Maybe they occupied "different curves—one going, one coming." Perhaps Jane should have stayed in Chicago, but that, Margaret knew, would only lead to expending herself—her talk—on people incapable of retaining it. "I was her best audience," Margaret concluded, and therefore she alone had to exploit her friend's unique gifts.

Gradually, Jane improved in spirits and joined Margaret in the inevitable house-hunting. First, they found a studio suitable for the *Little Review* at 31 West 14th Street, in the old Van Buren house; next they found living quarters at 24 West 16th Street, in a house that had once been the residence of William Cullen Bryant. Considerably restored by now, Jane selected her room and transformed it into a meeting place where "all *Little Review* conversation" would be conducted, a "special, haunting, poignant, dedicated room." In Jane's room, Margaret remembered, the *Little Review* entered its creative period.

No matter how uplifting it had been to find their flat, New York remained disappointing, if not quite the ugly reality it had seemed at first. The heyday of Greenwich Village, alas, was over. Among the first people they met was Max Eastman, editor of the *Masses* and a socialist; however, he lacked the "fire" Margaret had hoped to find in him and his ideas. Another disappointment was Carl Van Vechten, whose vacuous remark about Harold Bauer, one of Margaret's favorite pianists, drew from her a scornful rejoinder: "My word . . . don't you know anything at all about music?" The others gathered in Edna Kenton's apartment the night Van

Vechten irritated her—Ida Rush, Fania Marinoff, Helen Westley, Phillip Moeller—all "seemed to be exchanging book information rather than personal points of view." Their supply of anecdotes, gossip, "echoes of information, a cataloging of current impressions," and snobbish opinions produced a "singularly second-rate evening" for one whose object in talking was "neither to learn nor to convey but to enter into new emotional states."

The gatherings of poets, writers, and painters in Jane's room did more to kindle Margaret's blessed emotional states. Although it was Margaret whom most of them sought out, it was Jane who received them. Margaret was kinder, Jane told Alfred Kreymborg, but less hopeful than she. Both women soon gained a reputation as flippant, ruthless, devastating debaters, who sometimes sought resistance where none existed and who were then annoyed if no one deigned to rise to their challenge. They resented being regarded as just "simple sincere people with serious ideas." It seemed to be an easy way to grant them a victory without having to fight for it. When they did manage to inspire a debate, it often ended with Jane doing the talking for both and cajoling a silent audience with taunts like "Oh come on . . . a good answer deserves a good question."

Inevitably, Margaret relied on Jane for emotional invigoration. Together—and exhaustively—they speculated on the nature of emotion and its causes, the difference between sensibility and sensitization, the sine qua non that immortalizes objects, the power that goes into creating one's own image, the definition of the poignant human being. The harder they examined such matters, the more they dismayed the people they associated with. It was clear that these outsiders intended to remain outsiders. Both avoided bars and restaurants, partly because they cost too much but also because they preferred their own quarters, where they created what Margaret described as a "hearthstone." What so many had striven to avoid they were determined to build. "We were dedicated," Margaret explained, "to the ceremonies of living. We insisted upon living beautifully." It was a condition they perfected, despite unrelieved impecuniousness, by expending their energy maintaining a comfortable household and attending to their needs. They cut one another's hair, sewed, cooked, and made their own clothing. A suit Jane created for Margaret drew admiring remarks from a leading New York tailor. About all they did not do—and it was something Margaret later regretted—was to make their own shoes and stockings.

Through frugality and careful rationing of their funds, they were able to bring out the *Little Review* every month. They added more pages, increased the price from fifteen to twenty-five cents, and in November 1917, they were able to publish drawings by Gaudier-Brzeska, Wyndham Lewis, Jules Pascin, and Marie Laurencin. The length that month increased to forty-four pages. In December it swelled to fifty-eight pages. They had found the cheapest printer in New York, a Mr. Popovitch, to whose shop on 23rd Street they went Sundays to help correct proof, set type, and fold pages for the binders.

Real financial assistance, however, came only when the editors met Pound's benefactor, John Quinn, a noted Tammany Hall lawyer and book collector, who annoyed Margaret by telling her how to run her magazine and then agreed, subject to its being kept a secret, to contribute $400 to keep it going. Quinn raised an additional $1,200 from guarantors, including Otto Kahn, all of which, he instructed Margaret, he would place in a bank account from which she would be permitted to withdraw no more than $200 a month. Margaret fumed and protested to Pound that she would brook no interference with her magazine. That was exactly what Quinn wanted to avoid, Pound replied. No one in New York, he continued, was doing more for the arts. Quinn sent money to Wyndham Lewis, Joyce, Eliot ("an untried quantity"), and of course Pound. His advice to Margaret was to let some time pass before making up her mind about Quinn. "I wish there were one or two more like him," he added.

Pound's control over the *Little Review* extended to people other than its editors and patrons. In the June 1917 issue, he objected to a poem by Louis Gilmore (inferior language) and dismissed a letter from Max Bodenheim in which he revenged himself on Pound for dismissing his verse as unoriginal. Margaret had brought both authors to the magazine. In the aggregate, he informed Margaret, he preferred the editors' own contributions over all the other Americans' work. In August, with the magazine on a solid financial footing and with contributions from Ford Madox Ford, Lewis, and William Carlos Williams scheduled for forthcoming issues, Pound recommended that the slogan be changed from "A Magazine of the Arts Making No Compromise with the Public Taste" to one more irritating: "The *Little Review*: The Magazine That Is Read by Those Who Write the Others." The new flag was hoisted in October. The December issue contained a criticism of Eliot's "Prufrock" by May Sinclair, one of the two members of the London clientele—the other was Lady Randolph Churchill—who Pound believed would help the *Little Review* make its won way in England. Pound's major contribution, however, was *Ulysses*. In May he had told Margaret to announce that the serialization of the book would begin in

Georgette Leblanc, George Antheil, Margaret Anderson,
Bernardsville, N.J.

March 1918, and by January he had collected enough copy from Joyce for a first installment.

About the work that would bring her lasting fame as its first publisher, Margaret remained stubbornly defensive. Aware that Joyce was Pound's "private jewel" and that *Ulysses* "was being lent to the *Little Review* for the good of its soul," Margaret took steps to avoid being cast as an editor too unenlightened to recognize the genius of the author. Pound, she readily admitted, had recommended *Ulysses,* but Jane and she, on their own, had recognized its brilliance. That moment of recognition, as she described it in *My Thirty Years' War,* assured readers that they had both perceived that *Ulysses* was "the most beautiful thing we'll ever have." A more elaborate description appears in a letter to her friend Solita Solano. "We were terribly moved," she wrote, recalling the moment the first installment of the book arrived. Rushing through the pages and coming on the words "Ineluctable modality of the visible" brought her to the verge of tears. "We kept saying, 'What Art.'" It made no difference that the manuscript was filled with corrections. "We'll print this if it's the last thing we do!" Margaret cried. As their friend Allen Tanner, who witnessed the ecstatic moment, noted, "It almost was."

Disquieting intimations that *Ulysses* might create troubles with censors grew soon after the first portion appeared in March 1918. Almost no one shared the editors' enthusiasm for Joyce's opus, and some readers expressed shock and cancelled their subscriptions. Typical of the hundreds of objections Margaret received was this one: "I think this is the most damnable slush and filth that ever polluted paper in print. . . . There are no words I know to describe . . . how disgusted I am. . . . I reject thinking of you as part of this hellish business. . . . It has done something tragic to my illusions about America. How could you?" Such letters hurt Margaret as well as Joyce. Despite Djuna Barnes's insistence that it was not worth answering, Margaret did, arguing that not only ignorance but insensitivity had prevented the subscriber from appreciating "an epic criticism of mankind."

The *Ulysses* excerpts ran for three years. Twenty-three parts appeared, about half the book. Four times the *Little Review* was confiscated and destroyed for alleged obscenity by order of the U. S. Post Office. Each time, Margaret cried, "it was like a burning at the stake." It made the efforts she and Jane had taken to preserve Joyce's text intact and the worry over bills and the production of the magazine seem futile. Moreover, the anticipated support of the world's intellectuals never came. New York was particularly inimical, and she thought the *New York Times* was the "worst." It accepted no publicity about *Ulysses* and accused the editors of being "purveyors of lascivious literature." Others agreed, notably the Society for the Suppression of Vice, which moved against the *Little Review* in October 1920, when it served papers on the Washington Square Bookshop for having sold a teenage girl a copy of the magazine's July-August issue containing Episode Thirteen in which Bloom watches Gerty on Sandymount Strand. This, the most serious of the many run-ins the editors had had with various authorities, would require the services of John Quinn.

Although Margaret believed the main reason Quinn agreed to subsidize the *Little Review* was to make sure *Ulysses* was published in the United States, he scolded her and Jane for having thought they could do so. "You're damned fools," Quinn raged, for "trying to get away with such a thing as *Ulysses* in this puritan-ridden country." Fighting for them in a courtroom, he went on, was a lost cause. But when Margaret suggested that another lawyer might like to defend them, shrewdly recognizing that Quinn would never give up the privilege of defending Joyce in court, he changed his mind. He would take the case, but for Joyce, not for two people without an "ounce of sense."

Margaret Anderson and Jane Heap appeared before the Court of Special Sessions in December 1920. At their side was John Quinn. Also in the courtroom was John Sumner, head of the Society for the Suppression of Vice, whose "charm, sensitivity, and shyness" made his reactionary beliefs less offensive. Later, Margaret said that if she could have invited him to tea every day for a month, she would have made him as fanatical about a new set of ideas (presumably hers) as he was about his own. With him, Sumner had copies of the five other suppressed issues of the *Little Review.* Before three judges—two with white hair who slept during most of the trial and a younger man, a Norwegian, who told Jane later that if he had known she too was of the same descent he would have changed his verdict—Quinn argued the case of James Joyce. He cited Joyce's prestige as a man of letters, exploited his own standing in the legal world, and excoriated government officials who could not distinguish between literature and pornography. What he failed to do was describe the kind of person Joyce was. That, in Margaret's opinion, would have swayed the judges to dismiss Sumner's charges. But the only concern was obscenity. Was *Ulysses* obscene? The witnesses Quinn had gathered—Scofield Thayer, editor of *The Dial,* Phillip Moeller of the Theatre Guild, and the novelist John

Cowper Powys—were all less effective than Quinn believed they would be. Moeller confounded the judges by explaining the Freudian manner of revealing the subconscious and refuting the notion that Joyce's work was in any sense "aphrodisiac." Thayer thoughtlessly admitted that he would have consulted a lawyer before publishing *Ulysses*. In exquisite Oxonian tones, Powys declared that Joyce's beautiful work could never corrupt the minds of young girls. When the prosecuting attorney announced his intention of having certain "obscene" passages read, one of the sleeping judges awoke, and regarding Margaret with "a protective paternity," refused to allow the offensive passages to be read in her hearing. When Quinn pointed out that she was the publisher, the judge replied that she probably did not understand the "significance" of what she was publishing.

Throughout the trial, Margaret and Jane were as silent (Quinn had instructed them to be meek and quiet) as the New York newspapers, not one of which came to their defense, or to Joyce's. The *Ulysses* trial was clearly one to avoid. Quinn's spirited but misguided defense notwithstanding, the verdict went against them. They were fined one hundred dollars and led off to have their fingerprints recorded. Theirs was a glorious defeat. Art never claimed two more regal and pugnacious martyrs, as the clerks in the fingerprinting room soon learned. "For expecting ME to submit to such an obscenely repulsive performance," Margaret told Allen Tanner, who had witnessed the trial, "you'll see a scandal that would have brought Sarah Bernhardt delirious bravos." When asked to place her hand on an ink pad, Margaret drew herself up and, glaring at the clerks with furious disgust, declared she would never besmirch her well-groomed hands with their repulsive ink until they produced "a cake of very good soap, a bottle of very good Eau de Cologne, and a very clean towel" to wipe the black filth off her hands. Cringing and looking as though they regretted not only the existence of "such a filthy procedure" but the fact that they existed at all, they disappeared down the hall, and returned a few minutes later with the requested articles. With an expression of shattering revulsion, Margaret extended her hand over the ink pad, squirming with exaggerated disgust as each finger was inked and imprinted for posterity. The ordeal over, she stalked out of the room, giggling at her triumph over the legal indecencies of America. Only one person acknowledged her martyrdom, Mary Garden. "I'm disappointed in you," she said. "I thought you'd go to jail." Margaret shared her disappointment. Like Henry David Thoreau, who had the misfortune to have his jail sentence cut short, Margaret theorized later that she might have circulated "some intelligent propaganda" about

Ulysses if she had refused to permit payment of the fine and had gone to jail instead.

The successful action against the *Little Review* made the publication of any additional installments of *Ulysses* impossible. Joyce would have to wait ten more years before his book appeared in the United States. Meanwhile, however, it would be published in Paris, but before the appearance of Sylvia Beach's Shakespeare and Company edition in 1922, Pound and Quinn had agreed that a private edition, subsidized by private subscriptions, was Joyce's only recourse. Any attempt Margaret might make to commence reprinting sections of the book would not help Joyce's cause, Pound advised. Besides, printing only half of the book would increase the demand for the complete volume when it was published. The wisest course to follow was to come out with a new issue of the *Little Review* so good that magazines in and out of America would look poor by comparison; and to make sure it would, Pound had lined up Francis Picabia as guest editor for the next issue. As for the trial, Pound recommended that Margaret say nothing about it until after the Picabia issue had appeared. For at least a year, she must do nothing that might result in another suppression. The reproductions of Picabia's and Brancusi's (also scheduled) works forbade it.

Recovering from this latest and most serious suppression was not easy. Margaret felt restless again and hinted to Jane that the *Little Review*, to which she had devoted ten years, perhaps ought to be allowed to expire, gloriously, with "the epoch's supreme articulation," *Ulysses*. Jane disagreed, arguing that the *Little Review* had not come to its end and that if Margaret left it in her hands she would never be able to write another word. Only when she experienced Margaret's opposition could she write, and besides, she reminded her, what set the magazine apart from others was their intense conflicts.

Margaret gave in, but she won one concession from Jane. The *Little Review* would become a quarterly. In addition to Picabia and Brancusi, new contributors included Gertrude Stein, Jean Cocteau, Apollinaire, and the exotic Baroness Else von Freytag-Loringhoven, whom the editors mistakenly tried to present as a major writer. That she was not—not even a complete imitation of a dadaist, as they believed—became clear when they published a long piece by the baroness called "Thee I Call Hamlet of Wedding-Ring," supposedly a critique of William Carlos Williams's *Kora in Hell*. Margaret's misgivings gave rise to one of her most pungent observations: "The policy of the *Little Review* has always been: a free stage for the artists. There are moments when I believe this to be an uninteresting policy." Still, when Harriet Monroe recommended that the *Little Review* might consider dropping the baroness, Jane rushed to her defense: "We do not intend to drop the baroness—right into the middle of the history of American poetry. . . . When she is dada, she is the only one living anywhere who dresses dada, loves dada, lives dada."

The embranglement over the baroness was one of several signs that the *Little Review* had lost direction. Francis Picabia was Ezra Pound's last contribution, and without Pound, the main source of new work was gone. Gone also was the cohesiveness and continuity of thought and purpose that Pound and his literary friends provided. The tone from now on was increasingly narcissistic and frenetic. Of Picabia, even Margaret remarked: "We have never had anything from him except a Picabia number."

What finally brought an end to Margaret's restlessness and a release into something new was a meeting with William Butler Yeats, who was visiting in New York as the guest of John Quinn. When Yeats entertained her with stories of Joyce and Pound and others abroad, she found the explanation of her discomfort. The time had come to go to Europe. But how to get there and what to do once she arrived were questions left unanswered until after a second eventful meeting (arranged by her friend from Chicago, the pianist Allen Tanner) with the former companion of Maurice Maeterlinck, Georgette Leblanc, a singer whose beauty and mystery and legend had smitten Tanner as completely as they would Margaret.

At the age of eighteen, Georgette Leblanc had read Maeterlinck's essay on Emerson and, enchanted by the author's mysticism and the poetic quality of his writing, had given up her position at the Opéra Comique, in Paris, where she was a promising singer, to join this enchanting stranger in Belgium. "I had discerned a tendency of mind, a vision, ideas, and even a being whose secret inner existence corresponded to my own," she revealed in her memoirs. "I had not tried to find out what he was like, how he lived. . . . I had staked my life on a purely spiritual intention." In Brussels she arranged to attend a supper party at which Maeterlinck was a guest, and, wearing on her forehead a blue diamond she regarded as a symbol of happiness, she attracted his attention. For over twenty years— the most productive of the playwright's career—they remained companions and lovers, maintaining a liaison noted for its simplicity and intensity. Georgette acted in his plays, aided in his work, and her dramatic nature was a complement to his retiring and objective one.

The Chateau de Tancarville

Georgette Leblanc, Chateau de Tancarville

To Miss Leblanc's suite in the Commodore Hotel in New York, Tanner conducted his friend. From a meeting she went to without much interest, Margaret returned a transformed woman. It was love at first sight. To this woman with a dramatic sense of decoration, whose talk sounded like St. Just, who possessed "a strong heart and a clear head," who read the philosophers and wrote moral essays, Margaret lost her heart. If basic things seemed agreeable on first meetings, Margaret was fond of pointing out, then all was perfect. This was perfect. From Georgette, nearly twenty years her senior, Margaret was seldom separated. She accompanied her to musicales organized by Tanner, to dinner parties, to appointments. Georgette, although occasionally a little frightened by Margaret's enthusiasm and flamboyance, kept her in a state of continuous rapture. She transformed Margaret's life into a dream. Realities no longer counted or were even noticed. Only Jane was unhappy. Jealous of her friend's new companion, she pointed out Georgette's flaws, saying, for one thing, that Georgette was too practical. But Margaret was too mesmerized, too completely under Georgette's spell, to listen. As Jane saw less of Margaret, she struggled to control her feelings and maintain her dignity, but the shock of this sudden and apparently irrevocable twist of fate would not pass quickly.

Georgette strengthened Margaret's resolve to give up the *Little Review* and turn it over to Jane. Her abdication appeared in the form of a colloquy printed in the magazine.

> "I am definitely giving up The Little Review," I told Jane.
> "You can't give it up. You started it."
> "Are you mad? I started it. I can give it up."
> "You have no sense of responsibility."
> "Self-preservation is the first responsibility."
> "You certainly can't give it up."
> "I certainly can give it up. I'll give it to you."

Giving Jane the magazine may have been a compensatory gift, for Jane had refused to accept the "miracle of Georgette" in her friend's life and now faced a future without Margaret's company.

Not long after Margaret's eventful meeting with Georgette, the Hearst organization cancelled an agreement they had made with her to publish her memoirs of life with Maeterlinck. To recover from a blow that depleted her spirit as well as her purse, Georgette retired to rural New Jersey, where, near Bernardsville, she rented a large dilapidated mansion with a rose garden and a neighboring park. Margaret, certain that a rustic retreat would be the perfect place for their friendship to grow, eagerly accompanied her. So did Georgette's devoted *dame de campagnie,* Monique, an evanescent sort of "fairy-tale nurse"; the worshipful Allen Tanner; and (on invitation) the bumptious young composer George Antheil.

The summer teemed with sensual experiences. In the entrance hall Georgette wrote a passage on the wall: *"Tout est bien: il suffit d'être maître de soi"* (All is well: What is needed is to be master of yourself). She sang Debussy's *Mélisande* with Tanner, his voice creating a Pelléas that surpassed any she had ever heard. At dawn one day she discovered fresh meanings in Bach's deepest pages, and on a hot heavy night she and the others waltzed to *Rosenkavalier* until they dropped in dizziness. Margaret, indulging her love of nature, gazed at the distant blue hills that looked like smoke across the valley. Evenings she watched a rising red moon fill the opening at the end of the cypress-lined drive leading to the mansion. Everything was bewitching, particularly Georgette. Even Antheil's incessant banging on the piano scarcely disturbed the solitude and peace of their sylvan hideaway.

Again in New York, Georgette found it increasingly difficult to find work. It seemed that her career in America had run its course, that it was only a matter of time before she—it was now understood that Margaret would go with her as her accompanist—would have to return to France. The duration of that time was dramatically shortened by a program of extraordinary dances they attended that fall—sacred Tibetan temple dances, they were told, containing "exact esoteric knowledge" that the performers, as instruments, conveyed to the audience. The men responsible for this performance were even more impressive, a Russian-born mystic named Georgi Gurdjieff and his disciple and proselytizer, Alfred Richard Orage, former editor of the English philosophical magazine *The New Age.* In a single evening, Margaret reported, Orage had convinced her and Jane and Georgette that Gurdjieff's teachings would not just fulfill their hopes, they would exceed them. Gurdjieff himself remained behind the scenes, more of a presence than an interpreter, but on one memorable occasion he informed an entranced audience that his ideas were universal ("facts always known and always hidden"), that both a super-knowledge and a super-science existed and that he had found the way in which knowledge of both could be acquired. If Orage had seemed to be "a messenger between two worlds," a man who could interpret the world that scientists had revealed but not explained, then Gurdjieff was a sort of Hermes who would teach a supreme science of God, world, and man. When the women learned that Gurdjieff and Orage were returning to France, where they operated a school near Paris called the Institute for the Harmonious Development of Man, Margaret, Georgette, and Jane decided to follow, prepared to cast their nets.

Aboard the ship that carried Margaret and Georgette to France (Jane joined them a few months later) in May 1923 were John McCormack, Emilio de Gorgorza, and Vladimir Golschmann, the young Frenchman who would conduct Antheil's *Ballet Mécanique* in Paris. McCormack played host in his suite, sometimes singing with Georgette or with an overly sentimental Duchesse de Richelieu, and the last night at sea climaxed with a public concert and a champagne toast to the "eternal glory of France." The enthusiasm with which Americans drank to her country drew from Georgette an observation that would have deep, personal meanings for her companion. Why, she wondered, were they so eager to experience France when, unlike the French, who had learned to sit down, Americans were a people *en marche*?

Among the first people they met in Paris was Robert McAlmon, who took them to dinner and then to meet James Joyce. Joyce reminded Margaret of her father as a young man. He possessed the same gentle bearing, the same kindliness, "deprecating humor in the smile," the same feeling of personal aristocracy. Joyce's "strata of sensitization," as she put it, surprised her, however. She surmised it was produced by a recognition that certain irremediable things had and would continue to cause him suffering, two of which were his failing eyesight and the hardship of writing without his library and notes that he had been forced to leave in Italy. That Joyce spoke so little disappointed her, but his explanation she understood. He had given up conversation because he had become tired of people constantly interrupting him with trivial remarks or requests. There were occasions, of course, when he broke his vow and, stimulated by wine and an interesting subject, entertained guests with much convivial talk, until Nora (whom he would marry in 1931), exercising that spirit and independence she normally kept suppressed, reminded him that any more talk would doubtlessly impair his work the following day.

One meeting with Joyce took place in Ezra Pound's garden studio in the rue Notre Dames des Champs. The same mismatching of expectation and reality she had experienced with Joyce occurred with Pound. Not only his height, robustness, reddish hair, and high stentorian voice surprised her, but the man's nervous, self-conscious behavior was also amazing. He resembled a "large baby" performing "its repertoire of physical antics gravely, diffidently, without human responsibility for the performance." Puzzling, too, were a certain "slowness on the up-take" and a habit of personalizing the impersonal and, most annoying, a tendency to treat women as possessions—attributes that she would conclude later belonged to all established expatriates. Ezra, at thirty-eight, was an "academic type," someone she looked forward to knowing after he had grown up.

Another person Margaret visited was Gertrude Stein. Their meeting started badly when Gertrude reproached Margaret for not paying contributors to the *Little Review.* "You have no right to publish young writers without paying them." Margaret, extremely irritated, replied: "It's not a question of right, but of duty. No one else will publish them." That irritated Gertrude, and the visit went from bad to worse. There was much about Gertrude Stein that Margaret disliked. Her heartiness was repellent and the authority, serious self-love, and intensity involved in that heartiness were offensive. Gertrude, she concluded, "was a kind of commercial being, so practical, so implacable, so quarrelsome with the 'great friends' she loved and then detested." She was someone to avoid, as disagreeable as music one could not bear. A few years later Margaret made some constructive criticism of her writing: "To me, Gertrude Stein's style can be regarded as having two aspects. She has a way of saying things which presents perfectly her special matter; she has a way of repeating those things which detracts from her special manner." Implicit in the latter criticism is the flaw she found in all of Gertrude Stein's work: it was boring. Understandably, two dedicated egoists were bound to disagree. Each one's abiding belief in her own infallibility ensured this. When they found themselves together in the same room, as they occasionally did at Noel Murphy's home in Orgeval, outside Paris, it was Gertrude, according to Janet Flanner, whose psychology dominated. Against her nature and intelligent and splendid talk, Margaret was nearly defenseless. Reduced to relying on the opposing elements in her nature—violent agreement and violent disagreement—Margaret would strike out at everyone with taunts, punctuated by spiraling laughter. Her rather ponderous final assessment of her formidable foe combines astuteness and flighty mumbo jumbo: Gertrude Stein is "full of homely important knowledge of simple vital people, lack of knowledge of many of the human masks," and a paucity of imagination that makes it impossible for her to manage "even a preliminary examination of what [could be called] significant singularity."

For Alice B. Toklas, Gertrude Stein's alter ego, Margaret ironically felt an immediate liking, but not until after Gertrude's death in 1946 did the two women meet again. Alice admitted that her original impression of Margaret had been wrong. Immediately after her visit to the ladies' salon in rue de Fleurus, Alice remembered, she had turned to Gertrude and said: "She puts her hand on her heart because she is afraid it will jump away from her." That had been a crude statement about Margaret, she confessed, but not without a grain of truth. Later, Alice realized that what she had considered Margaret's excessive emotionalism and sentimentality were really simple spontaneous reactions.

In the early twenties, Margaret had published in the *Little Review* such French writers and artists as Louis Aragon, André Breton, Phillippe Soupault, René Crevel, Jean Cocteau, André Gide, Jacques Baron, Pierre Reverdy, Tristan Tzara, Francis Picabia, and sculptor Constantin Brancusi. One of the first of these Europeans that Margaret met was Brancusi. He lived in a stone studio in the rue de Vaugirard surrounded by stone benches and sculptures in various stages of completion. Everything was white, even his hair, beard, and blouse. He served chicken to Margaret and other guests. After dinner he prepared thick black Turkish coffee, sang Rumanian folk songs, danced, and at midnight took pictures of everyone and then led his party into the streets, to cafés where there was music, to the Bois, and finally to the Halles for onion soup.

As fascinating as Brancusi was Jean Cocteau, a catalytic figure, in Margaret's opinion, whose great charm tempered his immense vanity. In addition to his exquisite hands, which jutted from coat sleeves that he kept short with the tight cuffs turned back, Cocteau's talk entranced her. Neither his poetry or plays nor his translations accounted so much for his legend as his talk, his examination of "great ideas." The man's joyous participation in life seemed to be the opposite of Hemingway's. Where the former was spontaneous, nervous, and expansive, Hemingway struck Margaret as "simple." Hemingway was another whose reputation belied his nature. He seemed to be continuously afraid of falling in love, mainly, she gathered, because when it happened the experience was so absorbing that he was cut off from everything else, including writing. Ten years after meeting Margaret Anderson, Hemingway wrote to Janet Flanner that he had never met "a nicer or more flutter-brained legendary woman, nor a prettier one . . . than Margaret." According to Margaret, Hemingway had fallen in love with her soon after she came to Paris and had become so "gooey" that she had been forced to avoid him. Afterward, he had fallen in love with Duff Twysden (who became his model for Brett Ashley in *The*

Sun Also Rises), and while Jane and Margaret looked on, had taken to wandering around the Café des Deux Magots looking for her. The metaphor Hemingway had used in his letter to Janet to express his condition at that time—"a white rabbit with pink eyes dull with pain"—was actually Jane's, and was presumably an appropriate description of Hemingway when he pursued Margaret.

Paris, in the late spring and summer of 1923, provided a cultural feast that kept Margaret in that state of ecstasy without which, she believed, life was never worthwhile. She saw the Swedish Ballet, Stravinsky's *Les Noces* with the Ballets Russes, and Cocteau's *Les Mariés de la Tour Eiffel*. She introduced George Antheil to Erik Satie and Ezra Pound and arranged for Antheil's appearance in the Théâtre des Champs-Élysées during the filming of Marcel L'Herbier's *L'Inhumaine*. She attended the uproarious programs staged by the dadaists at the Théâtre Michel; the Comte de Beaumont's Soirées de Paris, where she saw Cocteau's *Romeo et Juliette*; and listened to American jazz played by black musicians at the Boeuf-sur-le-Toit. Paris was an endless treasure house of sights and sounds.

Surprisingly, her new life in Paris, although enriching and diverting, offered few opportunities for her to vent her combativeness. Certainly there were people and things about France that incensed her. She took to dressing down nosey concierges, discourteous railway officials, mashers who would follow her for blocks; she complained that French women were not protected or treated politely. She lambasted critics who lauded orchestras that she believed had played badly. She chided film directors who complimented their own work before the public saw it. Her discovery that in the nation renowned for chivalry there existed brutality and unrestrained boastfulness fueled her determination to fight against all that lacked a sense of perfection, against everything unintelligent. But the harder she fought, the more people disliked her—not just those she had "designated" to dislike her, but nearly everybody. By disagreeing, she became disagreeable. The only thing to do was to change, or, better, to give the appearance of change. Personal vanity, she decided, demanded it. For once, perhaps for the first time, she questioned her belief that she could stand anything, endure whatever existed. That it was not always necessary to endure had never occurred to her. She began muting her critical comments, speaking more politely, and adopting a diplomatic approach to annoying matters. Perhaps getting along in France would be easier if she considered the views of her friends rather than contradicted them.

Agreeableness was mandatory with Georgette's sister, the chatelaine of a spectacular eleventh-century château on the outskirts of Saint-Romains de Colbus, in Normandy—the Château de Tancarville—on whom the two women descended in the autumn after they had learned that a large sum of money a rich friend had promised Georgette would not be paid. Instead of being in a position to buy a château, they suddenly found themselves nearly broke and in need of a place to live. At Margaret's urging, they approached the chatelaine and asked for refuge. Living in a château used by William the Conqueror and Richard the Lion-Hearted and Charles IX and possibly by Queen Elizabeth satisfied Margaret's "long-established yearnings for a romantically framed existence." Although she, as editor of the *Little Review,* had been associated with revolutionary artists who impugned the art of the past, her psychic self, according to Janet Flanner, still consisted of "an elaborate, old-fangled euphoria." As a resident at the Château de Tancarville—the women were intermittent boarders for nearly twenty years—Margaret was now in the ideal place in which to accelerate her war against reality, although conducting it would involve her in some unusual battles.

The first deterrents to maintaining a life of luxurious pennilessness were the chatelaine and her husband. They were rich, very rich, but also very avaricious. The ten rooms in use were kept dimly illuminated and the salon always remained dark after dinner. At ten o'clock, the hour of retirement, the hosts and Georgette, but not Margaret, would don hats and heavy coats for the long journey through cold corridors to the bedrooms. Margaret, coatless and hatless and the object of alarm, led the ascent. From a position at the top of the stairs, she would watch the procession approach, candles in hand, "as if through the snow and ice of an Alpine night." Liquor and sex were two other commodities that were stringently monitored. Once Margaret asked a servant to bring a brandy for a guest of hers, and in jest handed the servant five francs in payment. The servant returned with the drink but not with the money. The master, he informed her, had retained it and measured out precisely five francs' worth of brandy. One branch of the family had three sons and three châteaux. For all of them as well as himself the father engaged one mistress. Economy of this sort shocked Margaret. "What would you have done?" the chatelaine asked. Margaret replied that she would have provided a mistress for each son, one with whom he was at least mildly in love, and as many for the father as he wanted. "Oh," the couple laughed, "it is not worth all that."

Tancarville provided a few places of escape from brutal French thrift.

Gurdjieff

Djuna Barnes, Margaret Anderson, Carl Van Vechten

One place was a cluster of Norman ruins filled with turrets, arcades, buttresses, spiral staircases leading nowhere, fireplaces suspended in air, windowseats in tiers of floorless rooms. Another retreat was in the recesses of the chateau itself. Only a few of the dozens of rooms were ever used. Wandering through the endless corridors and from room to room, occasionally meeting another houseguest, who would invariably comment on the weather ("The sun shines, it is gay" or, "It rains, it is sad"), gave Margaret a feeling of living in a world apart, a world where life lacked purpose but retained form, where the constant threat of boredom made watching the hours pass a distracting pastime. All the bedrooms faced the Seine, and each had a dressing room, an antechamber, and a canopied bed. Margaret's was done in Empire style, draped in gray-and-yellow silk, and from it she could gaze out on a white chimney, a large patch of sky, and a dark river below. Lace covered the marble mantlepiece. Candles glittered in a tall mirror, and on the bedside table burned a kerosene lamp with a pink shade. Even the most vicious miserliness could not touch her there.

Whenever they could afford it or had had all they could stand of the chatelaine, Margaret and Georgette returned to Paris and found modest quarters in small Paris hotels. Occasionally, Georgette was able to arrange concerts in Paris or tours that would take them to places like Monte Carlo. But in 1924 they went to live at Gurdjieff's Institute in Fontainebleau-Avon, which they had visited briefly on their arrival in France. It was Margaret's second château. Renamed by Gurdjieff the Château du Prieuré (it had once belonged to Mme. de Maintenon), it was a long building with large salons open to a court and formal gardens in front. Beyond was a forest. The floors above the salons were honeycombed with bedrooms, small ones for permanent pupils, large for transients. Margaret chose a room overlooking the garden where residents took their meals at individual tables. Georgette's room faced the forest.

Gurdjieff's routine required hard physical work. There were trees and underbrush to cut and burn, paths to straighten, food to prepare and cook, animals (donkeys mostly) to feed, rooms to clean, clothing to wash. Gurdjieff often seemed like a small boy overjoyed by something he had made. At other times, however, particularly in the study house where the residents danced against a backdrop of oriental rugs and furs and low-hanging red lamps, he presided like a Buddha. Except at meals, dances, and on occasions when he read from his manuscript, Gurdjieff was inaccessible.

As remote as the man was his teaching. It was completely different from what they expected. Rather than using the traditional devices of instruction and assimilation, Gurdjieff depended on his pupils' heredity and upbringing as well as their wish and will to provide the motivation for the self-examination that would make a new life possible. "I cannot develop you," he told Margaret. "I create conditions; you develop yourself." Hearing of how some of Gurdjieff's devotees had fared at Fontainebleau hardly increased her confidence in his method. The Americans, some of whom had been residents for some time, offered only naive generalizations; the comments of certain Frenchmen struck Margaret as gross; and from the institute's best known pupil, Katherine Mansfield, who had lived in a stable on Gurdjieff's property during her final illness, came only a few "vague spiritual interpretations." It was clear that whatever Gurdjieff imparted, either through manipulation of environment or through direct action, his precepts depended on the pupil's initiative. His process demanded action, not reaction, doing rather than absorbing. Whatever transformation occurred would be accomplished by the pupil.

The nature of that process soon became as formalized as a routine of attending school. Although most days were devoted to work and outdoor activities, the nights were given over to dance and endless discussion. After the evening meal, the pupils adjourned to the study house—an airplane hangar left over from the war—where Gurdjieff, seated at a piano, composed music for the dances that the students created under his and an assistant named M. de Hartmann's direction. Following the dances, the talk began; it was always geared to three audiences—guests, pupils, and Gurdjieff. From it, the Master learned about the pupils and guests; the pupils learned something about the guests and about themselves as they listened to Gurdjieff; and the guests would presumably wonder what it was all about. Afterward, back in their rooms, the real work began. Philosophizing, as Margaret called it, required a searching and impersonal self-examination, the object of which was self-knowledge. False starts were common. Gurdjieff's terminology, completely new, was less of a stumbling block than was the body of knowledge to which it could be applied: "a study of man's psyche from the standpoint of an exact science, illuminating the mystery of the processes by which a man can be said to be born again." Gurdjieff's message was directed to the person who, as Orage once told Margaret, had learned to act rather than be acted upon. Mere discussion or philosophizing led nowhere; doing was what counted. It was only much later that Margaret realized how easy it was to be convinced that they were going beyond philosophy and advancing toward self-knowledge, when at best they were comprehending the new knowledge only with their minds, not with their hearts.

At Jane's suggestion, Margaret pored over Gurdjieff's book, *Beelzebub's Tales to His Grandson*, but it yielded disappointingly little. What was it, she questioned, that she was not doing? She examined her reactions to the meetings and discussions and concluded that her exaltation came simply from the capacity to be moved. If that state was encouraged, apparently, she would end up a mystic and believe anything. For her, she vowed, there could be no rebirth, no new life, no new faith without science, without an identifiable substructure of human principles. Gurdjieff's values were meant to be applied to human behavior, not to the mystical.

Still, her determination to maintain a faith in the mind—in the power of talk and thought—often seemed to lead nowhere. Once when she had been arguing about right and wrong, Orage asked her why she persisted in doing so. "To convince people that certain ideas are better than others," she replied. "No one," Orage answered, "was ever convinced of anything by listening to ideas. . . . There are only three ways of influencing people—magnetization, competition, example." Orage tried to make her aware of the limitations of thinking in the attempt to arrive at truth or being. But how, she questioned, could one go beyond thought? What was the Master's "unknown doctrine"? What demands existed in Gurdjieff's immense cosmological abstractions? What could one do, beyond trying to "take impressions actively," to shape a new life in which one became a doer rather than a receiver? She believed that all her speculations might be figments of the imagination, and the imagination, Orage himself had said, was only "an excess of desire over ability."

It was Jane Heap, who had also become a resident at Fontainebleau, who finally came to Margaret's rescue. Likewise distrustful of the powers of thought but quicker than Margaret to perceive the ways one might attain Gurdjieff's ideal of super-knowledge, she formulated a set of questions, vital and comprehensible, designed to lead the others to greater self-illumination.

How much of your life is an illusion (the world as it appears to you through the distortions of lack of self-knowledge)?

How many failures or negative results (from well-intentioned, well-conceived, hopeful plans) do you think were caused by your illusion being too patent to others—with other illusions? Have you ever had a glimpse of the extent to which you rest under self-hypnosis? Have you ever been aware of the power of self-love as an hypnotic force?

Have you ever had a moment of realization of the spectacle of human beings going through life in a state of deep hypnosis?

Could you ever detach yourself enough from your illusory world to conceive a world of Reality—in which each person perceived Reality as one and the same thing—not interpreted by the whims, vanities, likes, and dislikes of a reacting animal? but perceived by a permanent, understanding threefold "I"—able to use the chemistry and vibrations of this type consciously instead of always being acted on from the outside (as we are)?

Years after her first association with Gurdjieff, Margaret admitted that she had been too much of a "doubting Thomas" to be wholly receptive to Jane's questions or the Master's teachings. Since anything she accepted at that time had to be literally exact, she had accepted very little. What she did learn, though, was that she had always reacted to things and that she had expended too much time and energy trying to attain one of the three states she considered blissful—liberty, ecstasy, and peace. The first, however, Orage had classified as an idea. So was ecstasy, and peace, she discovered, "had been a conscientious effort toward paralysis." When Orage rephrased his first injunction ("Act, don't be acted upon") in musical terminology ("Remember you're a pianist, not a piano"), he had issued a challenge that lasted, according to Margaret's calculations, for three years (from 1926 to 1929), during which she learned that the "quality of every life is determined exclusively by its position in relation to acting or being acted upon." That insight led straight to the conclusion that all the battles she had fought from the time she was fifteen had been reactions and that the moment had now come to reverse a course that offered no hope of moving her closer to her goal.

It would be some time, however, before Margaret assimilated the lessons of the past and began to make the adjustments in her life that her new association with Gurdjieff demanded. Immediately ahead was a period when she would drift with Georgette from Fontainebleau to the French Pyrenees, back and forth to Tancarville, to various hotels and apartments in Paris, to several exotic châteaux near the city, even to a rundown farmhouse in Brittany, and finally to an abandoned lighthouse along the Seine before she would rejoin Gurdjieff's circle in Paris in the midthirties and complete the reordering of her life that she had begun at the Prieuré.

From Fontainebleau, Margaret and Georgette moved south to the village of Cauterets in the Hautes Pyrenees. Whether because of its remoteness and solitude, or because she needed time by herself, Margaret fell into a reflective mood that yielded some disturbing thoughts about her past in America. For one thing, she realized how nervously cut up her life had been, how running the *Little Review* had drained her energies, and how it had kept her from developing. Allowing herself to become so fragmented had wrenched her away from what she really wanted to do, and that, she now knew, was never again to live under the compulsion that she *had* to accomplish something but to live simply and concentratedly for a "certain thing," aware that accomplishments would eventually come and without effort. Georgette's observation that although the French had learned to sit down, the Americans were still running had a larger personal meaning than she had guessed.

Attempting to understand the wellsprings of creativity, the processes that produced art, became a fundamental part of the process of reordering her life. Not art, but art's raison d'être catapulted her into an intense creative state. She examined her development as a musician. Whereas she had once practiced in a desultory manner and with virtually no comprehension of technique, she now began working harder at the piano, devising a procedure that made her feel that she might still become an accomplished pianist. Georgette's strict regimen of regular writing and practicing schedules and her insistence on putting work ahead of pleasure was an influence that helped Margaret clarify her goals and mobilize her energies.

What made Georgette an ideal mentor was her egoism. She was as great an egoist as Margaret. She, too, wanted certain things for herself, but she also wanted for Margaret the things that she desired. Neither would ever think of opposing the wishes of the other, since neither had wishes to impose on the other; in this way they avoided conflict and waste of time. The arrangement simplified life, gave it focus, steadiness, and interest. Above all, with Georgette Margaret found it was possible to be herself.

"Life is order for me," Margaret was fond of repeating. "Dirt yes, but not disorder." Eliminating the disorder of the past meant just as much in terms of reordering her living space as it did in changing the way she lived. When they took an apartment in Paris in the rue Casirir Perier, Georgette wrote a description of Margaret's room. "Our apartment is like a still-life which cannot move from its imaginary frame. Margaret has a tape-measure in her eye. Her own room is like a chord of music, each object a note that plays its part. Close to her bed are her mules, standing side by side like

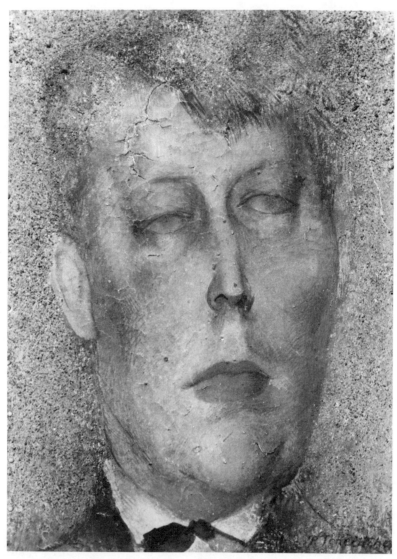

Jane Heap, portrait by Pavel Tchelitcheff

two steeds, harnessed and ready to go. She paints life as one paints a canvas. She not only arranged the apartment, she prepares the days. Each one must fit into the week like an object in its box. When all is in order, she is one with her surroundings. From her window even the branches of the trees in the garden look as if they had passed through her hands to decorate the sky." At Tancarville, however, Margaret could only admire or disapprove of what others had done. The chatelaine forbade any changes inside the château. Whatever Margaret found in her room would have to remain where it was, undisturbed.

The chatelaine inclined to slightly more liberality, however, with several other places she agreed to allow her sister-in-law and Margaret to use (at low rents) from time to time. One was a thirty-room château in Neuilly-sur-Seine called le Palais des Muses, which had once housed Louis XIV and later belonged to Robert de Montesquieu, whose fetes were still being talked about when Margaret and Georgette arrived in Paris. A wing of the château, Margaret decided, would make an ideal pied-à-terre. Another, half the size of the Neuilly château, was a garden house in Passy, much favored by Georgette for its spacious Peter Ibbetson gardens, which had a restorative effect on her. One other, with an even grander royal history, was a château-pavilion in the forest of Saint-Germain called La Muette, or La Folie d'Artois, in which, for intervals extending over two years, Margaret and Georgette shared the splendor once experienced by François Premier, Louis XV, Louis XVI, and Marie Antoinette, and by such literary luminaries as Voltaire, Madame de Staël, and Benjamin Constant. If their sequestered life at La Muette often lacked the amenities enjoyed by the former inhabitants—particularly irksome were shortages of heat and water—they never tired of such magnificent appointments as alcoved bedrooms, handsome fireplaces, and Jean Jacques Rousseau windows that opened to a forest of chestnut trees.

The place where they indulged their decorative fancies most fully was an abandoned lighthouse that stood on a cliff above the river Seine, close by the Tancarville château. For a rental fee of fifty francs, it became theirs. It looked a little like a country church. At the top was a tower with a glass dome in which they placed a windowseat. From there they surveyed the landscape in each direction—Le Havre to the west, Tancarville to the east, fields with grazing cows and horses to the north and south. Living there was like being in a balloon and observing life on earth as they floated by, meanwhile aware that their own life was the "most perfect kingdom" of all. Next to what seemed a worldly sort of routine at the château, living in the lighthouse transported one into the universe. From the château windows, Margaret rhapsodized, "the days look high and the nights deep, but at the lighthouse the days looked wide and the nights high."

Together they set about remaking this remarkable place. They furnished the terraces at the base of the tower with white tables, chairs, and colored umbrellas. They whitewashed the house attached to the tower, painting the doors and windows pink and the interior walls white. On the living room floor, they laid a dark blue carpet. They covered the divan in pale lilac, the davenport in pale green, and two armchairs in canary yellow.

From the lighthouse, Margaret and Georgette would occasionally retreat to Paris, usually in the winter, and install themselves in a small, inexpensive Left Bank hotel or apartment. As always, the city was an inexhaustible attraction, even for people who could hardly afford to live there. Margaret took a special interest in the cafés. At dusk she would change from the dark blue workman's jeans she wore during the day into an old, shabby suit that had become too decrepit to expose to the light of day, and walk through the shadowy streets, often stopping at a café in the neighborhood for a drink. It was a sensuously satisfying experience; as a place catering to the development of the mind and as a necessary refuge from domesticity, a Paris café was unequaled anywhere. What made Paris so alluring, such a wonderful city to live in, besides its sights and sounds and smells, was the easily retained belief that she had been "born" there and would never live anywhere else. Knowing so few Americans and being reluctant to venture to meet any more, she felt a sense of personal freedom that seemed to grow stronger when she knew Americans were close by. Expatriate, a word she abhorred, had no meaning, since she had never been conscious of being one.

Were it not, however, for one American woman with whom Margaret formed an intimate attachment, their sojourns in Paris would have been fewer, shorter, and certainly much less comfortable. A former journalist, Solita Solano had traveled around the world with her friend Janet Flanner before they settled down in Paris in 1922 to write novels. Solita, it turned out, was the more productive and produced three novels between 1924 and 1927, while Janet finished her first and only novel, *The Cubicle City*, in 1926. Except for a volume of poetry, *Statue in a Field*, which brought from Margaret the acclamation that Solita was "the most beautiful poet" she had ever known, Solita stopped writing in the late twenties and turned to reviewing and editing. Her interest in Margaret was as much emotional as it was intellectual. Although she had already companioned herself to Janet and would go on living with her for several years, Solita found in Margaret an immensely attractive person whose company she ardently sought and on whom she spent large sums of money from her family allowance. At least until the early thirties, Solita continued to help Janet while at the same time contributing to Margaret's support and buying her clothes. In letters to her sister Lois, Margaret listed the things Solita bought her. On one occasion they included "a heavenly dark blue Rasmus *tailleur*"; two satin blouses, gray and beige, and "all the rage"; a "beautiful black hat, à la Agnes, with one side way down." Solita also kept her supplied with *tabac blond*, lingerie, records, even a Pathé phonograph; in fact, without Solita, Margaret confessed to Lois, she would be reduced to workingman's suits for the rest of her life. As it was, she looked exclusively if not luxuriously dressed. The arrangement with Solita was not something she was proud of, but in return she gave of herself mentally, morally, and physically, so it was never one that shamed her.

In an autobiography Margaret had begun writing in the midtwenties, Solita took a professional interest. So did Janet. The book, appropriately entitled *The Autobiography of a Resisting Nature*, was the outgrowth of a plan that she and Georgette had formed to support themselves by writing books: each would write about herself and would try to make it amusing and saleable. Georgette had entitled hers *Souvenirs* (1895–1918). Neither progressed rapidly, although there were short periods, such as a summer they passed in a farmhouse in Brittany, when it seemed as though only days separated them from completion. Making do with three beds, a few chairs, and a long café table with benches—a spartan necessity that excited her—Margaret concentrated on practicing and writing, rising every morning at six and writing for two hours before turning to the piano. After lunch and a siesta, she worked until five and again in the evening. The discipline was invigorating. Life had order.

When she showed Solita and Janet portions of her book, both recommended that the story of the *Little Review* ought to run through it like a theme and that the book should also show how America had reacted to her efforts to give it Art. They also cautioned that her tendency to describe every house she had ever lived in was making her story tedious. "Your war with reality," warned Janet, "has momentarily become a thirty-year war with realtors." (Margaret had retitled her book *My Thirty Years' War*.) To assist the author in the last stages of her writing, Solita reserved a small quiet room for Margaret in her own hotel and furnished it with a red velvet armchair, three green lamps, wine glasses, and white muslin curtains. To keep her spirits up, she sent tulips every three days. Together they went to Man Ray's studio to have a photograph made for the frontispiece. "I've never seen a lovelier thing," Margaret exclaimed when she saw it. "It looks like a flower, or a cinema star of a charm equal to Greta's. Nothing like me (although everybody tells me I'm better looking all the time)." (What reaction Margaret had when she saw the portrait Berenice Abbott made of her in the late twenties is unknown, but in Miss Abbott's photograph, Margaret exudes an elegance and a redoubtable assurance not present in Man Ray's work.)

In 1929 shortly before the publication of her book, Margaret finally convinced Jane Heap that the *Little Review* had run its course. It was time to close it. Preparations for the final issue began in Paris. To artists and writers, many of them former contributors, Margaret sent a list of questions with a request for permission to print their replies. What were intended to be probing queries sounded sophomoric and were often either ignored or answered in a jocular spirit by some of the fifty-odd people who responded. Djuna Barnes found them uninteresting and the public an audience too disrespectful to address. Others including Bernard Shaw, Mary Garden, Picasso, even Joyce, did not answer at all, presumably as unmoved as Miss Barnes by questions like "What should you most like to do, to know, to be?" "Why wouldn't you change places with any other human being?" "What has been the happiest moment of your life?" To the last William Carlos Williams replied that he did not care to tell. To the final query, "Why do you go on living?" Janet Flanner responded that living was an instinct she could not conquer. Hilda Doolittle confessed that for years spite had been a reason for living but that happiness and a desire to extract all she could from life now kept her going. Marianne Moore found no reason to stop living, the surrender of it having never been demanded of her. In May the last and largest (nearly one hundred pages) issue of the *Little Review* appeared. Arranged in alphabetical order were the replies; next to most of them was a picture of the contributor.

In separate editorials the editors explained why after fifteen years they had joined to inter the *Little Review.* Margaret contended that the artist no longer knew what he was doing: "I can no longer go on publishing a magazine in which no one really knows what he is talking about." Jane Heap noted that the magazine had served "as a trial-track for racers. We hoped to find artists who could run with the great artists of the past or men who could make new records. But you can't get racehorses from mules."

The *Little Review*, she continued, had given space "to twenty-three new systems of art (now all dead), representing nineteen countries. In all of this we have not brought forward anything approaching a masterpiece except the *Ulysses* of Mr. Joyce. *Ulysses* will have to be the masterpiece of this time." There is no reason to believe that Jane had ever been disingenuous whenever she touted the singular merits of *Ulysses*. But as the era's one masterpiece, it had, she admitted, serious drawbacks. Besides being "an intense and elaborate expression" of the author's "dislike of his time," it was "too personal, too tortured, too special" to stand as a masterpiece "in the true sense of the word." Years later, when a professor cited her remarks in an article on the *Little Review* and concluded that Jane obviously did not like *Ulysses,* Margaret fumed. From the first moment, she reported, Jane "loved" *Ulysses*. "She also loved Joyce and Nora."

Margaret herself privately admitted that much of the manner and matter of *Ulysses* had displeased her, but in her public statements she always maintained that she too had immediately recognized the book as a masterpiece. What publishing *Ulysses* did for the *Little Review* and, in turn, for Jane and her was to create a powerful myth that obscured the magazine's obvious shortcomings, or as Margaret put it, veiled the "rot" they printed. "Of course," she confided, "we always printed some good things, but not enough for the immortality that has been bestowed upon us." That myth Margaret left undisturbed to the end.

Margaret and Jane, now accustomed to meeting only briefly, would drift apart even more in the midthirties. After 1948 they never saw one another again. Jane died in 1964 in England. Although friendship held them together, it was a mutual interest in Gurdjieff that had become their single common interest. Neither responded to the Master in the same way; Margaret remained skeptical of Gurdjieff's methods and was guarded in her openness to his teachings, but Jane became one of his staunchest disciples and instructors. Under his influence, she changed and became increasingly subjective, intellectual, mystical, and, some noted, even darkly pessimistic. But her immense vitality remained strong, and her trenchant truths, so often the source of Margaret's admiration, were as cogent as ever. Simply as a fount of verbal stimulation, Jane could never be replaced; and as an articulator of thoughts, which Margaret borrowed, quoted, and passed off as her own, Jane had no equal. "To me," Margaret said in 1967, "the expression, the formulation of [Jane's] thoughts amounted to genius."

The hardships of maintaining the life of art increased in the early thirties. Neither *My Thirty Years' War* nor *Souvenirs* (1895–1918) (Paris, Grasset, 1931) brought in any money, despite favorable reviews. As Georgette progressed with her work, writing several books at the same time—a volume of poetry, a treatise on love, and *La Machine à Courage* (Paris, 1947)—Margaret marveled at her ability to balance the beautiful and sensational, to permit just enough intimate detail to titillate readers and to keep her prose light and graceful. Even more admirable was her humility in regard to Maeterlinck; she blamed herself, rather than the actress Renée Dahon who replaced her in his life, for the dissolution of their relationship. The French publisher, Grasset, had written a disappointing preface, which Georgette feared might irritate Maeterlinck and prompt him to suppress the book. Although he accepted it calmly, Georgette did not. "I read it with the tips of my eyes," she wrote, "and the fact that my life's story should be associated with the vulgarity of soul that emanated from Grasset's pages made my life tremble." More disappointing news came when Margaret's local agent (W. A. Bradley) gave up trying to place *Souvenirs* with an American firm and when Pascal Covici, her American publisher, stopped sending royalties after paying only a few hundred dollars.

Without the income they expected from their books, Margaret and Georgette faced serious monetary problems. Fines and rent went unpaid. Furniture was taken from La Muette. They ate only brown bread and butter, lettuce, and soup. At one low point, Georgette was forced to sell a few pieces of her furniture and other possessions. Margaret sold her copies of *Ulysses* and Frank Harris's *My Life and Loves* to Paris booksellers for the best price she could get. Solita still bought some clothing for Margaret, but she, too, was not as well off as she had been. When they could no longer afford La Muette, they rented it out, hoping to bring in enough money to keep going until they could live in it again. Meanwhile, they lived in Solita's hotel at her expense. There was little to take their minds off economic struggle. Even Janet Flanner's offer to help them place still unwritten articles in *Vogue* and the *Ladies' Home Journal* seemed a remote possibility of relief. When in October 1934 Georgette came down with pneumonia and they went to live in the village of Vernet-les-Bains in the Pyrenees Orientales, their dream life came to a temporary standstill.

Fortunately, the peasant's house they found in Vernet was cheap, and it was small enough to keep Georgette warm. While Georgette rested, Margaret explored the region on foot. Along the paths that wound through the silent hills, she met the local peasants, who gradually became their friends. She and Georgette had nearly detached themselves from the rich bourgeoisie, favoring the company of artists, aristocrats, and, increasingly, peasants, whose nearness was reassuring and whose liking of one was a triumph. Vernet was a place for long talks; often they tried to determine what separated them from those people with whom they never felt at home—intellectuals, for example. Georgette found an answer. "We live for emotions . . . they live for events. In our relations with people, we wait on the development of personal atmosphere; they don't wait, they crouch. . . . They become critics."

Vernet was also a place for writing. Still convinced that it was the only way she could make any money, Margaret decided to write a continuation of *My Thirty Years' War* and to include funny stories about life in France. But what had formerly been a mostly pleasant task had become this time an irksome and frustrating ordeal. Disappointed with her work and slow progress, she sent drafts of two chapters to Solita and Jane, asking for suggestions. Neither provided much encouragement. Solita could find no charm or fun in the writing, and the tone, she observed, sounded too dictatorial. Jane scolded her for trying to write according to rules (Margaret had been following what she called the "art method"). Abandon them immediately and be yourself, Jane advised. Write spontaneously, without too much "brain," and go to it the way you drive a car. ("I drive a car so dashingly," Margaret once wrote, "that everyone says I look as if I were playing the piano.") "Keep it unreal, your value is illumination." Margaret understood Jane's words, but if she were to write the way she drove a car, she would have to find that "fixed point at which [her] life movement had revolved," and that would not be easy.

After a few months in Vernet, during which Georgette had recuperated, Margaret lapsed once more into a state of confusion. It was not because she was displeased with her writing. She had benefited from her friends' advice and had finished a sizable portion. Nor had she missed Paris so much that she felt she had to return. As in the past, her problem was an emotional and intellectual restlessness, and it was Solita, this time, who had aggravated it. In the late twenties, Solita had rejected Gurdjieff's teachings. ("I rejected his language, the suit he was wearing and his table manners [and] I decided that I rather disliked him.") Now, however, she had suddenly and quite unexpectedly experienced "a crisis of misery" of such grave proportions that she had sought out the Master for help. From

Paris Margaret received daily transcripts of her meetings with Gurdjieff and her valiant efforts, as Solita put it, to die to an old life. She also informed Margaret that after a long hiatus, Gurdjieff was again accepting a few pupils for special teaching.

Gurdjieff had given up the Institute at Fontainebleau and, while waiting for new quarters, had begun meeting pupils on the terrace of the Café de la Paix, near the Opéra, in the center of Paris. His massive presence attracted considerable attention and, from detractors like Robert Mc-Almon, considerable and often audible derision as well. To McAlmon, Gurdjieff was a charlatan who, unlike the Catholic Church, emphasized spiritual ferments too little and permitted carnal realizations too often. However, for many of his women followers, like Katherine Hulme, Gurdjieff was a messianic figure. Seeing him for the first time, Miss Hulme wrote: "He looked like a broad-shouldered Buddha radiating such power that all the people between him and me seemed dead." Kathryn Hulme, Solita, and a few friends formed the nucleus of the study group that Margaret and Georgette joined after returning to Paris in April.

Gurdjieff's way was self-transformation through self-knowledge, and Margaret was now in a mood to embrace it. Part of her trouble, she recognized, was that all she had heard or even experienced had been too vague to provide knowledge or understanding. All her beliefs, doubts, hesitations, struggles, efforts, and revelations, like Tolstoy's, had somehow failed to satisfy her craving for higher wisdom, for that "process higher than taking thought." She felt empty, incomplete; her physical, emotional, and spiritual lives remained unbalanced. Going back to Paris meant facing her dilemma, assuming a burden and thereby lessening the weight of it. She would call her return a "predestined accident." "I happened to be in the right place, at the right time, in the right condition, to begin all over again."

She could hardly have been more surprised at how this starting over again began. Gurdjieff, aware of the usefulness of shock and surprise as a means of inducing self-confrontation, had devised a culinary ceremony that included vast amounts of carefully selected foods and many bottles of a dry brandy called Armagnac. It was not the food itself—she liked it well enough—it was the unrelieved concentration on the food that annoyed her. Gurdjieff required not only that everyone know what was being eaten but why. The Armagnac was used in the ritual of toasts, which were repeated every few minutes. As soon as the bottles were emptied, more appeared. Each toast was made to a different kind of "idiot"—intellectual idiots, political idiots, compassionate idiots, ordinary idiots, superior idiots, ad infinitum. Gurdjieff once christened a guest named Bill Widney a "round" idiot, which, Widney learned later, meant that he was an idiot whichever way he turned. Drinking toasts to *idiotisme*, Gurdjieff explained to Katherine Hulme, was the result of seven years of study in which he had inculcated much "knowledge of human typicality [and] polarity." Toasting, Miss Hulme concluded, was an exercise in control, measuring, remembering, and certainly in keeping up with the Master, who consumed at least twice as much brandy as his pupils.

Toasting, like eating, left Margaret unmoved. She listened as impassively to the comments made after each toast as she did to the familiar simplicities that inevitably followed the meal. Nothing seemed to be happening. It would be some time before she recognized that nothing was explained in Gurdjieff's method. Everything, including the significance of toasting, remained "unknown" until the pupil himself discovered its meaning. The Master's doctrine of the "unknown" began with the person as an unknown.

Margaret moved from incomprehension and frustration into a second stage. Always rebellious (Janet Flanner described Margaret as "lawless by nature," one who always "practiced a variety of polite anarchy as her basis of conduct"), Margaret decided to challenge whatever she heard and saw. She prepared her protests in advance, hoping that the discussions would give her the opportunity to use them. Once, when Gurdjieff mentioned money, he turned to Margaret and said, "From you there comes a terrible vibration." Margaret answered: "But you know why." "I do not," Gurdjieff replied. "But you can imagine," she shot back. "Excuse," he said, "I cannot imagine. YOU can imagine. . . . Thirty years ago I could imagine, even was time I imagine I was God—or your Uncle Sam." Another time, when Margaret refused to eat green onions, Gurdjieff accused her of rejecting them because she believed only "small working people" ate green onions. When Margaret dismissed his explanation, saying she simply did not like them, Gurdjieff continued: "Nature cannot not like onion." Her idea was only "hypnotic." Margaret denied she held any bias toward working people. Unconvinced, Gurdjieff lectured her on the ancestors who had formed her and who, he assured her, all ate green onions. Margaret had presumably allowed her mind to tell her she did not like onions. She had denied her nature. Margaret remained silent, and then began to study Gurdjieff's face. "Why you look on me?" he asked. "Because I see some-

Georgette Leblanc in the St. Wandrille garden

thing in your face. . . . I like to study it." "Excuse," he replied, "you not see anything my face. For study me, you are too young. Three thousand years in your America, then maybe can study me." Rather than defeating her arguments, jousts with Gurdjieff strengthened them. Convinced that he avoided facing what she said squarely and either approving or disapproving, she descended into a third stage of quietude, fierce but also futile, in which she spoke just enough to show that she was still alive.

At one toasting ceremony, Gurdjieff asked Margaret to guess what kind of idiot he thought she was. "A zigzag idiot," she replied. "You cannot be zigzag," he answered. "But that is my condition now." "Condition?" Gurdjieff said, surprised. "Your condition has nothing to do with inner world. You defile zigzag. Wish go too high. Zigzag is high idiot, goes this way, that way. Struggles against *merde* he knows he is. Is as if you, a deacon, put on archbishop's robes." Margaret doubtless believed that zigzag was an appropriate designation for one who still vacillated between argumentation and silence, between assertion and withdrawal, and who still retained a faith in skepticism and investigation as a means to discover truth. Zigzag, according to Gurdjieff, meant fragmentation, allowing the mind to be continuously fighting something, disputing, criticizing, and attacking rather than struggling with oneself. Margaret moved between two positions: teacher and pupil. Too often, he contended, she wanted to teach and not to learn, to spoil the atmosphere in which learning could occur, and to blame others for her own obtuseness. No productive concentration on herself and her condition could take place as long as she persisted in being an angry, argumentative, unreceptive pupil. Behind her anger, she would eventually learn, was vanity and self-love. Behind her argumentativeness was a reluctance to accept Gurdjieff's knowledge without first being absolutely sure that it was literally exact. Margaret had not progressed beyond the point she had reached several years before.

A few months after Gurdjieff had begun seeing Margaret, he announced that her "outer animal" was a Tibetan yak, a cousin of the European cow. He explained that with each pupil he identified different creatures that typified their outer natures. Solita's, much to her distress, was a canary (because she quivered with animation), and Katherine Hulme's was a crocodile (because she overflowed so sentimentally). With these creatures, Gurdjieff maintained, the pupil had to remain friendly so as to help him achieve his work. "Help, not hinder" was his motto. "But in your case," he explained to Margaret, "you not look on door of new painted barn like cow which concerns itself only with question, 'Is that my home, or is it not?' You think like businessman, about quality of paint, how much cost, if will last, how react in rain—forget self completely." Margaret objected to both the yak and the Master's description. "Cows are placid. I don't wish to be a cow." "Not so," Gurdjieff replied. "Cows not always placid; sometimes yak go berserk. People run inside house, shut door. Something take the psyche of cow and entire being is wild—try break through wall—could even kill her children." Such fiery embellishments to the yak's nature mollified Margaret. The animal now seemed to fit what she believed she was and wanted to go on being.

Although it would be some time before Margaret would admit that Gurdjieff's identification of her "inner animal," a tapeworm, bore any resemblance to her, she could hardly ignore his perceptiveness. A tapeworm was a lazy animal that sought a comfortable place and fed on the labor and efforts of others. Even its food was brought to it. The implications were disturbing. Had she not depended on the work and talents and provisions of others for a long time? On Jane's and Ezra Pound's in the *Little Review* years; on Georgette's, the chatelaine's, recently on Solita's, and now Gurdjieff's? Had she not had her cake and eaten it too?

From Margaret's third stage—a spell of near muteness that lasted a year during which she groped to be "herself"—Margaret moved into a fourth— a long, silent period when she worked hard to destroy her old life as a lovely dream, beautiful though it had been, and to open herself increasingly to Gurdjieff's teachings. It marked the beginning of her recovery. The order of her life began to change. The old patterns she had followed dissolved. Although she felt she was living in a state of chaos, she slowly realized that it was the only "order" in which transition could occur. The four elements of her personal universe (music, love, nature, and ideas) were all affected. Orage had once broken into her rhapsodies on nature to say she was only in love with it, that she was an epicurean. Her reaction was to try to live without nature, to subject herself to the most noxious man-made conditions available. With music, so long the staple that made life worth living, she did the same thing. For two years (1936–1938), she tried to exist as though she had never heard the composition (Rachmaninoff's *Second Piano Concerto*) that had so often animated her life. Divorcing herself from music initiated a regimen she called her "D period." The "D" stood for depression, disgust (of self), despair, decrepitude, and destruction. Life had become a vast desert that immobilized her. She remembered what Solita had said about the pupils at the Institute: each was an egoist, studying for himself alone. Each had asked two questions: Why am I here? Is it worth my while to remain? Living in a state close to nonexistence made such questions painful to ask and more painful to answer. Even Georgette's cheerful predictions that each day would be better did little to relieve her gloom. The nagging question remained: What had all this to do with her quest for the "riddle of the universe"?

But Gurdjieff's way eventually yielded results. Still in the howling desert of nonexistence, stranded between two worlds, Margaret discerned certain flaws in her past that she had not detected before. Her imagination, for example, was merely an "excess of desire over ability," and intelligence was a "justification of this excess." Those intense emotions she had invoked and enjoyed she now recognized as an indulgent desire to experience the "pleasure of having emotions." And her penchant for glorifying art had been a "hope of repeating those emotions forever." Her personality, satiated with emotional richness, had prevented her from seeing these "facts." With devastating illumination, she concluded that she, as well as Jane and Georgette, had been almost nothing at all; like balloons they had floated to the ceiling and had stayed there because they could not go higher. "We had considered ourselves Nietzschean transvaluers of all values, but all we had really done was to act like Gabriele D'Annunzio."

Challenged, too, was Margaret's abiding ambition to ignore reality, to inhabit a dream. Gurdjieff had once said she rested in a dream, but she had rejected his perception until now. When one day Gurdjieff, or a pupil, spoke six words to her (Margaret never said what they were) that had the force of revelation, her defenses finally crumbled, her outer shell shattered. At last, she saw herself as she really was. What she saw was a stupid, vain, egoistic, and empty person.

Of the Biblical teaching that one must lose oneself to find oneself, Margaret became an example. "You must know your self-love," Gurdjieff instructed, "before you can kill it." "You must also destroy vanity," he added. "Are they not nearly the same?" Margaret asked. "Is sister," Gurdjieff answered. "Still not enough to know them. Must now have something independent." The "something independent" was Gurdjieff's term for one's "inner world, one's independent place." Whether Margaret ever attained the "something independent," at least in a sense that Gurdjieff would have approved, seems doubtful. Solita Solano came on the Master and Margaret on the terrace of the Café de la Paix soon after Margaret's disturbing insight. Only the day before, Margaret had told Gurdjieff that she feared she irritated him and had decided to drop out of the group. But here she was with him on the café terrace. After Margaret left, Solita asked Gurdjieff what had happened. Margaret, he answered, was "too light" to do his work, "too American." In life, "she perhaps have something good. . . . I thought when she first came that after she had contact with me, something would collect in her empty place, but now I see is not so. Such empty life leave empty place."

When Margaret recorded her experience with Gurdjieff in her second autobiographical volume, *The Fiery Fountains* (New York, Hermitage House, 1951), she remembered that at this point—1938—she was neither happy nor unhappy, but that she could rejoice because she understood that from now on she could only be helped, and that, regardless of dislocation, disadvantages, and debilities, she would always know what task was hers. What she did not record was that Gurdjieff knew from the start that she had no real courage or strength.*

For the events ahead, Margaret needed as much courage and strength as she could summon. On a cool quiet June morning in 1939, Georgette stood before her mirror and noticed a swelling in her arm. Her only too human effort to diminish its potential importance ended when a doctor at the American Hospital diagnosed it as cancer. In September, as France mobilized for war, a war that Georgette had been fearing for three years, she consented to an operation, as though surgery were somehow appropriate at a time of public slaughter. From the operation she emerged an incurable patient, notwithstanding the doctor's claim that he had removed the tumor. Georgette lived for another two years without knowing the gravity of her illness, or, if she did, without revealing that she knew. She took strength from Gurdjieff's teachings, remembering his lesson that one must always struggle against "dying before one's death."

Margaret assumed all responsibilities. After a short stay in Paris, she moved Georgette to Tancarville, leaving behind a city preparing for war. Georgette would never see Paris again, and Margaret was not to return to it until 1948. When the threat of German invasion grew, they drove south to Hendaye, near Biarritz, a few miles from Spain, through which, if necessary, they could escape to the sanctuary of America. Margaret busied herself rearranging the meager furnishings in a small house they found, covering a spacious worktable with emerald green wrapping paper and hanging curtains she made out of white tarlatan in the windows that faced the sea and where at night she always placed two lamps. Living in a "corner of the world," far from Paris and separated from their friends (Solita

---

*In her book about Gurdjieff, *The Unknowable Gurdjieff* (London, Routledge & Paul, 1962), Margaret tried to demystify him, to keep him simple, an assignment difficult for one who had perhaps looked on him as an extra-lover, godly, remote, and omniscient.

Solano and Janet Flanner had gone to the United States, and Jane Heap to London), they prepared themselves for a long period of instability.

Around Christmas Georgette's condition deteriorated. Then she rallied and for a while worked on her book *La Machine à Courage*. Early in the new year (1940), they drove to Cannes, on the Riviera, where friends had found them a flat in nearby Le Cannet. It was like reentering their dream life. In this flower-filled place, Georgette bloomed. The war seemed far away, and as summer approached they spent days sauntering in the olive country with baskets of wine, cheese, pâtes, and fruit. But in May when it appeared certain that Italy would soon enter the war and that Cannes would be vulnerable to bombings, they headed back toward Spain. For three months they shuttled from place to place. In Bordeaux, which over-flowed with refugees trying to leave Europe, they applied at the American Consulate for permission to go to America. During weeks of delays, their passports were lost. In Bayonne, where they waited, thousands of Frenchmen arrived from Paris. And when the capital fell to Hitler in June, Bayonne became part of the Occupied Zone. As soon as they received substitutes for their missing passports and exit visas to move to Unoccupied France, they returned to Le Cannet. Georgette was failing, and Margaret knew they would never go to America.

Georgette lived for nearly a year. In a little house in the hills above the sea called the Chalet Rose, Margaret, with the help of Monique, cared for a person who refused to believe she was ill. "I have only had an accident," Georgette would say. "I am not sick at all." She did all she could to relieve the strange "impasse" that had changed their life. She sang, she worked on her book, she began a correspondence with Jane Heap that lasted until she died, she spoke of going to America. When she was strong enough, she walked in the neighboring hills, and once she went to a concert in Cannes. To Margaret it seemed Georgette was showing her how to die after having shown her how to live. At times, though, living day after day with her in a world that was "always unreal" was a strain almost too great to bear. Georgette's courage was admirable, but her refusal to acknowledge her condition required Margaret to cling to a dead illusion. Georgette's brave suffering was like a tonic to Margaret. Her fear of death diminished. Her despair gave way to a sense of destiny. Her sense of personal tragedy faded into impersonal tragedy. "I know," she wrote later, "that our death-in-life was beginning its transmutation into the octave of life-in-death." Long before the day in October 1941 when Georgette died, Margaret was prepared for it, and it was Georgette who had prepared her.

"Is it possible?" Georgette asked near the end of her life. Is it possible

Margaret Anderson at the grave of Georgette Leblanc

that life was over? It was a startling question coming from one who had avoided mentioning death for so long. But more astonishing was Margaret's discovery that Georgette had already written about her own death in *La Machine à Courage* and had described her last great effort as being that of watching herself tear from her body "the core" of her being and throw it to "its new beginning." Georgette's depiction of how she once imagined this final transformation—rebirth—was so compelling that Margaret could hardly believe she was dying. In the final minutes of Georgette's life, Margaret held a picture of Gurdjieff against her cheek. Her face assumed a calm, a gravity and majesty. Gurdjieff had sent her a message saying that she had great courage and that he had always regarded her as a friend. "He said that?" Georgette asked. "Then we shall die without dying."

Jane Heap interpreted Georgette's final accomplishments. "I read and reread her last days as you tell them," Jane wrote to Margaret, "and I think I know what she was trying to do and say. 'As we go, so we come again.' Georgette will never perish. Die we all must, but we can hope that none of us who has 'eaten' of Gurdjieff's food will ever perish."

Of the friends who helped Margaret become a new human being, the most influential was Georgette Leblanc. From her Margaret learned that she could experience a life of art by perfecting the art of life. In her relentless war against reality, Georgette was a commandingly romantic figure, one for whom Margaret had both "real love" and "romantic love." In the former, one wants the other person's good, Margaret explained; in the latter, one wants the other person. Georgette became that "perfect human being" with whom everything had turned out to be "unbelievable happiness."

Margaret, by her own admission, was in love all her life. Her first "real love" was for her sisters, Lois and Jean. She had loved her father too, but only as an impersonal being who seemed too good to be true. Ironically, she hated her mother. At college, and later in Chicago, she discovered she could love people only if she admired them, and admiration meant having respect for their ideas and how they expressed them. It was an inflexible standard that may have had a hardening effect on her psyche. What drew her to Emma Goldman, whom she loved, was her anarchistic beliefs. It was another powerful and propagandistic personality, however, who became her first great love, Jane Heap.

Margaret tried many times to write about love and often succeeded. Edmund Wilson remarked that her description of love ("The Art of Love") was the part of *The Fiery Fountains* he liked best. Near the end of her life she wrote a novella (*Forbidden Fires*) in which she attempted to say "something true and beautiful" about lesbian love. For years she had complained that most lesbian stories distorted the subject, falsified it into a cliché. The characters were invariably miserable, tragic, doomed, or "evil" people, and, too often, the female protagonist, regretting the "evil" of her ways, turned to a man in the end for protection. *Forbidden Fires*, written to memorialize her emotional friendships with Jane Heap, Georgette Leblanc, and Dorothy Caruso (her third love) was an "authentically lesbian" story. Except for the idealized central character, modeled on an older woman with whom Margaret had had a brief flirtation, it avoided banalities.

As necessary as Margaret's friends were to her well-being (she believed she needed them more than they needed her), the motivating force in all she did remained self-love. She lived for herself, her nature, her individuality. "I always had strength *only* for what I wanted to do," she told Allen Tanner, adding that, although it was a shameful admission of self-indulgence and egocentricity, she had never knowingly lived under illusions. Margaret liked herself. Her happiness sprang from vanity as well as from her friendships. She enjoyed being called a "mysterious person," a "lovely freak of nature," someone "fearsome."

She never wavered from the belief that her tastes and perceptions and judgments were indubitably the "right" ones. When asked whether she had developed any critical standards that had enabled her to determine the importance of *Ulysses,* she became indignant. "*Mon dieu,*" she exclaimed, imperiously, "I had nothing *but* standards. Why would I have wanted to publish a magazine of art if I hadn't any standards? What were they? They were the standards of a 'touchstone,' which I considered myself to be. To me a touchstone is the kind of person who can prove that the despised terms 'I like,' or 'I don't like,' are important, authentic, 'right.'" Margaret never expanded on why she had published Joyce and accepted or rejected others (for example, Hart Crane's *The Bridge*), but she stoutly maintained that she always knew *when* writing was beautiful and when it was not. Knowing *why* it possessed beauty was less important and in the end made one neither richer nor happier. Nor would such knowledge endow the writing with any higher value; in fact, she pointed out, by absorbing oneself in the technique of writing, one might miss entirely the feeling it contained. Ezra Pound's pronouncement that she was the only editor in America who "ever felt the need of, or responsibility for, getting the best writers concentrated in an American periodical" was the kind of tribute Margaret loved to flaunt before the critics. It relieved her of having to mount her own defenses, bestowed on her the status of literary heroine, and joined her name forever to that of a great poet, patron, and propagandist.

Feeling, emotion, sensation, nuance, fine distinctions, and emanations were the qualities Margaret pursued and celebrated, none of which, in her opinion, intellectuals comprehended or considered useful. She prided herself on knowing what they did not know or did not care about. They had no interest in the discriminations she considered essential, and were incapable of having aesthetic experiences. Since they aspired to catch only the meanings of words, not to listen to their music, they would never be able to tell, as she would, when the sounds were being "hurt." They would simply want to hear the music, whether well played or not. To charges that she was uneducated and ill informed, Margaret readily agreed. Learning, she countered, had always been a dull activity next to understanding, which was possible to achieve without a lot of study. Dilettante was an appellation she accepted proudly.

Writers whom she classified as rarified intellectuals were as objectionable as the cerebral critics who touted their works. Not one, she believed, was capable of writing without passion, emotion, feelings. Not one was capable of moving readers. When Margaret read one of Djuna Barnes's last poems in the New Yorker ("The Walking-Mort"), she was horrified. It possessed not an ounce of "real emotion." It was false, forced, and ugly, a "blot" on all literature. Equally disappointing was Vladimir Nabokov's novel Mary, which Solita Solano had recommended. No atmosphere, Margaret complained, ever rose up from the book to flood the mind with "real emotion." Samuel Beckett and Robert Graves were in the same category. What was acceptable to Margaret was a composition one might ask to hear read or performed while waiting to die—James Wright's poem "Avenger," for example, or Rachmaninoff's Second Piano Concerto. Surcharged with emotion that could be experienced endlessly, they were among the rightful inhabitants of the realm of art.

Ceaselessly, Margaret celebrated the triumph of the created life, her own life, "unreal" but true, a life that contained what she wanted, needed, and demanded. She once called it "a life of emotions superimposed upon the emotions of life." It was in "a certain world next door," secretive, sheltered, sequestered, that she and her friends lived their "different lives." From Jane Heap she learned that to express the emotions of life was to live and that to express the life of the emotions was to make art. In Georgette Leblanc she had loved a person whose response illuminated and deepened her understanding of love. From her own being came that "mysterious energy" that made possible the miracles of her "extra life."

When all her friends had died or lived far away, Margaret chose to stay on alone in the same small house where she had cared for Georgette. As she grew older, she became reclusive, refusing often to be seen or to see anyone. To a friend she wrote that it was a thousand times better to remain alone, in the memory of the vivid, illuminated world of Georgette, Jane, and Gurdjieff, than to live in what Georgette once labeled "the dog-to-dog" of humanity. It was blessed to reside outside a world of politics, government, law, the vehemence of cities, the violence of events—to perpetuate the dream. Gurdjieff had said one could shun the pattern of human madness and impotence, and she had. Only occasionally did "reality" intrude, and when it did, for example after illness had forced her to leave the Chalet Rose and move to a nearby hotel, she beat it back with the indestructible belief that she had been more fortunate than most people, more protected, more befriended. Margaret approached death with as much equanimity as Georgette. "I shall die as I have lived," she said. "I shall just go into a dream."

Margaret Anderson died on October 15, 1973. Her life is a record of that "unreal" world she made for herself in France and into which she withdrew from the world around her. Her life was a crusade dedicated to making real what seemed impossible, to turning fairy tales into realities, to discovering exquisite emotion in experience. In her last years, far from Chicago where she had begun her life's adventure, Margaret may have remembered the words over the entrance to the Fine Arts Building through which she passed daily on her way to the *Little Review* office. "All passes, art alone endures." With imagination, intelligence, gallantry, will-power, and self-love, Margaret fashioned a life that possessed the grandeur, wonder, and durability of a work of art.